T0381030

William Y Chey, M.D., D.Sc.

# AMERICAN DREAMS,
## ~ *Still Alive.* ~

Memoir of an
# IMMIGRANT DREAMER

AuthorHouse™
1663 Liberty Drive
Bloomington, IN 47403
www.authorhouse.com
Phone: 833-262-8899

Because of the dynamic nature of the Internet, any web addresses or links contained in this book may have changed
since publication and may no longer be valid. The views expressed in this work are solely those of the author and do
not necessarily reflect the views of the publisher, and the publisher hereby disclaims any responsibility for them.

Any people depicted in stock imagery provided by Getty Images are models,
and such images are being used for illustrative purposes only.
Certain stock imagery © Getty Images.

This book is printed on acid-free paper.

ISBN: 978-1-6655-1985-4 (sc)
978-1-6655-1987-8 (sc)
978-1-6655-1986-1 (e)

Print information available on the last page.

Published by AuthorHouse  03/24/2021

**author**HOUSE®

# AMERICAN DREAMS,
## Still Alive.

# *Foreword*

T here is an old adage that states, "Like father, like son." My father and I do indeed share many similarities; for example, our physical characteristics are eerily similar—same height, same shoe size. Fortunately for me, my father had impeccable taste in clothing. Over the years, I "borrowed" quite a few of my father's sport jackets; each one holds a special place in my heart. Every time I see, touch, or wear one of them, I wonder what my father was doing or whom he met while wearing them. We also both chose to devote our professional lives to gastroenterology. In 2015, I was honored with an invitation to deliver the David Sun Memorial Lecture at the Annual Meeting of the American College of Gastroenterology. As I reviewed the list of distinguished gastroenterologists who had spoken before me, I was surprised and humbled to see that my father had also given the David Sun Lecture in 1987. It was fun to share this story with the audience at the start of the talk, though I didn't tell them the origin of the perfectly fitting sport coat I was wearing.

Though reading my father's story made me reflect on our similarities, it also provided me with a much more textured understanding of who he was and who he has become. He has so many stories of humiliation, loss, and sacrifice from the thirty-six years of tumultuous Japanese occupation, including WWII, followed by the fear and uncertainty propagated by the Korean War. Knowing that love of family is the salve that heals a thousand paper cuts makes clear how hard it must have been for my father to immigrate to the US. Like so many immigrants before him, he left his beloved family in the hopes of finding the American dream. It certainly wasn't easy to learn a new language, struggle to build a career in academic gastroenterology, and raise a family as an Asian immigrant; but he embraced, even relished, each of these challenges.

Learning of those events has helped me to better understand the sense of urgency that my father imposed upon and instilled within my siblings and me: "Do your homework, cut the lawn, go to the laboratory to help with an experiment, go on rounds to see patients with me. Don't waste time on things that don't have a clear purpose; do what needs to be done better than anyone else." While I was growing up, I resented this and, at times, even disliked him for it. The roller-coaster ride that my father—and, indeed, all Koreans—was forced to endure no doubt infused this feeling of "now or never": this sense of urgency. Growing up, I always wondered why my father worked so hard and seemed so hardened. I now realize he didn't have the luxury of leaving anything to chance; the only way for him to increase his chances of success were to work so hard that he determined the outcome. He had to earn everything, even if it meant having to work twice as hard as the next person.

In my original writing of this foreword, I wrote that my father's story is the quintessential American immigrant story. This statement is all the more important at a time when the American zeitgeist views immigrants as a problem rather than a critical part of the solution to many of our nation's problems. One need only consider the repeated scapegoating of immigrants for everything from "taking" American jobs to causing the COVID-19 pandemic to hear echoes of the American Party, which openly discriminated again Irish Catholics in the 1850s; the Ku Klux Klan, which terrorized African Americans and Jews over centuries; and the "yellow peril," a racist term describing the existential threat posed by Asians to Western culture. All that said, my original statement misses a very important point. My father's story isn't the quintessential American immigrant story; it is the quintessential American story—full stop. We are a nation of immigrants; to deny this immutable fact is to try to rewrite history. The richness of my father's story, and the stories of millions of others like him, adds to the complexity and depth of the American tapestry. American exceptionalism has been forged from the intelligence, empathy, sweat equity, sacrifice, and suffering of countless immigrants who wanted nothing more than a chance for a better life. As a nation, we overtly and implicitly benefit from the collective experiences and the resulting wisdom of people of diverse backgrounds. They have so much to teach us if we will only give them a chance and listen. For much of our nation's history, we have done just that. My father could not have left his mark on the American dream as a researcher, mentor, and doctor without the generosity and assistance of countless Americans and a system that offers the possibility of success based upon merit rather than only birthright. While we are "making America great again," let's not lose sight of what made America great in the first place.

William D. Chey, MD, FACG, AGAF, FACP, RFF
Timothy T. Nostrant Collegiate Professor of Gastroenterology
Professor of Nutrition Sciences
Michigan Medicine

# Preface

T his book was planned originally as a short story for my children and grandchildren about my roots, where I came from, and how fortunate I was able to come to the United States of America and become a proud naturalized citizen of this great country.

As I was planning to write this book, however, I realized that I have had three different names in my short life time. For each name period, I have stories to share. I was born in South Korea with a Korean name, which was changed to a Japanese name until Korea was freed from Japanese colonialism when World War II ended in August 1945. After the war in Korea that ended in the summer of 1953, I had the opportunity to come to the United States of America for advanced studies in medicine, and I have had an American name since. I have shared the stories of my life from each of these periods in hopes that my life story may be interesting and instructive to not only my children but also the general public. I have had a dream, an American dream, and I am proud of it. To me, that dream is still alive today in this country for everyone. Thus, I mention the dreamers in my family, special friends, and my mentors who inspired and nurtured me.

The book has seven parts, in which I describe my childhood, my life in elementary schools in small rural towns, and my middle school days with my Japanese name in South Korea. As World War II ended, Koreans were freed from Japanese colonialism on August 15, 1945, and my own Korean name was restored, along with my new hopes for the future (Part I). However, the new hope was soon shattered by the cruel North Korean army invasion of South Korea on June 25, 1950. My family survived in Seoul during the atrocious North Korean occupation of Seoul. Then I fought in the front-line combat zone as a proud Republic of Korea Army medical officer against Chinese and North Korean invaders. With the kind help of friendly American medical officers in a nearby US mobile army surgical hospital (MASH), I came to the United States of America for my postgraduate education in medicine (Part 2). It was an incredible opportunity for me to come to the United States from a combat zone in Korea in August 1954. Since then I have had my American name, William Y. Chey, in the new country, the United States of America.

I wished to share my life experience in this great country. Having worked hard in several medical learning institutions, I achieved my goal and my dream became a reality—an American dream. I have had a wonderful and proud family. I had the fortune of having excellent graduate training, receiving two advanced medical degrees from the University of Pennsylvania, a world-class university in Philadelphia, Pennsylvania. My hard work paved my way to becoming a physician scientist and physician educator in higher learning institutions (Parts 3 and 4). I believe that the American dream is still very much alive and not dead today in this great country. The story I tell is not only for my family but also for many American people who believe in this great country. Not only my family but also all Americans should be proud of America and should also cherish real American traditions and values (Parts 3 and 4).

The door was open for my further advancement in a reputable university's exceptionally good medical community in Rochester, New York, where I would organize and establish a successful academic digestive disease program that included training not only for clinicians but also for physician scientists in gastroenterology who combine both clinical work and meaningful medical research. In the latter program, many postgraduate trainees came to our research laboratories from all over the world (Part 5). Part 6 describes my gratification for being a clinician-healer and physician scientist and for having my happy family and lifetime friends. I believe my original American dreams are realized; I have a good and wonderful family and a successful career as a physician healer and educator, a physician scientist, and a mentor for those physicians and scientists who came to our institutions in Rochester, New York. In my last chapter (Part 7), after telling of my retirement from the university, I share with you my life of joy and honor as a physician healer, again in a medical practice setting—a rare and delightful opportunity for a retired professor. Also I describe my proud family—my American dream.

I would like to thank Mrs. Ok-Hee Nam, my dear sister and a recognized artist and painter, for an abstract creation of my image for the front cover of the book; Ms. Bethany Wilson, BS and Ms. Crystal M. Rothfuss, BS, for their help in the preparation of the manuscript; and my editor from Authorhouse for the editorial help.

This book is dedicated to our parents, Chey Kee-Bok and Lee Meung-Gwon; my wife, Fan; our children, Bill, Donna, Richard, and Laura; Late Dr. Harry Shay, my mentor and guardian; Dr. Alvin L. Urelese, my longtime friend and mentor; and my late dear friend William Konar. Without them, I would not have realized my American dream.

# Contents

*Part 1*

# My Childhood and Middle School Days

# Mother Waits for Father's Return Home

In 1936, I was six years old. We lived in a small rural town, Pyeongrim, in South Gyeongsang Province, South Korea, about fifty miles away from Busan, which was the provincial capital. Busan is the second-largest city in Korea and is the largest harbor close to Kyushu Island, Japan. The town's population was less than a thousand. Most people's homes were built with walls made of mud mixed with bits of dry straw, small stones, or both. The small rooms had smooth clay floors covered with thick, oil-treated, tan-colored paper, small wooden floors, and each had a small separate kitchen. The roofs were mostly thatched. About 10 percent of the houses were small-scale Western-style buildings, including a small primary school with a playground the size of a soccer field, a township office, a police station with a small jail, a district bank, a small post office, and two general stores, one of which—the smaller one—was managed by a Japanese family.

There was one main dirt road in the town that connected to other neighboring county towns and small cities five to ten miles away. A passenger bus came to the town twice daily, in the early morning and at dusk. The town was surrounded by mountains, hills, and open plains mostly occupied with rice plants. In part, it opened to vast rice paddies that merged into wet fields and swamps. Tall poplar trees stood on both sides of the main dirt road, which eventually passed through the rice plants along the outskirts of the village and reached the main road connecting to neighboring towns. The road extended to a mountain road that was the only transportation route we could see in the distance from our home. Our house was built on a small hillside from which we could look down at the village and the road cutting through the mountain surface until it curved to the other side of the mountain, out of sight.

In a chilly dusk of late autumn, my mother stood on the edge of our front yard, holding our baby sister, Su-Ok, in her arms, and anxiously watched the road, visible on the edge of a distant mountain, that crossed over the town and the rice plants. The road was connected to the main road in the town. We waited for the last bus to appear on the edge of the mountain road. She was waiting for our father to return from Haman, a district capital that was one hour away by bus. Father went to Haman bank headquarters once a month for business. My mother was hoping to see a small shadow of the bus on the dirt road in the distance.

The bus finally appeared on the distant dirt road, raising a blanket of dust behind it. Mother and I then went down to the gate of our house and waited for Father. But Father did not return home that evening. Both Mother and I were disappointed and worried. Mother and I had a quiet dinner with my younger brother, Woo-Gyeung, and younger sister, Sang-Ok. No one spoke at dinner, because everyone in the room was worried and missed Father. After dinner, Mother went out to the front yard again and spent time by herself. When I went out to find her in the yard, her eyes were full of tears.

"What's wrong, Mother?" I asked.

After a deep sigh, she replied, "Your father must have worked so hard that he missed the last bus home."

"Don't worry, Mother," I told her. "He will be all right and will return home tomorrow morning. You wait and see." I then suspected that there were other reasons for her worry. We did not have a telephone at home in those days. Through winding dirt roads in mountains, plains, and small towns, a slow-moving bus usually took more than one hour to arrive in our town from Haman.

The Chey family in 1935. *From left:* Mother, baby sister Sang-Ok, Father, older brother Woo-Jik, younger brother Woo-Gyeung, and the author.

About 2:30 a.m., we were awakened by the noisy barking sounds of our dog, Ellen. Then Ellen made a friendly noise. The entrance door quietly opened, and Father entered the house, avoiding the dog's friendly jumps. We all welcomed Father, who had red cheeks and ears from exposure to cold weather.

Sang-Ok, who was only three years old, ran to Father with both arms raised and her hands open wide, saying, "Daddy, Daddy, we were so worried!"

Father lifted her with his two hands and held her to his chest and smiled. The front parts of his leather shoes were scraped in patches and covered with dust and dirt. He explained that because he had been busy with work at the regional headquarters, he had missed the bus. He said, "I decided to walk to return home tonight; otherwise, your mother would worry very much."

Mother told us that she had heard about bandits on mountain roads and worried about robbery, and that it must have been very cold in that terrain. Only later did I learn the real reason he had missed the bus that day.

During World War II, Korea was liberated from Japanese colonial oppression on August 15, 1945. Until that time, I did not know that at the age of nineteen, our father, then a local high school student, was incarcerated as a political prisoner for one year. He was a student leader who organized a student protest march for Korean independence in his hometown of Gijang, near Busan. On March 1, 1919, Korean people in villages, towns, and cities throughout the entire country rose up and protested on the streets and in parks for independence and freedom. My father was arrested and suffered harsh punishments, including torture. Following his release from prison, the Japanese government did not forgive him, and he had been under relentless surveillance by Japanese police agencies. He had not been permitted to complete his high school education. Without a high school diploma, he could not have a decent job.

I found out later that his monthly visits to Haman headquarters were not to his company's headquarters but to the regional police headquarters, where he underwent hostile and humiliating interrogations by police detectives and inspectors. Some of them were pro-Japanese Korean nationals. The real reason he missed the bus on that day was an extended interrogation by the police officials. Mother told me years later that each time he reported to police headquarters, she feared it might be the last time we would ever be together again with him at home. But even with such fear and stress in our daily lives, neither Father nor Mother hinted at his incarceration and the constant surveillance and interrogations by the police until we were freed on August 15, 1945, a glorious and historical day for all Koreans.

There were fourteen Japanese people living in this small town, including schoolteachers and their families, two policemen, and the owner of a general store and his family. The policemen wore dignified black uniforms and carried shiny sabers at the left sides of their waists. They looked intimidating. One early morning, one of my mother's assistants in the kitchen, a sixteen-year-old girl, did not return on time from an errand she usually accomplished in fifteen minutes or less—a trip to the open market to purchase fresh vegetables. On this day, it took half an hour or longer, and when she returned, she looked frightened. She apologetically explained that on the way to the market, she had come upon a black-uniformed Japanese policeman standing on the bank of a small stream and urinating into it while smoking a cigarette held in his mouth and reading a newspaper. She was petrified and made a detour to reach the market and return home.

This kind of misbehavior was not acceptable in Korean culture. My youngest uncle went to a college in Japan and told me that the Japanese are very courteous and polite in Japan. It was obvious that this man was misbehaving because he was in Korea, a Japanese colony. From time to time, young boys in town stood on the road near the police station and heard screaming coming from the police station. The screaming sounds came from suspects of thievery. There were rumors that the chief policeman tortured the suspects to get confessions. The worst story I heard was one about the policeman attempting to pull nails from the hands of the suspects during interrogations. But the cruel and violent behavior of the policemen may not have represented the majority of Japanese living on the main Japan islands. In civilized Japanese society, even during World War II, I believe—and, in fact, I am sure—these were not acceptable behaviors. Many Koreans in town resented the arrogance of local Japanese who behaved as if they were superior to Koreans.

# Our Home and Family

My father and mother had eight children: five sons and three daughters. My father was the deputy manager in charge of a branch office of a Japanese banking organization, a subsidiary of the colonial government in a small town, Pyeongrim. He was born in Gijang, near Busan, and was a highly intelligent, good-looking, and hardworking manager with ten coworkers. He was certainly the most handsome man in town. Unfortunately, he could not be promoted to the position of manager in the bank headquarters because of his political crime. My mother was a former elementary school teacher with a graduation diploma from Jinmyeong Girls' High School, a well-known school for girls in Seoul. She was an intelligent, beautiful, caring, and devoted wife and mother. However, she was also a stern and strict mother. She was the disciplinarian for us children at home. Father was a responsible provider for the family, and his primary goal in life was for his children to have the best possible education. There was no compromise with his children's education throughout his life. Unfortunately, during the six years of my elementary school education, the family had to move to two different locations in the same province. My father had been under constant surveillance by intelligence officers of the district Japanese police headquarters. This was one way for them to prevent our father from becoming involved in the underground anti-Japanese movement.

The bank provided us with a good-looking Japanese-style house built by Japanese workers, including carpenters. Father built a garden with a small pond in the front yard of the main house. In the pond, it was always nice to see a dozen goldfish swimming between lilies with pinkish white flowers. We had pets also, including one cat, rabbits, one dog—mainly for protection—and several white goats that were housed in a fenced yard. The dog, Ellen, a lovely, seventy pounds heavy female German shepherd had a good-looking little house of her own. She was strong, loyal, friendly and protective of not only our family but also our pets. At home we always had breakfast and dinner together with Father, Mother, and my little brothers and sisters.

My father, brothers, and I used to go fishing in the nearby river or mountain stream when my elder brother Woo-Jik returned home during his Summer vacations. He was a student of Busan Second Commercial High School. The Busan First Commercial High School admitted Japanese Students only.

Using either fishing poles or fishing nets, we enjoyed catching brook trout in a clear water stream in a mountain valley, or carp or other freshwater fish in the river, where we used a small rowing boat. Sometimes we spent all night long catching trout under a floodlight. Sometimes, when we identified a group of several trout in the stream running along the rocky bottom, Father quickly threw the net over the stream and Woo-Jik and I jumped into the stream to catch trout under the net with our hands. We returned home at dawn and were all exhausted, but it was unbelievable fun. These were precious moments for Father and us brothers to be together.

During cold seasons, we enjoyed flying kites on the hill behind our house. Father made beautiful kites, spending most of a night on each one. To make a kite, he started with a dried bamboo stalk, cut longitudinally, and meticulously carved with a sharp knife to make a slender frame for the kite. It took hours to construct a good kite. We were proud and showed them off to our friends, because our father's kites were better looking and flew higher and were more mobile in the sky than any kites sold at local stores. Father used to spend all night making such beautiful kites while we were in bed. In retrospect, I don't know how he could work at the office the next day after so few hours of sleep.

# My First Elementary School

There was one small elementary school that was a one-floor building made mainly of wood. It had windows, and the roof was made of black ceramic plates. The school had a total of about three hundred students. The schoolmaster was Japanese, and there were ten teachers, consisting of four Koreans and six Japanese. These teachers rarely smiled either in the classroom or on the school grounds. In addition to regular classroom work from Monday to Saturday, each student was assigned to one of several sports, including kendo, judo, and field sports, which were carried out on an outdoor area as large as a soccer field.

My elementary school, second-year class, 1937;
the author is four from the right on the second row.

There was no school transportation system, so all the students commuted on foot every day. Many of them walked on small, narrow dirt roads from small rural villages as distant as four miles from the school, even on rainy or cold winter days. None of them had bicycles. After regular school hours, class members cleaned their own classroom, scrubbing the floor with soapy water and cleaning the glass windows. The schoolyard and flower beds in front of individual classroom windows were kept clean. When the assigned work was completed, the class teacher inspected the students' work, including the classroom, flower beds, and schoolyard. Then the students were dismissed.

Late one afternoon, when the school was about to close, I was called to the office of my younger brother's teacher. Here I saw my younger brother, Woo-Gyeong (who was called "James" in his later years), standing scared in front of the teacher's desk. I knew he had done something wrong. My brother was often undisciplined and playful. As the teacher, a Japanese man about thirty years old, saw me entering the room, he got up from his chair and stood in front of both of us with his arms crossed over his chest. He scolded my brother and said, "You took small pears from a wild pear tree in the garden in front of my office." Then he pointed to me to look for them.

Indeed, he did have two small pears in his trouser pocket. My brother's face was flushed. I apologized to the teacher and told him, "This is my own fault, and he shall never do it again, sir." He ignored my plea, and he bent forward toward Woo-Gyeong and slapped his right face loudly. I was embarrassed, humiliated, and angry, but I was helpless. My little brother, only an eight-year-old boy, burst into a loud cry in defiance. On returning home, I could not tell our father about the incident. I was afraid that he might become very angry and protest against the teacher's unacceptable behavior. I wondered what this teacher would have done if the student had been Japanese.

At the school, we were forbidden to speak the Korean language, and then we were forced to change our names to Japanese names around 1940—a humiliating event for all Koreans. I, too, lost my identity as a proud Korean student when I was in the fifth grade. My Korean name, Chae Woo-Yoon was changed to Japanese name, Oyama Hiro-Masa. How could this sad situation happen to Koreans who had done nothing to provoke or hurt the Japanese? It was an unforgettable experience that has caused painful humiliation ever since. My proud father was speechless at home and had to change the name plate on the gate from his original Korean name to a new name—a Japanese name. On the day when the elders in the town changed their names to Japanese, many were angry and humiliated. Some of them visited their ancestors' cemeteries to seek their forgiveness from the ancestors and wept, pounding the ground with their fists.

For sport, I was assigned to exercise kendo, a Japanese martial art that is a Japanese form of fencing with two-handed bamboo swords; it was originally developed as a safe manner of sword training for Japanese samurai. The head, face, body, hands, wrists, and arms were protected by kendo armor. The exercise was closely supervised by a Japanese kendo teacher in the gymnasium as two players attacked each other like ancient Japanese warriors. In kendo, as one attacks by hitting the opposing player with the sword, he must scream very loudly to scare the opposing player and gain a psychological advantage over him. I had to work hard every day with a bamboo sword whenever I had spare time. When I was in the sixth grade, at the all-school tournament, which lasted all day, I was the champion after winning over five opponents, although I was not physically larger or stronger than the opponents. It felt good to show my skills and brave act to the crowd and my parents. My father looked so proud of me. At the end of the day, I was exhausted, with bruised, swollen, and tender elbows and sore wrists. But it was a worthy lesson and experience that I have remembered ever since. It is indeed an unforgettable memory

# My Grandparents

As an adolescent, our grandfather left his home in Gyeong Ju for a job opportunity in a small southeastern city, Gijang in South Gyeong Sang Province. The city was located near a seashore town, Samseong, about one mile Gijang and about 30 miles away from Busan, the capital of the province . He started as an assistant at a small business store where he worked hard with strong work ethic. He earned recognition and praise from the owner. He saved his hard-earned money and started a modest but profitable copper mining business. With that money, he invested in a fishery business with good returns. Before he was 30 years old, he was a rich man. With his very supportive wife, they bought farmland and built a magnificent home with a creek running along the front yard.

Here they raised seven children, four sons and three daughters. My two uncles were elementary school teachers and after graduating from middle school, my aunts became kindergarten teachers. They would later marry and have children. My youngest uncle achieved the highest education and studied in a respected University in Tokyo, Japan. This was available to him due to my grand parents' wealth. During his college days, he became a champion of Japanese martial art, Judo. His skill and hard work resulted in a 4th degree black belt winner in Judo in his senior year. He was honored to become the prestigious university's Judo Team Captain. We were so proud of him.

One of the joys in my childhood was visiting our grandparents' home during summer vacations. It took all day by bus and train to get to their home in Gijang. We enjoyed staying in our warm grandparents' home with my cousins—as many as twelve at one time. We went to the beach every day, which was only one mile away from my grandparents' home. Grandmother and her helpers always prepared delicious lunch boxes for everyone. The beach was clean and was covered with fine, flaky nearly white sand, and the seawater was blue and crystal clear, so the bottom of the sea was readily visible. We ran on the beach, swam, and played volleyball, soccer, and baseball. We caught clams and crabs on the rocky part of the beach.

When we returned home in the dusk, Grandma and helpers would be waiting for us with freshly prepared delicious meals including steamed rice, steamed fresh fish, vegetables, and seaweed or vegetable soup mixed with small chunks of cooked beef or clams, which we all enjoyed so much. The mackerel were kept alive until the fish was prepared for cooking. Then we had a feast of desserts, including fully ripened and sweet yellow melons, watermelons, and rice cakes. Grandfather enjoyed watching his grandchildren eating with ravenous appetites. After a week, we had to sadly say farewell and return home. We all missed the warm grandparents' home that had many rooms in two wings of the house, a beautiful courtyard, a closing gate, and a large yard outside of the gated house. The yard was surrounded by a five-foot-high wall with an open gate to the narrow street on the low bank of a creek that contained clean running water. I have always cherished my warm visits to our grandparents home.

# My Brother Woo-Jik and I

Woo-jik, my old brother, and I were very close, and we both loved each other unconditionally. He graduated from the Second Commercial High School in Busan. This was the best trade school for Koreans in South Gyeongsang Province. The Busan First Commercial High School was reserved for Japanese only. It was no mistake that the "first" schools were mostly meant to be for Japanese and the "second" schools in big cities were for Koreans, although all the students had Japanese names and spoke Japanese. The "first" … schools were better equipped and had better-quality teachers, including athletic teachers. In order to enter the highly competitive school, Woo-Jik had to study in a better elementary school in the Busan area rather than a school system in a small town where we lived.

When summer and winter vacation time approached, I used to count days starting a week before Woo-Jik returned home. On the day of his return, we would wait for the last bus to arrive in the town, and my smiling brother would step out of the bus to hug us and hold hands with us. In the evening, we would talk about his life at the school and any notable events that had taken place in town while he was away. Then we would be in a sad mood for several days before his vacation was over. We sobbed under the blanket at night for days. I would have warm tears as I saw him off at the bus stop. His eyes would be red and filled with tears. I always missed him during those days. Although he wished to advance to a college education, our father could not afford his college tuition and other expenses in Seoul or in a city in Japan.

As Woo-Jik graduated in March 1943, he was drafted as a forced laborer and was sent to Yokosuka, Japan, the largest Imperial Japanese Navy shipyard, near Tokyo. He suffered from physical and mental hardship, just as many American POWs did in those days. I remember those days. When Father wrote a letter to him, encouraging him to work hard, he dropped tears on the letter, which he hoped my brother would recognize. The letter was left with dried traces of smudged words written with an ink pen.

We were so glad to see Woo-Jik back again when Japan surrendered on August 15, 1945. But he was not feeling well. After receiving a surgical operation on his digestive organs by an incompetent Japanese doctor at the shipyard, he had been disabled, although he worked hard to become a top insurance company president in Seoul until his retirement at age seventy-one.

# Good Times with Father

As my brother's vacation began during his commercial middle school days, it was a fun time. We went to the nearby river for swimming and fishing and visited golden yellow melon and watermelon farms to pick fresh, sweet, and delicious melons, and we then climbed up to a small bungalow, looking down the vast melon field. We enjoyed cutting open as many melons as we could eat. Mother told us that Jim, a younger brother, ate so much watermelon that his wet bedsheet appeared mildly pink. One of the joys for the entire family was fishing during weekends, using fishing rods and hooks with earthworms, or throwing fishing nets on the river or mountain stream. It was fun to watch many shining fish with rainbow-colored scales caught in the net during sunset. When we came home exhausted, Mother and her helpers were waiting for the fish to arrive. Then the entire family had a feast in the evening.

Fishing became one of the traditions of our family years later. When we had family gatherings in Rochester, Ontario Lake, the Finger Lakes area of New York, or Lake Michigan, one of the fun things we did was fish.

Fishing Family on Ontario Lake near Rochester, New York (circa late 1990s).
From left; Cameron (grandson), Author, Dale Hoellrich (Cameron's Dad),
Samuel Chey, William (sam and Rusty's Dad), and Rusty Chey

My son, Bill, and my grandsons, Samuel and Russel, now enjoy fishing in Florida as well. The most memorable times are those we spent fishing in Ontario Lake using a modest-size chartered boat. Sam, Rusty, and Cameron were particularly excited when we caught big lake trout or salmon. My son, Bill, caught a salmon in Ontario Lake near Rochester, New York, circa 1990.

Bill caught a large salmon in Ontario Lake

# Flood and My Father

When we lived in our first small town, Pyeongrim, the town was always flooded in early summer—a monsoon season. Many days of storm and torrential rain produced an overflow of muddy water from the tributaries of the Nakdong River, which runs through the southeastern part of Korea. One year, brown floodwater slowly covered rice paddies on the outskirts of the town; and on the next day, the only road that brought buses and other vehicles to the town was submerged under the water; and then the entire part of town across the road was flooded. Within five days, virtually all of the homes in town were submerged under brown water, with only the tops of many houses showing. From our house, which stood on a hill, we could see the town submerged under the floodwater for days until it receded.

Many people living in town fled their homes and stayed on the hill behind our house. They sat and watched the roofs of their houses above water all day long. When their houses crumbled and they could no longer recognize them, they pounded the ground with their fists and cried. My mother and the wives of my father's coworkers were busy all day long without rest for days, preparing food—mainly cooked rice balls, vegetables, and dried fish dishes—and distributing it to hungry people in the worst despair and agony of their lives. They were consoled by my mother, my father, his coworkers, and their wives. After the floodwater receded, it was clear that entire rice farms had been wiped out, many houses had been destroyed, and good parts of the roads had been washed away. Our father told us that the only way one could prevent massive flooding like this from the river was to build a large dam upstream of where the river branched from the Nakdong River. He prepared a proposal and asked for the support of the town superintendent, a kind and gracious Korean gentleman. They and other people in town, with the help of construction engineers, developed a plan to construct a dam with the approval of the manager of headquarter office in Haman, the capital of the county. He spent six months raising enough funds to construct the dam. He told us that this was one way of helping our people. In fact, the Japanese officials couldn't have cared less. Almost fourty years later, his contribution was recognized and appreciated by the people in the area, and he received a hero's welcome when he returned to the town. By then we lived in Seoul, and my little brothers and sisters were unaware of the hardship we had endured in our early years.

# Father's transfer and Death of Ellen, our beloved dog

In the late autumn of 1941, our father received a transfer notice from the bank headquarter in Haman to Inbo, a small town located in a northeastern part of the province. Inbo was about five hours away by bus. My father was not consulted on the timing of this relocation. Preferably, it would have taken place during winter vacation time instead of in the middle of my 6th grade academic year. This was my most crucial preparation time for the difficult entrance examination into middle school, spring of 1942. I was angry and heartbroken to leave our lovely home and friends in Pyeongrim. At the new elementary school, I had to settle into the new school environment, different teachers and classmates. This resulted in my studying for the middle school entrance examination without guidance or help from the teachers who were unfamiliar with my scholastic status. In retrospect, it was another rude decision on father's transfer made by the bank's managers who were mainly Japanese. To me, it was another harassment of my father.

In the early morning, when we were about to leave our home for the new town, it was unusually cold for the season. The ground was covered with a thin layer of snow, the first snowfall of the year. When we were ready to leave, we called out for our well-trained dog Ellen, but she did not respond promptly. Usually, our beloved German Shepherd Ellen rushed to see us with her tail wagging. To our dismay, she was found dead in her doghouse, her furry body still warm. I was shocked and profoundly sad. She had been a part of our family for over five years and was my close companion and loyal friend. She was a lovely little puppy when she joined us and lived in our house until she grew up and went to live in her own doghouse. In Korea, dogs do not live in the main house with their human owners. Ellen was 70 pounds full-grown and unusually territorial. In one late night under moonlight, our fully pregnant white mother goat came out her wooden cage house that was supposedly closed and locked. The hungry goat must have been eating grass on the ground of corral. The corral's gate had also been carelessly left open. Ellen bravely and fiercely fought against two wolves and chased the beasts away to the hill, leaving the goat fatally wounded. The two baby goats were still alive until the next morning but without their mother, they did not survive. We were devastated by Ellen's untimely death. My father and his co-worker buried her on the sunny side of the hill behind our house. I was very sad traveling to our new town, thinking about her.

Ellen used to wait for me at the gate of our house when I returned from the school every late afternoon. She was always glad to see me, jumping over me. Then I quickly left my school bag on our small garden and both of us ran slowly climbing up the hill. Then we sat down on the grass and played by throwing a soft base ball as far as I could. She always ran fast and brought it back to me for a reward. She used to love to eat sweat Korean rice cookies. The beautiful memories of Allen was very difficult to forget. Since then, I had never had another pet dog. I still don't understand this mysterious tragedy.

# The Japanese Imperial Navy Air Service Attacks Pearl Harbor

In the early afternoon of December 8 (December 7 in the US), 1941, the Japanese school superintendent, a tall, skinny man with a deformed jaw who rarely smiled, spoke to the entire student body in the school auditorium. He was excited and unusually cheerful. He told the audience that "our brave Japanese Imperial Naval Air Service pilots successfully bombed Pearl Harbor in the Hawaiian Islands and destroyed virtually the entire American naval base and their warships in Pearl Harbor. Many ships were sunk. Many American soldiers were killed." He then raised both of his arms sky high and screamed "Banzai!" several times, and the entire audience, students and teachers, followed his example. He went on to say that the Imperial Japanese soldiers would soon invade the American mainland and enjoy the victory. He came to our sixth-grade classroom afterward and again praised the brave Japanese Navy Air Service and said, "I am looking forward to going to America someday and enjoying a Western-style life with white women." We were dismissed thereafter, and the school was closed for the rest of the day for celebration. It was difficult for me, a twelve-year-old boy, to understand the reason why the Japanese military airplanes had attacked the American naval base in Pearl Harbor, Hawaii. I had heard that many Japanese and some Koreans had emigrated to the Hawaii Islands in the early part of the twentieth century. There had been no declaration of a war between the Japanese Empire and the United States of America before the Japanese attacked the beautiful Hawaii.

When my father returned home in the late afternoon, I asked my father, "Why did the Japanese Navy Air Service attack Hawaii? The schoolmaster was euphoric".

Father looked at me sternly and then advised me gently, "Son, don't repeat that question again to your friends or other acquaintances." He did not answer my question, but I could sense that he was quite disturbed and was in silent and deep thought.

# Boarding House at Age Thirteen

For my middle school education, I aimed to apply for the best public middle school, which was in Dongnae, now a district of Busan. The school was the best known for Korean students in the entire South Gyeongsang Province. There was a Japanese middle school in Busan, which did not admit students of Korean origin, although the school was known as a better school with better-qualified Japanese teachers. The local primary school in Inbo, where we had recently moved, offered no program or course relating to preparation for the entrance examination, as did many other schools in urban areas. In order to be accepted to Dongnae Middle School, I studied hard day and night in order to pass the entrance examination. On the day of the entrance examination at the middle school campus, I had to face fierce competition from well-prepared and better-educated applicants from primary schools throughout the province, including my cousin, Woo-Myung. He studied at Gijang Primary School, a far better school than mine. Gijang was located about ten miles east from Busan. I did my best at the entrance examination, which lasted all day. The next morning, I looked closely at the list of accepted students' names on the school bulletin board, examining it again and again, but my name was not on the list, although my cousin's name was. I was profoundly disappointed, embarrassed, and humiliated. My father and mother, too, were deeply disappointed, and my father later expressed his guilt for not having provided me with a better primary school education. In fact, as I mentioned before, my education had been compromised when our father was transferred to a new town in the middle of my final school year.

After a long discussion with Mother and Father, Father decided to send me to Dongnae and repeat my sixth-grade education at Dongnae Primary School, one of the best primary schools for Koreans in the province. I was fortunate to find an affordable small room—five feet long by five feet wide, with a low ceiling and one small paper window—in a small house with a thatched roof owned by my mother's older sister, who was about sixty years old and had been a widow since the age of twenty. She followed old Korean tradition, which held that she was to remain a widow for the remainder of her lifetime.

When she went shopping at the market, she always wore a concealing hat made of thin bamboo strips in order to hide her face. To become a widow was supposedly a disgrace.

In the house, there was a small dirt yard. There was no running water or well, and a small open toilet facility covered with a thatched roof stood across a small yard. Father could afford to pay for only this boarding room arrangement every month. There was a main room in the house that was larger than mine, and both my aunt and a twenty-six-year-old distant cousin shared the room. He had become an adopted son of my aunt when he was a child. He had graduated from Dongnae High School and had a job in a local business firm. He was often depressed and sighed because he was not able to secure a higher education in a college. His father had migrated with most of his family to an industrial city—Kobe, in Japan—to get a job in order to support his family. This cousin, however, was separated from his family and was brought up by the widowed aunt and educated at the middle and high school by the same aunt, who earned money by sewing clothes. Every time I saw him depressed and down, I was inspired to study harder, hoping that someday I would have a college education. In those years, many poor Koreans moved to Japan to live in impoverished areas of major cities. I missed my family so much every day but was also grateful to my hardworking father with limited income.

Dongnae primary school was indeed a very good institution with excellent curricula and outstanding teachers who were friendly and communicative. I enjoyed learning and loved academic challenges in the classroom every day. I studied hard until midnight or one o'clock in the morning, and in three months I was selected by the class teacher to become the class leader. I had determined not to fail again. The following year, when I took the entrance examination at Dongnae Middle School, I was far better prepared than the previous year and was accepted by the school. My parents were so delighted and proud of me.

# My Late Sick Brother, Woo-Weon

While I was boarding in the small room, my five-year old brother and my mother came from home to stay with me because my affectionate little brother, Woo-Weon, became very ill and needed an expert medical evaluation and care by a physician who had been educated at a Western medical school system. In the small town where we lived, there was no doctor who had been educated at a Western medical school system. My little brother was pale and weak. He had a marked swelling of his face, including both eyelids; arms; hands; legs; feet; scrotum; and abdomen. He was not able to pass urine well. Mother bought fresh watermelon from the open market for him every day. Watermelon seemed to improve his urination. The doctor told us that he was suffering from a severe kidney disease. His condition became steadily worse. Our hearts were torn apart each time this little brother begged me and Mother, saying, " Brother and mom, please help me; I don't want to die. Don't let me die." After one month of suffering, he was so exhausted he couldn't even cry. One night, he passed away peacefully. He was such an affectionate child whom everybody used to adore. Father, Mother, and I were devastated. Father sobbed and repeatedly said, "This is all my fault to lose such a wonderful child." What he meant was that because he had to live in a small rural town, he had not been able provide Woo-Weon with the proper medical care the little brother deserved.

Father told us he had wished to pursue a medical profession if he could have such an opportunity. He said a profession that helps the sick is noble. I promised my father then that I would study hard and try to enter a medical school. Father's eyes welled with tears, and he squeezed my hands. I had two uncles, one from my mother's side and one from my father's side, who were healers skilled in Asian herbal medicine. Among the five siblings then, he and I were the closest, and I always loved and protected him. The little brother still remains in my heart and I miss him.

# My Middle School Days and World War II

I entered Dongnae Middle School in April of 1943 in what is now in the Busan District. It was the most competitive middle school for Koreans in the province. The students enjoyed some degree of prestige and pride at attending the school. Except for a few teachers of Korean origin, the majority were Japanese. These teachers were rude and unfriendly. Some of them behaved as if they were superior to Korean natives. Many of them lacked the passion for teaching, which I always considered a noble profession. Most of them rarely smiled in the classroom. One art teacher even insulted us on his first day by saying that we were "sons of a lost nation." He made this remark when he saw one of my classmates dozing. He was never forgiven or respected by the entire class.

# Daily Routines and Bullying
# on the School Campus

School started at eight o'clock every morning from Monday to Saturday. As individual students passed through the open gate of the school campus, they had to stop and stand at attention and turn left to bow toward the Shinto shrine in the well-manicured garden. The shrine housed the Japanese god Amaterasu Ohkami. Many Japanese people today still seem to worship this god. As we walked through the campus to enter the classrooms, all students had to stop and salute senior students and teachers as they passed through. It was a spectacle to watch and salute liaison army officers (usually first lieutenants) strolling the school walk. They wore colorful officers' uniforms and carried samurai swords in leather sheaths on the right sides of their waists. One carried a shiny, rattling saber because he was a tank officer in reserve.

At eight o'clock, all the students and teachers assembled in formations on the football-field-sized school grounds. The officers often inspected students at attention and picked on the students with slight deviations of posture or uniform code. I always felt tense as the officer walked through in front of me and looked at me. Some of the students were slapped on their faces when an officer found any irregularity of uniform code or undesirable behavior, such as moving eyes. Then the students and teachers would turn toward the east and gave a deep bow to express respect and appreciation to the emperor of Japan in Tokyo. The superintendent routinely talked about the war, the greatness of the Japanese emperor and imperial Japan, morality, disciplined life, and good behavior. This was followed by ten laps of jogging around the football field in formation while wearing uniforms and leather boots. Those who could not run the entire course were severely reprimanded. They were ordered to scrub and clean the classroom floor or windows, although the rest of students cleaned also the classroom and schoolyard in turn so that teams of students contributed once a week. Then assigned teachers inspected the cleaned rooms and yard. In the classroom, when the teacher entered and stood on the podium, the students stood and bowed toward the teacher. Teachers rarely smiled in the classroom or gymnasium, or on the school grounds, but they insulted students verbally whenever the students slightly misbehaved or strayed from paying attention. Certainly there was no fun in attending the school, but we had to attend for our futures. Every morning as I left the boarding house for the school, I was anxious because I feared the unpleasant events I might have to face because of the teachers at the school. Many classmates had similar fears every morning.

As World War II became intense in the Pacific theatre, the school treated us as student military personnel. We had to wear greenish brown uniforms with rolled gaiters on each leg, short leather boots, caps, and leather bags on our backs even in the hot summer. Students were expected to salute teachers and senior students when we passed them either in or out of school areas. If one failed to do so, he was summoned by a group of ten senior class members in a half-empty classroom at night in which both desks and chairs were moved to the back area of the room. While nine of them sat on one row of chairs, one representative would stand up and call the accused in the room. The representative senior would then mention why the accused had been summoned. Those accused would be physically punished and humiliated, and they would be left with swollen cheeks or faces. Similar punishment was meted out to those the seniors considered to have behaved arrogantly. The accused were not allowed to argue or debate. The only permitted response of the accused to these seniors was apology, whether or not they were right or wrong. These seniors were mostly bullies, and teachers knew about the seniors' unacceptable behaviors as an acceptable part of student life at the campus. Apparently this egregious culture was copied from the Japanese middle school system. This kind of behavior, needless to say, was acceptable then. Why would Korean students, just because they were seniors, justify punishing the juniors and beat up their own Korean brothers? There was no appeal system for the students who were unjustly punished, but this unacceptable and ugly culture faded away slowly as Korea became a free nation.

The curriculum, besides lessons on Japanese and other foreign languages, mathematics, history, and the like, included semiweekly physical education and military training exercises in full uniform. We were taught to use military rifles with bayonets, which many of us hated. The reserve military officer told us so often that the students ought to be ready to fight the enemy if and when the enemy soldiers invaded the country. They physically and verbally harassed students during military exercises.

Among the many classes we had to attend, I hated physical education the most. The teacher never inspired the class or was friendly, and he never smiled. On one hot summer day, the classmates were all standing in formation in the schoolyard. While he was inspecting students row by row, he suddenly stopped in front of me and slapped my face at full force without warning, and my glasses flew into the air. Then he scolded me: "Your lip is red. You are a sissy like a girl." He accused me of painting my lower lip with a red lipstick. My lower lip was very itchy in those days, so under the hot sun I used to frequently scratch the lip with my upper teeth. I tried to explain, but he slapped my face again, saying, "No excuse." The only way to avoid his further abuse was to apologize—but apologize for what? My left cheek was swollen and streaked with the red lines of his finger marks.

I have had an itchy lower lip since my elementary school days. My father took me to several different doctors for consultation without a clear diagnosis or improvement. This agonizing condition continued until I came to the United States. For some time, I forgot I even had such a condition with my lip in the past. It was apparently the result of a sun allergy. I no longer have the issue, because I have not been exposed to sunlight as much as I used to be in Korea. My parents were so pleased when the problem disappeared.

Most of the teachers in our middle school seemed to be not as good in quality as those who taught in the Japanese schools in the same city. The students in Japanese middle school in Busan advanced to high schools on the main islands of Japan at a much higher percentage than the Korean students educated in Korean schools. Entrance examinations were required to enter the reputable high schools. The attitude of the teachers was rather obvious: they were in colonial Korea, and the teachers in Korean middle school were not as good as those in Japanese schools. Even now I still bitterly remember the unjustifiable physical punishment that I, a fourteen-year-old boy, received in physical education class. I wanted to know then, and even now, why I deserved such unacceptable physical abuse from a teacher. In those days, students could not enter the teacher's office and ask the teacher why they had been physically punished.

# Student Laborers and a Japanese Kamikaze Pilot

As the war became fierce in 1945 and the American heavy bombers destroyed major cities on the islands of Japan, they began to bomb Japanese air force facilities in Korea. The heavy bombers dropped bombs on the airfields, usually at night, creating huge excavations on runways.

Starting in April of 1945, we did not have regular class or other educational activities in the classroom or physical education or military training in the schoolyard. Instead the students all worked in a mountain valley about four miles from the school campus, digging out stones and dirt, which were transported to the nearby Japanese military airfield. A railroad was hastily constructed between the valley and the airfield, located near the seashore about two miles from the valley. The students slept in their classrooms daily after their hard work. About this time, the supply of food was significantly limited, so we often had only one steamed rice ball the size of a fist with vegetable soup diluted with fermented bean paste (known as miso soup in Japan). When an empty open cargo train reached the valley, we were forced to fill the cargo train in a hurry, using shovels as quickly as we could. Some students were beaten on their backs by Japanese teachers who were reserve army officers, using dark brown leather sheaths that held long swords inside. The students were from fourteen to seventeen years old, and most of them lost weight and were often dehydrated. The condition of my lower lip grew worse, and every day, I was exhausted and anorexic. We were told that the dirt and rocks were being transported to fill deep and large craters on the runways that were created in the night by US Air Force bombers. The level of the ground in the valley near the railroad gradually became lower day by day until the level of railroad was higher than some students' heads. It required strenuous, hard work to pile dirt and stones with shovels in the cargo train in a timely manner as the ground level became lower and farther from the surface. The runways had to be hurriedly repaired by filling craters with the dirt and stones or rocks that we piled on the cargo train.

One day, some of us were asked to visit the airfield where we sent the dirt and stones. For the first time, we saw it. It so happened that there was a short ceremony that day for a kamikaze pilot in full pilot uniform. He was holding a sword with a leather sheath in his left hand and had a white silk headband with a round red symbol on his forehead—a sign of the rising sun. He was a young man wearing the insignia of a second lieutenant, and he must have been about nineteen or twenty years of age. He saluted the two superior officers—a major and colonel. Then he shared a small cup of sake and then yelled, "Banzai, Emperor!" three times. He climbed into an old airplane with a single engine. The plane took off from the runway with a rattling noise and slowly disappeared in the distant sky. I, for the first time, understood that our laborious work in the mountain valley was being done so kamikaze squads could take off using the repaired runway.

It was late in June 1945, and the weather became humid and hot. We had been doing intensely laborious hard work for three months. I lost more than ten pounds; most of the students lost substantial amounts of weight. One day, while several of us were having lunch under the sun with a Japanese teacher who was respected by students because he was gentle, soft-spoken, and fair to us, he quietly asked us while eating, "Do you think we can win the war?"

We were stunned and looked around to make sure no other Japanese people were nearby. One of us answered, "Of course, sir."

He puffed on a cigarette and quietly said, "Don't say bullshit."

He was an excellent teacher of Japanese language and was a graduate of Tokyo Imperial University, the most prestigious and best university in Japan. Graduates of this high-caliber university were rarely assigned to a colonial middle schools for Korean students. At the moment, we all quietly realized that not all Japanese believed in winning the terrible and cruel war. Apparently he knew more about the status of the war in Pacific theatre than we did. We promised each other to keep this unexpected talk of an honest teacher to ourselves. He must have trusted us because we had worked together as a team since the laborious work started.

# My Father's Unexpected Visit

In the last week of June, my father unexpectedly visited our working site in the mountain valley. The sun was very strong, and our skin had become dark in color. He appeared to be very disturbed by looking at me. I looked at him, too, but I remained silent. He was the only parent to come to see us since the work started. I was afraid of his visit, fearing that the Japanese teachers might be offended. Without saying one word, he nodded and gestured good-bye with his eyes looking wet.

The following afternoon, I was told to see the teacher who was assigned to my class. I was quite anxious, though I didn't think I had done anything wrong. Sitting on a wooden chair with both his feet on the desk in the tent, he looked sternly at me, and I became more anxious and frightened. He asked me, "Why didn't you tell me if you were ill?"

I didn't know how to answer because my father did not tell me anything and, in fact, could not phone me. I told him hurriedly, "We are in the war, sir."

He said, "You should see the school doctor right away. Go." When I saw the Japanese doctor in town the next day, he briefly examined my chest with a stethoscope and handed me a letter to the school superintendent stating that I had early tuberculosis of the lungs, and he advised me to rest at home for three months. I was pleasantly surprised. Did I really have tuberculosis? Of course not.

The next day, I took a morning bus to return home. It usually took about three hours to get to the small city, Yangsan, where my family lived. This was the third place our family had moved to in nine years. The bus drove over winding dirt roads through mountains and hills. On a steep mountain road, the bus could no longer move and climb as it had one year earlier, when the bus's fuel was gasoline. Now all the buses and civilian trucks had to use gas fuel produced by the burning of charcoal in a large, cylindrical metal tank attached to their rears. The Japanese military trucks passed us as if they were privileged, leaving dense dust clouds on the road and in the air. The military trucks were Nissan made. All the passengers had to leave and empty the bus and push from behind to reach the peak of the high mountain road. Down below in the valley, we could see small farmers' homes with thatched roofs and many rice paddies in the distance. We had to repeat the pushing of the bus on several mountain roads. It took five hours or longer to get home. My uniform was drenched with sweat when I arrived. As I returned home, my parents, my little brothers, and my sister were so happy to see me, and I was so glad to see them.

At a later date, my father told me that he was angry and agonized when he saw me in the valley in such poor physical condition. He decided to rescue me from hard labor and the potential danger of fighting against invading American soldiers if the war became more intense and the Japanese military needed more manpower. He decided to negotiate with the school doctor in his private practice office and bribed him with a small bag full of cash. Father was courageous to do this, jeopardizing himself by committing a serious crime. He said, "Son, if I lose you, there is nothing left in my life. I took a chance to test the Japanese doctor, and I won." I asked my father where he had gotten the money in such a short time. After he saw me that day, he immediately went to town and borrowed the money in cash from the local bank, using his home as a collateral. I later learned that after he was incarcerated at age nineteen for the Korean Independence protest on March 1, 1919, my grandparents had learned how to bribe the Japanese prison officials to decrease his imprisonment to one and a half years from three years.

He also told me that the war would end one way or another in the not-too-distant future. He knew more about the situation regarding the war in the Pacific than I did. There were rumors that Okinawa islands were already occupied by American military forces and Tokyo had been totally destroyed and flattened by repeated massive bombings that had resulted in over ten thousand deaths and numerous casualties.

After that, I ate three delicious meals every day that my mother personally prepared, and my stomach was always uncomfortably full. I began to get my strength back, and I gained weight and enjoyed being a part of my family again. Every day, my little brother, my sister, and I went to a nearby stream or river for fishing. In early August, local newspapers published that an atomic bomb carried by a US B-29 bomber had been dropped over Hiroshima on the main island of Japan, and another one a few days later over Nagasaki, on Kyushu. At home, father did not mention the news of atomic bombs or the Okinawa invasion by US military forces. He might have feared such news may irritate local policemen, who were already edgy and frightened.

*Part 2*

# Imperial Japan's Defeat, Free Korea, My Medical Education, North Korean People's Invasion, Escape from The People's Volunteer Army and My Service in Combat as a ROK Army Medical Officer

# Imperial Japan's Defeat and Free Korea

On August 15, 1945, father hurriedly returned home just before noon, perspiring. He turned on the radio in his workroom. While listening to the radio announcement, he sobbed quietly, his fists tight and trembling. We heard, for the first time—like most Japanese people—the voice of Emperor Hirohito of Japan. He announced his unconditional surrender to American military forces and the United States of America. The dreadful war was finally over, and we Koreans were liberated from the oppressive Japanese colonial rule that had lasted thirty-six years. We were ecstatic, and we all regained our original Korean names with pride and joy. Father then told me about his imprisonment at age nineteen for his so-called political crime. On March 1, 1919, he participated as the leader in a student protest march for Korean independence in his hometown, Gijang. On that day, there were uprisings for independence throughout the entirety of Korea, including cities and small villages. Many student leaders, students, and civilian leaders were injured by Japanese police forces and arrested, tortured, and imprisoned. My father was sentenced for one year and a half. In the prison, he was brutally tortured and humiliated not only by Japanese prison guards but also, shamefully, by pro-Japanese Korean guards and detectives.

The prison cells were about six feet square, and six inmates were held in each. There was no running water, and on the cold concrete floor was a hole in the center large enough to dispose of waste, including urine and feces, in front of roommates. Only my father's hands covered his private area. During the night, they were prey to numerous bloodsucking bedbugs that had hidden themselves in the cracks of old, dried wooden pillows and cracked concrete walls. One of their routines in the early dawn was to hit the pillows on the hard floor, which caused the bedbugs to drop to the floor, where the inmates would killed them with their hands before the bedbugs ran into the cracks in the cell walls. The killing of the bugs smeared the floor with blood. Indeed it was a human hell for a nineteen-year-old lad who was brought up in a well-off family.

Soon after the Japanese emperor's announcement on August 15, 1945, large crowds of Korean people flocked out on the streets from everywhere and screamed "Manse, Manse!" (long life), and some of them held in their hands Korean national flags that they had hidden in their homes for many years. The crowds became larger and larger and marched on the main streets, banging gongs and blowing flutes. The Japanese policemen had run away so quickly from the streets and the police stations that they were no longer in sight. The same happened with the pro-Japan Korean collaborators. We could no longer see them anywhere. Many in the crowds marched to Japanese Shinto shrines and destroyed them and burned them to ash. People on the street spoke the Korean language and felt free at last. Indeed this is a day to be remembered forever by the freedom-loving Koreans. I remembered this historical day—August 15, 1945—every year, even after I came to the United States. I celebrated this day every year and shared the Korean history with my colleagues and workers in my offices and research laboratories by offering lunch gatherings. Few of the Americans I spoke with were aware of this history and the significance of the date of August 15, 1945, which changed world history forever.

Unfortunately, however, Korea was divided into two countries along a border at the thirty-eighth parallel near the Imjin River, which runs from east to west in the central zone of the Korean Peninsula. The northern portion of Korea was occupied by Soviet military forces, whereas the southern portion was occupied by the military forces of the United States of America. Then southern Korea was governed by the US Army Military Government in Korea, and northern Korea by the Soviet Civil Administration, until the Republic of Korea was established in South Korea by free election on August 15, 1948, and Mr. Syngman Rhee was elected as the first president. In the North, Mr. Kim Il-sung, a former military officer and a major of the Soviet Union Army, was chosen as the Premier of the Democratic People's Republic of Korea. The dream of having a unified Korea soon faded away in the midst of many ugly and, at times, brutal political upheavals.

Middle school education was resumed in the fall of 1945, and we all returned to the school campus. We were so happy to meet with classmates and friends in the school. We all proudly had our original Korean names, used our own language, and had our own Korean teachers. I moved to the school dormitory from the boarding house. It was a delightful experience with so many friends. I then advanced to the freshman class in high school. Because of curriculum changes made by the Ministry of Education of the US Army Military Government in Korea, students were eligible for the entrance examination for premedical college when they completed their freshman year.

I and those classmates interested in pursuing a medical school education were excited. This meant that both those in the upper class (junior year) and my classmates were eligible for the entrance examination as qualified candidates, though this did not include the Seoul National University College of Medicine, which did not follow the new curriculum. Severance Union Medical college in Seoul, the oldest and most outstanding medical school in Korea, was my choice. For the entrance examination, I worked hard day and night, sleeping only four to five hours at night. Five students from Dongnae High School applied and had entrance examinations in the spring of 1947. I was the only applicant in my class; the remaining four were from the sophomore class. It was one of the happiest days in my life when I received an acceptance letter from the premedical college. I then found out I was the only one who had been accepted from among the five from our high school. Once students entered the premedical college and completed the two years of premedical education, they advanced to four years of medical college to receive a doctor of medicine degree. My father and mother were so happy to hear the news. My father said his longstanding dream had finally become a reality. He congratulated me and said, "I am very proud of you, son. Now we have a real doctor in the Chey family. You have fulfilled my dream." My opportunity for medical education would not have been possible if we were under the colonialism of Japan; nor would it have happened without my father's firm determination to help me with my medical education.

# Father's promotion and his transfer to Dongnae

As the Japanese withdrew from Korea, my father was transferred to the same bank organization in Dongnae, one of the desirable cities to live in South Gyeongsang Province. He was appointed as the general manager of the bank. We were so happy to be together again as a family. Moreover, my high school was in the same city, and I commuted to the school from home every day. It had been a long time for me to be together with my family. My baby sister, Ok-hee, was born there. Dongnae was a suburban city near Busan, and electric streetcars provided traffic convenience between Dongnae and Busan. One mile away from the city, there was hot spring resorts which were connected by the same electric streetcar system. In this town, there were both one of the best elementary schools, good girl's middle and high schools and one of the best boy's middle and high schools in the province.

# Moving to Seoul

As I had to move to Seoul for my medical school education, my Father decided to move to Seoul with our entire family for many good reasons. The most important reason was for better education of his children. Of course, Seoul had—and still has—the best educational system in Korea. It was the dream of parents for their children to be educated in Seoul. Fortunately he was appointed as the general manager of a well-recognized insurance company in Seoul. Our entire family moved again with new hope in free Korea. Of course it was very convenient for me to attend the campus of Severance Union Medical College from home, using either bus or streetcar.

In our first-year class of premedical college in September 1947, we had fifty friendly classmates who came from every province of Korea, including those in the North whose families had migrated to the South in defiance of the brutal and oppressive Soviet regime and better opportunities for the family. Both premedical and medical colleges were in the same campus which were built on the southern hill side of Namsan (South Mountain) about a half century ago by a Presbyterian Christian Missionary. I was one of the three youngest ones in the class. After two years of premedical college education, we all passed the final examinations and advanced to the first-year class of the medical college. Of course, all of us in the class of 1953 were happy and proud to be medical students in one of the two top medical schools in Korea, Severance Union Medical College. We were happy and proud of our comradely relationship with classmates until the day of the North Korean army invasion and occupation of Seoul, an unforgettable nightmare and human tragedy.

# The North Korean People's Army Invades South Korea

Just before dawn on June 25, 1950, our entire family was awakened by sporadic bursts of gunfire and machine gun fire and the noise of rattling metallic chains in distance. These noises came from the main street with streetcar tracks in the northeast part of Seoul, where our family lived. I rushed to the street and found a large crowd already lined up on the sidewalk of both sides of the main street. On the street were several dead bodies of Republic of Korea Army soldiers. The street was completely occupied by Korean People's Army (KPA) infantry soldiers holding Russian-style semiautomatic guns, machine gunners, many tanks, and other military vehicles carrying artillery guns. I saw one dead soldier whose body was run over and over again by tanks. We, for the first time, witnessed and realized that this was a real war between North and South Korea. The entire city was suddenly paralyzed and there was no transportation in the city for several days.

Our family was stranded, and like many people in Seoul, we could not escape the city. There was no transportation system, and one main bridge over the Han River that connected Seoul to its southern suburb and southern Korea was destroyed by explosives in the early dawn by Republic of Korea (ROK) Army engineers to slow down the advancement of North Korean invaders beyond the Han River. Many uninformed civilian drivers and families plunged into the deep river and died. Thus the major transportation route to southern Korea was disrupted. Our family had no choice but to be detained in Seoul. The immediate crisis was the shortage of food supplies. All the markets were empty and closed. People had to push and shove the crowd aside to purchase fresh produce from farmers' markets and rice from street vendors. It was indeed a chaotic scene everywhere in such a short period of time.

I walked to the medical school campus, which took about forty-five minutes. The city transportation system, including buses and streetcars, was completely paralyzed Several days later, when we returned to the medical school campus and the medical college hospital, all the student friends and faculty members of North Korean origin were no longer in sight. Most of them had escaped Seoul and fled to southern cities—mostly Busan, my former hometown. I realized then more than ever before that they were keenly aware of the totalitarian North Korean regime and their unacceptable behaviors. Most of them fled Seoul before dawn, when North Korean soldiers entered Seoul. The medical college hospital was taken over by North Korean soldiers. We could smell a strong stench from these soldiers that we could sense from the distant ends of the hospital's floors and stairs. I was told that they did not bathe or shower for months, nor were their clothes and shirts washed.

In the classroom, the remaining classmates gathered, but our friendly gestures and smiling expressions were no longer present. We became suspicious of each other, as if we were being watched by communist sympathizers among my classmates and it was difficult to discern who they were. I couldn't believe that in only in a few days, the smiles were gone and no one was friendly anymore. It was even more disheartening to realize that we could no longer trust each other. There were no regular class lectures for basic sciences, such as anatomy and biochemistry. Instead we had talks by Communist Party officials on the revolutionary history of North Korea, Russia, and the lives of Kim Il-sung and Stalin. We learned songs from their so-called heroic and victorious revolutions. On the streets, people no longer cared about their appearance, and many men did not shave but had unmanicured mustaches; nor did they exhibit friendly expressions anymore.

One day, as I walked on the sidewalk to return home, I was stopped by a North Korean policeman near a police station, and I was frightened. He looked at me and said, "Comrade, show me your identification card or document." He then checked not only my hands but also my shoulder areas. He said, "Come to the station." I felt quite uncomfortable by this time, but I followed him to sit in front of a desk on the dusty floor. "You have not done hard work in your lifetime, because you don't have hardened calluses on your shoulders and your hands are soft," he said while another policeman was watching me. I explained to him that I was a medical school student and I did not do hard, laborious work. He said, "So you belong to the exploiting and ruling class of American capitalism." I did not respond to his sarcastic remark, and they let me leave. I had feared for a moment that they might detain me in the jail. When I returned home, I discussed the incident with my parents. They, too, feared that I could have been jailed. My parents insisted that I should stop attending the school and stay away from the streets where the policemen patrolled. Young people were slowly disappearing from the busy streets as days went by.

The streetlights in the city gradually disappeared, there was no light on the street any longer, and the surrounding neighborhood became dark at night. Pet dogs in the neighborhood were no longer barking. Dogs were disappearing from the street, and we all suspected North Korean soldiers were stealing people's pets for their meals. At my parents' suggestion, I decided to hide in a small community of Buddhist temples inhabited strictly by female monks in a mountain valley near the eastern suburb of Seoul. This arrangement was made with the help of one of my distant aunts, who was an influential female Buddhist monk. I was embarrassed initially to sleep in the same room with several young female monks. During daytime, the monks (and I myself, wearing the female monks' clothing) were told to participate in daily road repair work to fill potholes created by US Air Force bombing raids. I felt chills when I was watched suspiciously by armed North Korean soldiers on the road. In a week or so, a senior monk came to the room to inform me that she had heard the local communist officials were suspicious of male dissidents hiding in the temple premises. When I peeped down the valley, indeed two soldiers holding automatic rifles were inspecting a temple building. I immediately took off the monks' clothing and escaped the community and hid on the mountain behind the temples until it became dark. Then I returned home on back roads.

While I was hiding at home, one of my close classmates, Lee Yoo-bok came to see me at night and said, "There is a rumor that some students are hiding on the campus of the medical college and hospital. They are waiting for the opportunity to escape together to the southern part of South Korea, behind the battle line, to join the ROK Army and fight against North Korean invaders." It was already the last week of July.

One morning at the campus, we were told to have a general meeting in a small auditorium for those students and remaining junior faculty members who had missed the chance to escape on June 25. A school communist official updated us on the Korean People's Army's victorious advances into southern Korea. Suddenly one of my classmates standing to the right side of me raised his right fist high in the air and loudly claimed, "We can't sit here while our courageous comrades are fighting and sacrificing their lives against bloody Yankees and South Korean poppets." Another schoolmate in the left corner of the room screamed, "Agree! We, too, must join this heroic fight of the People's Army." In a few seconds, the entire crowd roared, "Agree! Agree!" and chanted revolutionary songs and praised Kim Il-sung. I was bewildered, shocked, and disheartened that many of my friends and I could not express our opinions. One self-proclaimed leader in the crowd whom I had never met before raised his voice, stating that we all agreed to join the volunteer army. I then recognized that some of my classmates were Communist Party members or their sympathizers. Also I realized that this meeting had been prearranged and well planned by Communist Party members and their sympathizers. We could no longer trust each other. Such brotherly and friendly relationships were no longer present among us.

Soon we were told to assemble in a platoon formation on the schoolyard, and we left the school campus and marched along the main street out of the college campus. After passing the South Gate of Seoul, we headed to the center of the city, chanting revolutionary songs. I sang along to assure others that I was with them as an enthusiastic comrade. We entered the schoolyard of a local high school campus. There were already several hundred student comrades in military formations, like us, in the schoolyard.

# Detainment in a High School Building

We were assigned to stay in an empty classroom on the second floor of a building. I did not have a chance to say good-bye to my family, particularly my father and mother, who did not know that I was being detained in a school building in the city. Many other classrooms were also occupied by many young people and students from other schools. Then we were indoctrinated by officials wearing civilian communist uniforms to become volunteer soldiers, and we again started listening to Communist Party members' lectures, which included statements like "Great hero, Great leader Kim Il-Sung, sacrifice of heroic patriotic partisans …" This went on and on to brainwash us. In room with me were several classmates, including one of my dear classmate friends, Lee Yoo-bok (who later became a senior vice president of medical affairs at Yonsei University, one of the top universities in Korea). There were also several instructors of basic sciences at the medical schools, and high school teachers whose families would not know what had happened to them or where they were. One of the teachers said, "There is nothing to eat at home, and I have two small children and a wife." He looked sad, sighed, and often had tears in his eyes.

We were able to see the street and sidewalk through the windows. On the morning of our third day of detention (August 3, 1950), I found my parents sitting on the sidewalk just beyond the street near our detention room. It was like a miracle. I was told later that many detainees never had a chance to let their families or loved ones know until they had been kidnapped and taken to North Korea in similar circumstances. We waved and nodded our heads when we saw each other. We were forbidden to talk. While receiving daily indoctrinations from the Communist Party officials, we heard rumors that we were to be sent to the southern front line area to join the Korean People's Army training camp. Many of us thought that this would give us a chance to escape from the Korean People's Army to the Republic of Korea Army line. In retrospect, it was certainly a naive wish. Without proper training, it would be almost impossible to join soldiers of the ROK Army defense line.

It was heartbreaking to see my parents looking up at the windows of the building in which we were detained. So often, we were just looking at each other without words. My eyes were filled with warm tears that kept streaming down on my cheeks. We had already lost the most precious right of human mankind—freedom. Even my father, who was so brave in his youth as to protest against Japanese colonialism and be a patriot for the Korean independence movement, could not argue with the brutal and totalitarian North Korean regime. They should have allowed parents or loved ones to converse and say at least good-bye to each other. Now I was about to lose my parents and the rest of my family. They told me later that they felt so sad when they came to look for me the next day but found that the buildings were empty and their son was no longer in sight. They felt they had lost their precious son after all of their sacrifice and hardship ever since I was born twenty years prior.

# Forced March toward North Korea

In the early dawn of August 8, 1950, we all were awakened and ordered to assemble in a military formation on the schoolyard. The shirts and trousers we had were already more than one week old, and of course we had not been permitted to wash our bodies. One high-ranking partisan official wearing a beaten brownish-green uniform and a round donut cap announced loudly, "Comrades, we are leaving here as you hoped and will advance to the South to join our heroic and courageous People's Army at the southern front."

My anxiety was partially relieved with a hope that some of us could escape from there to join the ROK military forces. As the troop passed the South Gate of Seoul, instead of marching farther south, the front column turned west and marched toward the North. I said to a Korean People' Army sergeant, "Comrade, the partisan leader on the schoolyard mentioned we were to move to the southern front." He looked at me and replied cynically, "You guys are not well-indoctrinated communists. You need more intensive mental and physical training in North Korea to become a real People's Army soldier."

At first, I felt shock run from my head through my entire body, but soon I said to myself, "I am not surprised, and somehow I will survive this nightmare." The entire column of so-called volunteer soldiers, over one thousand of them, passed the West Gate area of Seoul, having realized that we were indeed heading toward North Korea. From then on, my mind struggled while advancing step-by-step on the dusty road that led to North Korea. I was completely preoccupied with the idea of whether I should try to escape at the risk of being shot dead or obey their order to march toward the North. Every step of the way, I dreamed of my affectionate and caring mother and father, who had worked so hard to bring us—particularly me—up as a family. My father had wished his son would be accepted to medical school, and he was so happy and proud of me. He wished to become a physician, but he had never had such an opportunity. Then I thought of my brothers, Woo-Jik, Woo-Gyeung, and Woo-Shik, and my sisters, Sang-Ok and Ok-Hee, who were part of my life, remembering recently fishing in a nearby river before the invasion; it had been so enjoyable. We so often laughed together, cried together, and cared for each other.

The volunteers in my platoon were mostly college students and schoolteachers. Among them, there was one very close classmate and two assistant professors of pharmacology that happened to be brothers. I whispered "Must escape" in English to my friends every time I had a chance, avoiding the platoon leader's attention. They heard and nodded. We continuously loudly chanted communist songs to pretend as if we were patriotic People's Army soldiers. In particular, I made more effort to sing loudly in hopes that the platoon leader would recognize my feigned enthusiasm and passion for communism, Kim Il-sung and the

People's Army. The long marching column of many platoons raised blankets of dust on dirt roads, and people living in houses on the roadside could hear loud tramping sounds day and night.

We were ordered to stop and rest on roadsides for five minutes every hour. As we approached North Korea, I became more and more tense. As we reached a small town called Geumchon, several miles south to the border, our platoon members sat on the roadside near an old woman vendor who was selling golden yellow melons, watermelons, plums, and other fresh fruits. Everybody bought fruits and gorged on them as if they had never seen them before. Their behavior suggested that they wanted to spend all the South Korean money they had in anticipation that we all would soon cross the border, the thirty-eighth parallel, to enter the territory of North Korea. Indeed we were just a few miles south of the parallel. I felt sad and disappointed. I had not spent money until then, although I probably had the largest sum of money in a brown envelope hidden in a special belt that my father had given to me some time prior in case I was caught by the enemy and had an opportunity to escape. The hot sun was right above our heads, and it was very hot at noon without a breeze. I was still constantly struggling in my mind as to whether I should escape or move on to cross the parallel at their mercy. The latter thought brought me again the images of my father, mother, brothers, and sisters, who, I imagined, were very sad at home. At the last roadside stop for five minutes' rest before crossing the parallel and the Imjin River, I bought the largest fully ripe watermelon, which I cut open readily and offered the communist sergeant, the platoon leader, to enjoy.

# Escape at High Noon Near the Thirty-Eighth Parallel

While the sergeant, a sun-tanned dark-skinned soldier, enjoyed the melon immensely, I asked him if I could take off my trousers because it was so hot. He nodded and looked at the trousers in envy. Some time back, before the invasion, my father bought them for me in a local black market in Seoul. The stylish trousers, designed for US Navy officers, were tan and wrinkle-resistant. I hung them on a branch of a pine tree right near the vendor. He looked at them once again while munching a cut watermelon and spitting out melon seeds. I had short pants extending to the knees under the trousers in case I needed to run away at a high speed when such an occasion arose. I gambled that even a hard-core communist noncommissioned officer may still have a desire for materialism and may be corruptible if I offered him the pants when I found them and returned. Less than five minutes after the resting time started, I suddenly stood up in a hurry and told the sergeant, "Comrade! it's the time to depart right away; the time is up." Without finishing another piece of the melon, he stood up promptly and ordered the platoon members to assemble quickly in the same formation. We marched north on dusty dirt roads, chanting again and again revolutionary partisan songs. At the same time, I kept thinking, *Will I ever see my family again? And will I ever have the freedom that I took for granted?* My heart was pounding in my chest, for this was the last time for me to make my life-changing decision to escape and return to my family and my free world, knowing I might be shot in my back. *I cannot possibly be dragged to hell full of evils, as the communists are. I would rather be shot dead before I become another of the victims in their atrocious society. No freedom? Unthinkable and unacceptable in any circumstances.* The sergeant was tramping forward near my right shoulder. Suddenly I looked at him and spoke to him. "Oh, comrade, I forgot to put my pants on." He responded instantly without hesitation or a moment of second thought. "Go right away, comrade, and find them before someone gets them."

I ran back slowly about half a mile as if I were a liaison to a platoon or company at a distant front. I concentrated my mind and focused to accomplish my intention to escape in the midst of tramping noise and advancing volunteers' chants. When I reached the vendor's site, my trousers were still hanging on the pine tree branch. The woman vendor was so glad to see me, and she asked me, "Do you want another watermelon?"

"No ma'am, I came here to get my pants. Thank you." She appeared somewhat disappointed.

My heart continued pounding in the chest. I muttered, "Should I return to my platoon in order to save my life? No, I should not." Some of the officers leading platoons and companies looked at me, but no one stopped and asked what I was doing there. I was amazed. There is a Korean proverb my grandfather used to tell me: "When you are searching for a thief, think of an old wise saying: 'It is dark right below a bright candle light.'" The pine tree was at the foot of the mountain northeast side of a mountain, and the village houses were lined along the roadside across the street and faced southward. I was drenched with sweat and waited for the chance to cross the road to enter one of the houses. The gates of houses were closed, but my first step in the escape was to cross the road. While hiding behind the vendor, I found a distant gap of about one hundred feet between the two marching platoons.

I crossed the road without looking at the advancing troops and pounded the closed wooden gate on the other side repeatedly with my fist, asking with my loud voice for drinking water for my strong thirst. After several attempts, the gate opened with a squeaking sound. Two elders, a couple about seventy years old, came out in traditional Korean summer clothes; the frail old man, who had a long silvery mustache hanging below his chin, was holding a wooden jar full of water in his hands. I gently pushed them inside the gate and closed the gate. I begged, "Grandpa and grandma, I know you have a grandson like me. I am running away from the People's Army. Please help me. Can you hide me?"

The old man's face suddenly became pale, and he dropped the jar holding the precious water on the ground and said, "What am I going to do? We, too, ran away from Seoul and rented this house." Looking inside of the house, I saw there was a small courtyard surrounded by a wall higher than five feet that was made of mud and small stones. I ran swiftly through the yard and jumped over the wall to land on the bank of a canal full of running water that was about over 50 feet wide. After a hard fall of my back on the ground, I oriented myself, and I sensed somebody was near me.

I found a young man near my age sitting near my side against the wall. I was instantly frightened to see him. He appeared even more frightened than I when he looked at me. No young man of my age should have been around at this time, more than one month into the North Korean invasion, in either a rural area or a city, unless he was a partisan or a North Korean government agent. I was prepared to fight to kill him. Suddenly his eyes were open wide and shining, and he said in a quiet voice, "You are a student of Severance Union Medical College. I feared you were coming after me to arrest me."

I asked, "How do you know I am a medical student? And what are you doing here?"

He said, "Your belt buckle shows the emblem of Severance Union Medical College. I trust you, brother." He shook both my hands as tears came to his eyes. The majority of the faculty and students of Severance Union Medical College were Christians, and he must have been quite relieved of his anxiety.

Mr. Park B.G. was a North Korean refugee and a student of Seoungyunkwan University in Seoul. He had been hiding there for more than two days, and he was afraid of crossing the canal because when he tried to climb up the bank across the waterway, he was exposed to the marching soldiers toward the north on the road from which we both escaped. He said thousands of soldiers like us had been marching continuously during day and night. I said to him, "I must move on, because People's Army soldiers will look for me any minute." About one hundred feet away northward, the opposite bank was covered with pumpkin vines, with beautiful yellow flowers scattered over broad dark green leaves. Park reluctantly followed me. We moved in the running water, which reached my neck; crawled under a dense network of leafy pumpkin vines on the opposite bank of the waterway; and crawled slowly and carefully. If we climbed up to the upper edge of the bank, we would expose ourselves and could be readily detected by the marching soldiers. My heart was pounding again, and we both were drenched from head to toe. The sunlight was strong and hot, but the pumpkin leaves gave us a comfortable shade to hide under.

While we were hiding under the broad leaves for a while to figure out our next move, an old farmer in his midsixties walked near the edge of the bank, carrying a wooden barrel on his back that contained old liquid human waste to be used as a natural fertilizer for his crops in the field. I thought this was a good opportunity to ask the old farmer for an accurate direction to run in to move toward the south. I whispered to the man, "Grandfather, (Halabeoji in Korean)" while hiding under the leaves and peeping at him between them.

He stopped walking and turned around to look for someone talking to him, but he couldn't find me. Then he muttered, " Strange, I thought I heard someone whispering at me." When he was just about to move on, I whispered at him in a somewhat louder voice. He found me at this time and gave me a mild smile on his tan face, which bore a thick gray mustache. Some of his front upper teeth were missing, and that made him look cute. He stopped walking further and unloaded his heavy fertilizer barrel onto the ground from his shoulders and back. He opened the cap of the barrel and poured the liquid fertilizer into a wooden jar attached to a wooden handle and gently poured it over his crops, which turned out to be soybean bushes. He apparently realized that we were seeking help from him.

We were still hearing soldiers' chants and their tramping noise in the distance. I asked him quietly, "Which direction is south, sir?" He pointed south with his eyes and he then mounted the barrel on his shoulders and back and moved away. We did not have a chance to thank him. We planned to hide until nighttime. It was about 1:30 p.m. A short while later, the sky was suddenly covered with a thick and dark cloud, and it became virtually black. Soon a severe thunderstorm with heavy blankets of rain battered the entire field. Loud thunder and frequent lightning frightened us, but we took advantage of this sudden weather change. We ran as fast as we could toward the south, passing many farm fields, until we reached the foot of a mountain. We climbed the mountain and found a valley that led to a distant small village.

Down in the valley, about a quarter mile distant, there was a small thatch-roofed house with a tiny open yard. A chimney in the roof emitted white smoke. We were exhausted, thirsty, and hungry. Without one word, we both stood up and walked and crawled down to reach this little house, which had a squeaky wooden floor and two small connected rooms. I called "Hello, excuse me." A small dog began barking at us. An old man in his sixties came out of one of the rooms. I said to him, "Comrade, we are government agents, and we are heading toward the southern front for a special mission." He welcomed us with a mild smile and invited us to one of the two rooms. The room was connected to a small kitchen, and I showed him a small bag containing rice and asked him whether someone could cook for us. I told him, "I will pay for your service. I have plenty of South Korean money." While we were waiting for the meal, we heard a young teenage girl peep at us through a narrowly opened paper door with a wooden frame, and we heard her singing in the next room, which had a small, thin paper window. She started to sing some of the familiar revolution songs we had sung so frequently until I escaped.

The meal was served: warm cooked rice with an incredible aroma, kimchi and cooked dry fish in a bowl of soup mixed with Korean fermented bean paste, and chopped steamed pumpkins, which tasted sweet and delicious. The elder, while smoking finely cut tobacco leaves with a long bamboo pipe, told us, "It is not nice to tell an old man a lie. You two are carrying rice belonging to a People's Army ration."

As we heard him, I noticed that the young girl was no longer singing the marching songs. My friend, Park, asked the old man, "Where is she who was in the other room a moment ago? I cannot hear her singing."

The elder said "she went shopping in the village. You two may rest here and have supper with us."

My friend, Park, gently stood up and said, "I am leaving because I like to get home before nightfall."

I told him, "You can't walk Seoul streets before dark."

"I will leave here alone then," He insisted. I reluctantly agreed to follow him.

As we reached the peak of the mountain, he turned around and looked down into the valley. "See, this is exactly what I was afraid of." We saw two People's Army soldiers with semiautomatic guns on their shoulders following the young girl we had met in the house.

While hiding behind bushes and watching the valley, Park, a refugee who had fled from North Korea several years earlier, told me about his first attempt at crossing the thirty-eighth parallel. Just before his first try, he was so thirsty and tired that he stopped at a nearby house to ask for water in a border town. While drinking water, he was caught by communist sympathizers from their neighborhood communes and was imprisoned for six months. It took another six months for him to escape his hometown and succeed in crossing the border. It was this experience and his instinct that saved both of us from being caught in the valley. We crossed more hills and mountains until we reached the outskirts of a small village about thirty minutes away from Seoul.

Although it was such an unforgettable, comradely friendship, we had to separate for our own individual safety. I decided to enter a village in the western part of Seoul, the Sinchon area, to stay for the night at my distant cousin's home. As I entered the city proper, it was an early dusk. I was limping like a crippled man, using a wooden cane that I had made from a pine tree branch while hiding on the mountain. Healthy young men were rarely seen on the street after the communist occupation.

When I entered the house through the gate, my sister-in-law was stunned to see me limping. She looked at me without a word for a short while and then said quietly, "Dear cousin, what has happened to your leg? What did they do to you?"

The moment I entered the room, I no longer limped. She was pleasantly perplexed. I told her, "I faked being a crippled young man in order to avoid suspicion by police or communist sympathizers."

My cousin went to a southwestern province for official business regarding a private company. After eating her delicious dinner, I went to bed on a soft mattress and slept under a thin blanket. I felt as if I were in heaven. Soon, however, I felt so sad that all the innocent members of my platoon must have crossed Imjin River and the thirty-eighth parallel. I knew they had little chance to escape and return to South Korea. They were students, schoolteachers with families, medical school faculty, and my dear classmates. Particularly, I lost my dearest friend, Lee Yoo-bok, whom I would never see again. We would live in two different worlds: a harsh communist country, North Korea, and free South Korea. I would miss him for a long time. He was brought up by his hardworking widowed mother. His success in becoming a medical student was solely attributable to his mother's iron will and hard work. I was deeply saddened to lose a close friend that I had had ever since we started our premedical education. He was three years older than I was. My other concern was his elderly mother, who depended on her only son.

# Returning Home

The next day, I waited until well into dusk, when nobody could recognize me without streetlights. I walked along back roads to get home. When I heard footsteps or someone's voice, I limped using a cane. I could not reach home until the next day, August 10. In ordinary circumstances, it should have taken about three hours. In order to hide my identity during daytime, I hid in a vacant building halfway to home. At dusk on the next day, I finally returned home. I rang the street gate door, and our housekeeper, Jeung Ja, a seventeen-year-old girl, came out to open it. She seemed almost shocked to see me. She quietly opened the second gate and ran to my parents' room to inform them I was alive and here. My father stood on the main wooden floor and appeared stunned and frozen, not uttering a word. I was standing on the courtyard, right in front of the entrance to the main floor. Mother stepped down hurriedly to the courtyard and looked at me awkwardly as if she were wondering whether I was her real son. "Mother, this is your son Woo-Yoon. I am alive and came back home." She took one step further toward me, hugged me, and touched my face, shoulders, arms, and hands. I saw that her eyes were filled with tears, which were also streaming down her cheeks. "You are alive and real. Welcome home, my son. We thought you were killed on the battlefield. We heard the rumors that so many soldiers died on the battlefield because of heavy bombing by many, many American airplanes." We all—Father; Mother; my two younger brothers, Woo-Gyeong and Woo-Shik; and my two sisters, Sang-Ok and Ok-Hee—sat by the dining table and had dinner quietly so that the neighbors could not hear my voice.

My father told me that on the morning of August 8, when he and mother went to the usual site of the sidewalk near the high school building where we were detained, they found the buildings empty and quiet. They felt sad, disappointed, and empty in their hearts. Then they saw an arrow marked with white chalk pointing toward the south on the wall below the window of the room where I stayed. They heard from the people on the street that all of the volunteer soldiers had left the campus in early dawn and headed south. After the enjoyable dinner, I told everybody that I must hide somewhere in the house premises. This would be better than going elsewhere to hide. By this time, I was frightened, and everybody in the neighborhood was suspicious of each other and hid from communist sympathizers, even my trusted and close neighbors.

The most secure place I could think of to hide was a foxhole to be made under the main floor of the house, where even a cat or rat could not get in. In order to get to the ground surface below the main floor, which was made of thick and firm wood, I had to break a small part of the low concrete wall below the narrow wooden floor, which extended throughout the entire back of the main house. The wall was made of concrete and carved stones that were one to one and a half feet square, with a thickness of about one foot or less. In the wall near my parents' bedroom, there was one stone block that was slightly loose and could be moved very slightly. Using a small shovel and iron bar, I was able to move the stone, open the hole, and then push the stone back into the wall to hide the hole. Through this small hole, I barely managed to slide my body to enter the dark space, where I could barely manage to move my body, which at the time weighed only 125 pounds. I constructed a foxhole measuring three feet deep by six feet wide and one and a half feet deep. Then I placed a thin blanket over the hole. The entire back of the house was protected by a five- to six-foot-high wall made of concrete and stone, leaving only a narrow walkway for one person. Across the wall, there was another house similar to ours.

This foxhole became my security nest until courageous United Nations armed forces—mainly US Marines, US Navy, ROK Army, and ROK Marines—landed at Inchon harbor and eventually occupied Seoul on September 29, 1950. Until that time, I listened to, at the lowest possible volume, a small portable radio I held close to my ear, which was the only friend that kept me sane and gave me hope every day. I frequently monitored the news from the UN Allied Forces Headquarters in Tokyo, and North Korean propaganda through the local radio station. Although the enemy broadcast repeatedly that their so-said victorious People's Army was about to push the bloody-handed Yankees and South Korean puppet army to the sea, the gallant UN forces and South Korean military forces successfully held the enemy within the Busan perimeter. The post was tenaciously defended and held by the brave fighters of both the ROK Army and the UN Forces to save the Republic of Korea.

# Life in a Hidden Foxhole and Nightly Raids of Terror

I came out of the hidden shelter that I called a foxhole once daily, through the small hole in the concrete wall, in the early evenings, to have a quick and quiet meal with my parents and any other available family members. Once in a while, I took a short nap on my mother's comfortable mattress. During those precious rest periods, my mother went to a room in the south wing of the house near the middle gate with my little baby sister Ok-Hee in her arms. I still remember my adorable baby sister Ok-Hee looking at me and smiling. When I retreated to the foxhole, Mother and Ok-Hee returned to their bedroom. In this manner, Mother listened to the sounds coming from the street and sidewalk, and she looked through a small hole made in the paper window to watch outside the gate and guard me.

Around midnight every day, the outside gate was knocked upon and then banged upon loudly by North Korean secret policemen, usually two of them, and the squeaky sound from the middle gate frightened everybody inside the house. Our housekeeper went out as usual and opened the middle gate. The policemen quickly walked into the courtyard and yelled, "Comrades, we are here for inspection." Soon I could hear the noise of their tramping boots on the floor right above my head. My heart trembled. Once in a while, I could hear nasty remarks made by these bastards: "I smell the air of the ruling class, like you people. Are you hiding any young men or antirevolutionaries in this house?" They checked every part of the house, including the attic, storage spaces, bathroom, and garage for any hidden spaces. Until they left the house, I would be sweaty, my heart was racing. One man once entered my sister Sang-Ok's room and checked all the picture albums page by page, questioning my beautiful sister about all the family members, particularly her brothers and cousins. He was apparently enjoying conversing with her, an attractive young lady with charm. He asked, "Why are your adult brothers not at home?"

She told them, "They are serving in the People's Army, but we haven't heard from them yet."

My anxiety level climbed higher and higher as this night of horror passed by.

Two days after I returned home, while hiding in the foxhole, we had an unexpected visitor—the mother of my closest classmate friend, Lee Yoo-Bok. My mother met her in our courtyard without inviting her inside of the house. I was listening closely to their conversation from my foxhole. Mother was quite cautious about what Mrs. Lee told her. She said, "My son, Yoo-bok, is back home today from the People's Army. Is your son Woo-yoon back too?" My mother answered, "We were told that our son is fighting on the southern front."

Mrs. Lee said, "My son is back home today. When his platoon was about to cross the Imjin River, they were suddenly attacked by several Australian jet fighters' machine guns, and the troop was dispersed into the plains."

Apparently most of the platoon members escaped without crossing the river, including my friend Yoo-bok. I was quite relieved. Mother could not trust even Mrs. Lee, the mother of my closest friend. Mrs. Lee sounded quite sad that I had not returned home. I was thrilled, though, to hear this incredible news. Yoo-bok was alive and back home.

In these days of despair, the only thread of hope and comfort came from the radio news from Tokyo's General MacArthur Headquarters. I heard on the morning of September 15 that US Marines had landed in an Inchon-area bay. Days earlier, I thought I had heard artillery sounds in the distance from the western part of a Seoul suburb near Inchon. During the following week, the artillery attacks became more intense in the southern part of Seoul and the Namsan area, where our medical school campus and Severance Hospital (the college's major teaching hospital) were located. Also, UN air force jet fighter attacks over the area became fierce and readily audible even in my foxhole. The nightly surveillance on our house became more intense and aggressive.

# One Unexpected Frightening Night Raid

O ne night, two friendly uniformed officers inspected the house at 10 p.m., an unusually early inspection, and left without much conversation with my family. Since it appeared that their routine inspection was done for the night, I decided to sneak out of the foxhole and the narrow concrete wall opening and lie down on the mother's soft and comfortable mattress in my parents' bedroom, the closest room to my foxhole below. Mother, with baby Ok-hee, moved to the room in the south wing of the house. I had never felt so comfortable and relaxed, and I fell asleep. It was one o'clock the next morning when suddenly I was awakened in a hurry by my mother, who was holding my baby sister in her arms. I told Mother, "Don't worry, Mother. They were here already tonight. They don't come twice on the same night."

Father whispered, "Someone jumped down from the roof of the south wing of the house." They had not come through the gate this time. The moment I heard him, I jumped out of the bed instantly, and mother and Ok-Hee lay on the same bed. One secret policeman with light sneakers on was already standing in the courtyard with a bright floodlight illuminating the main floor and the paper door of the bedroom, where father stood with his arms stretched to both sides to block the intruder.

The policeman said to father, "Comrade, what the hell do you think you are doing?" and he pushed father aside and stepped into the bedroom and screamed, "Where is he? Whom are you hiding?"

Father was bewildered and stiff, and he remained speechless. But mother and Ok-Hee were already in bed, pretending to be asleep as usual, and the empty bed was Father's. He answered, "There is nobody in this room."

The man checked the attic immediately using the flashlight and quickly ran through the small paper door in the back of the room and moved to the narrow wooden floor in the back of the house. About that time, my head, body, and legs were already below the main floor behind the concrete wall, except for my right hand and wrist. I was pulling the edge of the loose stone block in order to close the entrance to my foxhole. The bright floodlight was flashing throughout the back of the house and across the entire length of the narrow floor and below the floor. I stopped pulling the stone, and my hand on the edge of the stone was exposed to the bright light. When the light passed over my hand and the moving stone, my hand appeared red, as if my hand were a red-hot iron bar. I remained in this awkward position without motion until the man left the area. Miraculously, he overlooked my hand. Apparently the man did not think the suspect could escape fast enough to disappear from his sight. He and his companion searched inside the house again and again. This is indeed a horror I will never forget.

Then the high-ranking man told my father, "Comrade, we need to ask you more questions. At ten o'clock this morning, we want you to report to the nearby local police station." He gave him a slip of paper—a sort of summons. My father told me that when he was pushed aside by the man with floodlight, he thought that was it; he assumed he was about to lose his son. He acted like a catatonic man, standing in front of the bedroom door like a zombie, and spread his both arms to both sides in order to delay the man's entry into the bedroom. To enter the courtyard without going through the two gates of the house, they climbed the front wall and jumped up to the roof of the front wing of the house. With the sneakers on their feet, they could jump down without obvious noise.

As the intruders left the house, the immediate concern was how to protect Father from having to report to the police station at ten o'clock. I recalled a lecture given by a professor of pharmacology at the medical school about the severe side effects of an antimalarial drug called quinine sulfate. An excessive dose of quinine can cause chills, fever, nausea, vomiting, abdominal pain, and sometimes jaundice. I remembered that my father kept various medicine bottles in the medicine cabinet. Miraculously, an old bottle with a quinine label was in there. He took four tablets with water in the early morning. About nine o'clock, he started to experience chills, followed by fever, sweating, nausea, and vomiting. He looked severely ill. My mother was so worried and said, "Here we send you to medical school to become a doctor. Instead you are killing your father." I could not seek medical help under the circumstances. He covered himself with a thick blanket, although the weather was quite warm.

About eleven o'clock, two armed policemen walked into the house and asked, "Where is comrade Chey? He didn't show up at the station."

Mother responded, "He is very ill, with shaking and chills. I think he caught a bad infection. Come and take a look." The two peeked into the room through the narrow opening of the paper window, and one fellow said, let's leave here quick!"

Father recovered from the side effects over the following few days.

During the same round of late-night raids, several innocent men were caught in our neighborhood and were jailed. At a later date, they were found shot to death as the enemy cowardly escaped from Seoul.

# Cruelty and Atrocity

The enemy soldiers and partisans ran away from the Seoul area through roads off the busy or main streets during the last week of September. Some of them even ran without their weapons. Often they hid under the roofs of roadside houses to avoid low-flying UN jet fighter planes. The people found out the police station's jail was packed with dead bodies. Many of the corpses were in standing positions. The people living in the vicinity had heard machine gun fire from the station throughout the night. I felt chills. Had my father been arrested and jailed during the raids the night before, he could have been one of those many unfortunate victims. Behind a large rock on the top of the hill that we used to see when we left home every day for the schools, several dead men were found abandoned. All of them had been executed. One of them, a radio station announcer, had been shot in his forehead, and his mouth was tightly closed, his lips having been sewn shut with copper wire. The executioner probably performed this horrible crime as revenge for the man's pro-government commentary through the radio. So many hundreds of men, their hands and arms tied behind their backs, were dragged to march north through Mihari Height, a road near the northeastern border of Seoul in the district where we lived. Many family members of the victims stood on the roadside and watched as their loved ones were helplessly dragged away from their hometown. The atrocities committed by the North Korean enemy agents were prevalent throughout Seoul and its vicinity before they were chased away by the United Nations military forces and ROK Army soldiers and Marines.

# The Ugliness and Brutality of Civil War

Our medical school buildings, hospital, and official residential housings for faculty were destroyed by heavy UN artillery attacks and air force bombings on the Namsan (South Mountain) area. Several faculty members and their family members were the victims of the bombings. Many students and faculty members returned from Busan, where they had stayed as refugees. They were mostly those who had fled North Korea previously, when Korea was divided by the thirty-eighth parallel in the late 1940s. I was disheartened to witness that those faculty members and students, including many of my classmates, who had fled to the South did not appear sympathetic toward those like me who were detained in Seoul. Of course, those who migrated to South Korea from the North after Korean independence in the summer of 1945 knew much more about the cruelty and atrocity of the inhumane North Korean regime, which southerners like us had not experienced.

The majority of students who returned turned out to be the members of so-called Western Youth Organization (Seocheungdan), which was a recognized radical anti-North Korean organization and was thus a staunch left-wing anticommunism group that exercised violent behaviors toward right-wing conservative youth groups and students. On the medical school campus, this left-wing student group set up interrogation rooms in their offices. They began to interrogate their schoolmates, and even their teachers. They asked about political beliefs and view, and in many cases they used sticks or baseball bats to elicit responses. Even some of the faculty members who taught us were verbally insulted and beaten physically. Only four months prior, they were all friendly classmates and teachers. Although some of us were not interrogated, including me, most of us were totally dismayed. I was also very disappointed in my left-wing classmates and faculty members who fled from North Korea before the war. This was one of the ugly and cruel behaviors committed by both extreme right-wing and left-wing political groups during, and even before, the war in Korea.

# Medical School Education Resumes in Seoul

In October 1950, the unprecedented Combined Medical School Education Program was established on the campus of Seoul National University's College of Medicine, which had suffered no significant structural damage by US and Allied air force or artillery attacks from Inchon harbor. Eligible students were from four medical schools in the Seoul area, including the host institution, Severance Union Medical College, Seoul Women's Medical College, and Ihwa University Women's Medical College. The lectures were given for the first time by a pool of professors from the four schools, although the majority were Seoul University professors. It was a new experience with a coed system. Unfortunately, however, this combined medical education in Seoul was short-lived because of the unexpected insurgence of Chinese People's Volunteer Army soldiers into North Korea. In less than two months, the school had to be closed and we all had to retreat to the Busan area, at the southern end of the Korean Peninsula.

# Chinese Communist Army Insurgence and Our Escape from Seoul to Busan

On September 27, 1950, the Republic of Korea Army and UN forces, mainly brave US Marines, chased North Korean soldiers away from South Korea and freed Seoul. They advanced to North Korea and reached a part of the Yalu River, the border between North Korea and China, in the later part of October. The Chinese People's Volunteer Army decided to cross the river to invade North Korea, and they advanced toward Seoul in the later part of November. All the people in Seoul were anxious to leave their homes for freedom and safety in the South. On December 15, my elder cousin Woo-Jeon, my most respected and closest cousin among many, walked into our house without advance notice, wearing a thick winter coat and hat. He was a midlevel executive of South Korea's railroad system who worked and resided in Busan. My father and the rest of us were pleasantly surprised to see him for the first time in a long while. Father said, "Why are you coming to visit with us so suddenly?"

Woo-Jeon said, "Uncle, we were told by government officials that the Chinese Communist army is advancing toward the south and may enter Seoul's perimeter in the next several days. I wanted to make sure you and the entire family in Seoul were able to return to Busan by cargo train. We don't have much time, sir, and we must leave today to have space in the cargo train that I arranged. Otherwise, we may have to stay on the roadside of the railroad in this very chilly weather and wait for the next one, not knowing when it will be available."

We could not have second thoughts for a moment. We each packed a trunk and walked about ten miles to pass a temporary Han River bridge and reach the vicinity of Suwon, a southern city on the outskirts of Seoul. Cousin Woo-Jeon carried little Ok-Hee on his back. Woo-Jeon was tall, muscular, and strong. He was the most responsible and respected among our twenty cousins. He had a fourth-degree black belt in judo.

It turned out that these cargo trains were used to transport the military equipment and supplies of UN forces and South Korean military forces from Busan harbor to the battlefield, where they could be used to halt Chinese People's Volunteer Army advancement. On returning to Busan, they carried refugees from the Seoul area. There was no assigned train station or schedules for arrival or departure. Passenger trains were no longer available. There were at least ten cargo trains on the track. All the refugees climbed to enter each cargo train without step ladders. Everybody struggled to enter, particularly elders, women, and children. My cousin helped our family first and then others to board the train. The inside was completely packed. It was freezing cold, but those who could not enter climbed up onto the roof. It was so cold that some men's mustaches and whiskers were frozen with icicles. As the train moved on, many wiggled and adjusted themselves to sit in available spaces. Little Ok-Hee was in the arms of Mother and Father throughout this hard trip.

Within a few hours after departure, people began screaming on the other side of the train car we were in. We saw that many women were hysterically scratching their hair. Somebody yelled, "Many lice are crawling on my head and neck!"

With the noise of squeaky wheels, the train stopped. The place was in the vicinity of Daejeon, a city in the central part of South Korea that is the regional commercial and transportation center. The heavy door was opened, and people jumped out of the cargo train. Soon a US Army ambulance arrived, and American soldiers sprayed white powder (later found to be DDT) in people's hair and inside of their clothes. A moment later, there was a rumor that several North Korean refugees had merged into the crowd and entered the cargo train together with South Koreans. They certainly benefited from the DDT spray, and people no longer complained of itching. The train stopped and started to depart many times, with bumps and noises. It took two and a half days to arrive at the Busan train station, although the trip normally took less than six hours by an express train. My cousin, being a railroad system official, arrived in Busan one and a half days earlier by official train. He was waiting for us with a smile. He took us in a taxi to our temporary residence in the western part of Busan. Father, Mother, Ok-Hee, Sang-Ok, Woo-Shik, I, and a female housekeeper had to accommodate ourselves in a single room that was about eight feet by twelve feet with a ceiling height of six feet. We had an open kitchen. Many felt we were lucky to have a room of this size in this highly crowded city with so many refugees.

Seoul was recaptured by Chinese Communist forces on January 4, 1951. Unlike the first occupation by the North Korean army on June 25, 1950, virtually everybody in the Seoul area left for southern Korea this time. One newspaper reported that even stray cats couldn't be found in Seoul, meaning that even small animals had fled. The Chinese army's advancement was, however, slowed by gallant UN forces headed by the US Eighth Army and the ROK Army. The enemy could no longer advance beyond the northern third of South Korea. Although our family originated from the Busan area, now, within three years after we moved to Seoul, we became refugees, and our lives were compromised like the lives of other refugees. Father was employed as an executive of a local industry company, and I had a part-time job as an English translator for textbooks in an ROK Army engineering school in Dongnae. As my family settled, my brother, Woo-Gyeung, was drafted into the ROK Army and served on the front lines of the battlefield. It was painful to see him off as the train carried him away in an army uniform after combat training in a military camp.

# Wartime Medical Education Resumes in Busan

My primary goal was to resume medical education as soon as possible, although we were in very difficult circumstances as refugees. I thought of the combined medical education I'd had at the Seoul National University campus in Seoul the previous October. I visited the dean of Seoul National University's School of Medicine, Lee Chae-Koo, professor of pathology, in his small temporary office and volunteered to search for a vacant school building in the city. Because so many families had been dispersed because of the war even in Busan, some school buildings were vacant. I met with my maternal uncle, who was the city education commissioner, and asked for help to obtain a vacant high school building where we could have lecture rooms for medical students. Professor Lee was very pleased, and he expressed his great enthusiasm to organize the education program. Thus a wartime combined medical school was reestablished in Busan. Professor Lee became my most respected teacher, role model, and mentor. The professors of Seoul National University (Seoul University) and their families were located one by one, and one big classroom was emptied in order to accommodate temporary housing for professors' families who had endured difficult and inconvenient living conditions. We several students who initially started attending were deeply touched by the professors' dedication, personal sacrifices, and efforts for our education in such difficult circumstances. Professor Lee and his family shared the same difficult times as his colleagues and their families .

Students from several medical schools attended our third-year medical school class, including Seoul University, Severance Union Medical College, Seoul Women's Medical college, Iwha University Medical college, Gyeongbook National University, and Jeonnam National University. Without these dedicated professors, mostly from Seoul University, we couldn't possibly continue the medical education. I was honored to serve as the class liaison person in helping and coordinating the class members and the school administration. We had clinical education at ROK Army General Hospital, Gospel Hospital, and clinical faculties' private clinics. In addition, I elected to attend the US Army Evacuation Hospital, which was like a general army hospital. Only a few of us had permission to enter the hospital and interact with young American army medical doctors and nurses. They were friendly, and we followed the team on rounds in medical wards. I attended and enjoyed their weekly clinical pathological conference, which was not in our curriculum. There was so much to learn. I wished for better command of hearing and conversation skills in English so that I could interact with them to learn more effectively.

My most memorable and valuable learning experience was when I rotated through Busan Gospel Hospital. The outpatient clinic, operating rooms, and inpatient facilities were made of tents. This was where I received the personal tutelage of professor of medicine Dr. Chun Jong-Hee and professor of surgery Dr. Chang Gil-Ryeo. Both were superb clinician teachers who were totally dedicated to their professions. Professor Chang, a graduate of the former Seoul Medical College, was a refugee from North Korea and a former professor at Kim Il Sung University Medical College in Pyongyang, the capital of North Korea. He fled to South Korea when UN Forces retreated from Pyongyang. This skillful surgeon did not use blood transfusions for patients who needed major surgical operations, such as subtotal gastrectomies, with uneventful good outcomes. I often shared this experience with American surgeons in the United States.

My time at this temporary medical school elapsed quickly, and the entire class graduated with doctor of medicine degree (M.D.) on March 23, 1953.

It was very sad to find about one third of my classmates of Severance Union Medical College were missing because of the war. Moreover, before we moved to our senior year, the Severance Medical College Administration decided to move back to the original medical school campus in Seoul from Busan to resume it's own medical school education including both didactic lectures and clinical work at the medical college hospital. This move by the Severance Administration devastated me, because I could not think of leaving my family again while the enemy, both North Koreans and Chinese soldiers were still aggressively engaged in active combats in the north, only about 100 miles from Seoul, against the defending forces of the United Nations and South Korea. In fact, the South Korean Government forbad such a move for all the medical schools to return to Seoul. My sincere request to the Severance Administration on behalf of my several classmates who wished to remain in Busan as Severance students was denied. I was deeply disheartened to be separated from my dear Severance classmates and lose my identity as a proud Severance student. Nevertheless, it was unthinkable to be separated again. I was reluctantly transferred to Seoul University College of Medicine. Very fortunately, I was told recently by my dear friend and former classmate, Choi Byung-Ho, M.D., that most of our classmate had graduated the Severance in subsequent years. Dr. Choi was a former professor of pathology, an outstanding teacher and researcher at University of Rochester Medical Center.

Immediately after the commencement, we were commissioned to become ROK Army medical officers with the rank of first lieutenant. In one week, we were admitted to the army training camp for two months of intense and harsh military training. Although I was advised by Professor Lee, the dean of the medical school, to stay as an assistant member of Pathology at Seoul University College of Medicine as a civilian, I respectfully declined the offer because the majority of my classmates were drafted and assigned as medical officers serving and fighting in combat on the frontline. I, too, wanted to contribute my service in the combat area and fight against the enemy advancement.

# ROK Army Medical Officer in Combat

After a two-month period of intense training to become a real soldier in the training camp of the ROK Army Medical Corp, I reported to the ROK Army Headquarters in Daegu, North Gyeongsang Province, in early June 1953. In an army officer's uniform with first lieutenant badges on the collars and a hat bearing a lieutenant's badge, I looked like a proud army officer. I was assigned as the Third Battalion surgeon, Third Regiment, Seventh Infantry Division, positioned on the northeastern Front. An army ambulance driven by a corporal carried me along highways, villages, and rugged mountain roads, taking more than eight hours to reach the Seventh Infantry Division Headquarters. While passing through the rural areas, I noticed that the farming workers in the fields were young and middle aged women, intermixed with male elders. Certainly the landscape of farm workers had changed. It appeared that virtually all young male farmers had been drafted into ROK military service, previously kidnapped and brought to North Korea, or killed by the North Korean regime. As we passed through the outskirts of Chuncheon, the capital of Gangwon Province, which was the regional cultural and commercial center, I noticed that the city had been completely replaced by US Army barracks, tents, and airstrips after having been mostly destroyed by the North Korean invasion in 1950. Decades later, the city had not only recovered but had also become an enviable modern and beautiful city.

A modern, beautiful, Chuncheon—Korea, 2020
(courtesy of Professor H. J. Park in Chuncheon).

The monotony of travelling in the car on a long, winding mountain road was relieved by listening to and enjoying popular Korean songs broadcast by Seoul Central Radio Station. My favorite song was "Moonlit Night of Silla," sung by one of the most popular male singers of the time, Hyeon-In. As we approached the combat zone, we began to hear occasional enemy artillery shells exploding on distant ridges that had black smoke rising from them. We could no longer hear songs or music through the radio. I realized then that this was it; I was in the combat zone.

I put on my metal helmet and bulletproof jacket. The headquarters of the ROK Seventh Infantry Division was positioned in the northeastern mountainous region north of Yanggu, near the northeastern area of the DMZ. We arrived in the division's medical company about noon. The commanding officer of the medical company was Lt. Colonel Kim, a former practicing physician who appeared to be in his midfifties. In his tent office, I saluted and reported my arrival. He responded to my salute and said, "I have been waiting for you." I was thirsty, tired and hungry. I needed a short period of rest and some water or tea.

Soon he and I were in a small jeep driven by a corporal. While driving on a narrow and winding dirt road, we heard artillery explosions and saw smoke in the nearby hills and ridges. I was in combat fatigues with a bulletproof jacket and iron helmet. I then realized I was in a real combat zone. The jeep stopped about thirty minutes after we left division headquarters. Colonel Kim said, "Lieutenant, your battalion's aid station and bunkers are over there," pointing his right index finger toward a small hill on the right side of the road. He did not mention what to expect, but one thing was certain: I was walking right into fierce combat on the front where our battalion soldiers and so-called People's Volunteer Army soldiers were fighting. I arrived at the aid station, which was about fifty yards away from the road. There were a dozen wounded soldiers lying on cots and the ground.

My most seriously ill soldier was a twenty-year-old private who was in shock and had a half-inch-long open wound in the left side of his chest. The young man, in agony, said, "sir, I can't breathe; help me." He was gasping for air. He was indeed in agony; he looked pale, and his lips were dry and blue. I suspected pneumothorax resulting from a chest-wall wound that must have collapsed a part of the lungs. I started intravenous infusion of fluids while Lt. Park called for an ambulance to evacuate him to either the division medical company or a nearby MASH. I was the new battalion surgeon in charge of the battalion's medical aid station; I had one liaison officer, Second Lieutenant Park, and twelve medical aides with ranks ranging from private to sergeant. Wounded soldiers were brought mostly on stretchers by medics who had been on the front. In the one hour after my arrival, there were two dozen casualties lying or sitting on the ground in front of the first aid bunker before they were transported to either a regimental medical collecting station or division medical company. The casualties were young soldiers with gunshot wounds, fractures, and wounds to their arms or legs caused by shrapnel. On the front, the ROK Army infantry division and the People's Volunteer Army had been engaged in fierce combat for days, especially the two days after my arrival. Both camps wanted to gain more ground before the peace negotiation in Panmunjom was finalized between the ROK Army; UN forces, including the US Army; and the communist forces, including the Korean People's Army and Chinese People's Liberation Army.

I was told by the wounded soldiers that their battalion advanced to reach the top of the strategically important high mountain called Palgong-oh-koji (805 feet in height). After the fierce fights with the enemy soldiers, who were mostly Chinese, including hand-to-hand fighting for days, they found many wide and deep trenches filled with badly wounded and dead soldiers from both sides. Unfortunately, the Chinese soldiers flooded into the trenches and fought back to reoccupy the lost ground. Both sides suffered heavy casualties, and the fight became a stalemate for days. Many of our soldiers were wounded and slaughtered. Even a battalion commanding officer was killed, and the entire battalion (about 750 soldiers) was wiped out. They also found many tunnels connected to trenches. For two days, my team served over one hundred casualties, most of them wounded soldiers whom we gave first aid, and they were evacuated. I saw one young soldier with a helmet on who was sitting on the ground who appeared confused and was speechless. His metal helmet was extensively scratched and had several readily visible small dents on it. As his memory returned, he said he and a Chinese soldier were having a hand-to-hand fight in a trench. The Chinese soldier hit his helmet repeatedly with a grenade with a handle. Apparently he did not have a chance to pull the pin to detonate the grenade. The Chinese soldier ran away through a nearby tunnel. The Korean soldier was confused and was rescued by his platoon members, who found him wandering near the trench.

I had not had time to rest or have one decent meal since my arrival. I realized for the first time that I was indeed engaged in real, very fierce combat against tough Chinese People's Volunteer Army soldiers. I was proud of being an army medical officer of the ROK Army with the brave soldiers around me. Any one of them could have been my brother or cousin. I did not feel hungry or terribly exhausted.

**Cold, cold winter in a northeastern combat zone of the Korean War, 1953.**
**The author (a first lieutenant) is on the left, standing in front of his bunker.**

I felt honored to be with these young brave men, who were fighting for the same causes as I was, instead of remaining in the medical school as one of the graduate students or assistants in a basic science department who were exempt from the draft via waivers. Having experienced humiliation and horror under the North Korean regime's terror in my Seoul home, even though mine was a short period of experience with them, I felt it was worthy to fight in combat against my mortal enemies.

A week after my arrival, I was transferred to the regimental collecting station. The commanding officer of the medical company with a junior doctor Son who was a first lieutenant at the station, Captain Lee, had been drafted like me but had been in general practice in a town in a southwestern province. The collecting station, with thirty-five medics, had several tents containing portable medical equipment, supplies, medicine, and stretchers, which were located on the premises of the regimental headquarters. This medical station, which housed a company, received casualties from three battalion medical aid stations on the front. The casualties usually received their first aid treatment from battalion aid stations in the infantry regiment, consisting of thirty-five hundred soldiers. The soldiers with minor injuries or other light medical problems were treated by medics at the station, and those who required further treatment were triaged to either the division medical company or a MASH. In early July, 1953, the entire Seventh Infantry Division was suddenly mobilized from the northeastern region to the central region of the front line, called the "Iron Triangle." The military movement took all day long. The Chinese aggression was so intense in the central combat zone that an additional ROK Army division was needed to defend against the enemy insurgence. If this defense line had been broken by the enemy, Seoul might have been reoccupied by the enemy.

A new regimental medical collection station in the regiment headquarters was built on the southern side of a hill, and it faced the enemy line in the north below the ridge of the hill. Thirty-six medics, including two medical doctors, worked in the station. Another hill in the south was separated from our location by a valley with a creek at its bottom. Our infantry regiment was flanked by allied forces in the vicinity, including combat soldiers from the Philippines, Turkey, and the United Kingdom, in addition to the ROK Army and US Army. We were receiving casualties from our three fighting infantry battalions on the frontline, which was about one to two miles away from our station. The wounded soldiers were mostly carried to us on jeeps or three-quarter-ton trucks on either stretchers or vehicle seats. The station was not as busy and hectic as the battalion aid station on the northeastern front near Heartbreak Ridge during my first forty-eight hours after my arrival.

**ROK Army medical company members (First Lieutenant William Chey, commanding officer, is fourth from the left, second row) in a northeastern combat zone in the Korean War, 1954.**

Early one afternoon, some sporadic enemy artillery shelling began on the hill and ridge across the creek. Soon the enemy intensified the shelling, with explosions covering the entire hill. Then the artillery rounds began passing just above the roofs of our tents and our heads. We all lay flat on our stomachs on the surface of the hill and were afraid to raise our heads even one inch above the ground. Explosions began to occur near us. My heart was pounding, and my breathing became faster and faster; I was exhaling hot air. I could not control my rapid breathing. I muttered, "Dear God, please help us." We all covered our heads with helmets. One three-quarter-ton truck from a nearby US artillery battalion, while moving on the narrow road below our collecting station, was hit by artillery shells, and three soldiers were seriously hurt. One soldier was screaming, "Help! Help! Doc where are you?" in English. I could not raise my head or move an inch for several minutes until the artillery attack slowed down. An American soldier about twenty years old from a nearby US artillery battalion base had been hit and was in shock. He was bleeding profusely from an open wound in his right leg, which was almost severed. I applied a tourniquet to his right thigh to slow down the bleeding, and a US Army ambulance arrived and carried him away on a stretcher. Many ROK Army soldiers were severely wounded, and several soldiers were killed. The area was really chaotic for a while. The enemy's aggressive attacks on the front line, including our area, were contained eventually by effective aerial attacks of UN air forces, as well as our friendly artillery attacks.

The reason for the massive artillery attacks was that there was a US artillery battalion on a distant hill more than one thousand yards away from our medical station. There was a rumor that a reconnaissance officer from the artillery battalion had been caught by the enemy soldiers at the front, and he had apparently revealed the location of the artillery battery. Although the artillery attack lasted for about two hours, I felt we were attacked all day long, and I was extremely exhausted afterward. I felt as if my lips were burning with hot air, and they were so dry. My inflamed lower lip was covered by a thick crust and partially cracked.

In early July, I was promoted to the position of regimental medical company commanding officer. Late one morning, my liaison officer entered my tent office and, with a surprised expression, informed me, "Sir, a three-star general is looking for the company commander; that's you, sir." I was bewildered to find a three-star general in clean combat fatigues and shiny dark brown leather boots holding a dark brown leather crop in his right hand. He was standing in front of the entrance to my tent. He said, "Lieutenant, there are about one hundred wounded soldiers trapped in a valley between two hills at the front that are exposed to the enemy's artillery units on a higher hill north of the two hills. We have to rescue them as soon as possible. The casualties have been hiding there for several days without medical care or even drinking water." First I was stunned to hear this distressing and terrible news. No intelligence officer or commanding officer of the regiment had mentioned this at the early-morning regimental chiefs' meeting. Undoubtedly it would be a very risky operation to evacuate the wounded soldiers, because there was one dirt road in the wide-open plain, the valley was about one and a half miles away, and the road was readily visible to the enemy soldiers dug in on the high hill north of the valley. I felt they needed prompt evacuation in a short period of time.

The ambulance, which was no larger than a regular van, was not suited for the mission. I proposed an alternative to the general: "General, in order to rescue that many soldiers, could you send us five or more full-size GMC trucks?"

The general said with a mild smile, "No problem!" He then ran off to a fancy jeep and disappeared in a cloud of dust. In less than one hour, five new empty military trucks arrived on the premises of the medical station, ready to go. I put on my helmet and bulletproof jacket and hopped into the jeep. Three medics were assigned to each truck. My jeep led the caravan of five trucks. We passed the dirt road between two small hills and drove at full speed on the bumpy road that ran across the plain.

There were several destroyed vehicles on the roadsides, including abandoned jeeps and military trucks. As we drove across the plain, I felt it was strange that there were no enemy attacks using short-distance artillery guns, although I sensed that the enemy artillery soldiers were watching us through their binoculars. When my jeep entered the corner of the valley where the wounded were hiding, we began to smell the stench of decomposed human bodies. About two hundred yards away from the corner of the entrance, there were many wounded soldiers with dirty wounds exposed to numerous flies; some had lost arms or legs. Many of them were extremely dehydrated, helplessly lying on stretchers. Some were standing with canes they had made from pine tree branches. Several battalion medics who had been taking care of these soldiers were so glad to see us, and they saluted. I feared that the enemy soldiers might well be watching us from the nearby hills and mountains. I stood in front of the crowd and yelled, "Hear me, everybody. We don't have much time. I want you all—I mean everybody—to climb up onto the trucks. We will leave here in five minutes." Miraculously, everybody was on the trucks on time, including several soldiers with broken legs on crutches, and heavily wounded soldiers on stretchers.

As we turned the corner of the valley, we were assured that no soldier had been left behind. I asked the driver to go as fast as he could. I said, "Come on, faster!"

The driver replied, "Sir, I am pressing the accelerator to the floor."

About the time the convoy approached the central zone of the plain, the first artillery explosion took place on the right roadside, ten yards in front of my jeep. The second shell exploded a few yards from the car, and it shattered the front window. I said, "Come on, go faster! Let's go, dammit!"

"Yes sir, but this is all I can do."

Then the artillery attack hit the third truck behind my jeep. The truck behind the hit truck pushed the hit truck forward. About this time, we were approaching the corner of the hill from which we had entered the plain about one hour before. The hill certainly protected us from the enemy's artillery attack. The wounded soldiers were transferred to the waiting ambulances, there-quarter-ton trucks, and jeeps for immediate medical care at division headquarters. The Chinese artillery force must have watched when we entered the plain and waited until we drove out with our wounded soldiers in trucks. In a way, they were not as cruel as the North Korean soldiers. They could have caused much more heavy damage while we were crossing the plain. I and my company medics rescued more than ninety wounded soldiers in this very dangerous situation, and I was very proud of my men's bravery and sacrifice. In hindsight, I realized that the Chinese People's Volunteer Army might have been reluctant to take these wounded soldiers as their Prisoners of War, hoping that the ROK Army would rescue them.

It is still difficult to comprehend this incredibly risky mission. The order of the mission was directly given by the commanding general of an ROK Army Corp; there was no regimental commanding officer in sight. When we returned to the medical station after the mission was accomplished, there was no phone call from either the general or the regimental commanding officer. Our operation should have been covered by our friendly combat air force. I felt that, at the very least, each of us who rescued these wounded soldiers deserved to receive a citation as recognition for this risky and difficult task. In retrospect, I still cannot understand this strange event that I experienced in combat in July of 1953. Good leadership includes the ability to recognize and reward subordinates for their bravery and meritorious conduct.

# A Chinese Volunteer Army Prisoner of War

One hot midafternoon, a frightened, skinny, and exhausted Chinese People's Volunteer Army soldier was brought to my tent for medical examination. He was accompanied by a military police sergeant, an intelligence officer, and an interpreter. The emaciated prisoner was forty years old, five feet eight inches tall, and weighed 125 pounds. He wore an old ragged uniform and old black cloth shoes with rubber pads, his toes peeking through holes. He had tied a pair of brand-new sneakers to the left side of his belt on his waist. The interpreter asked him. "Why don't you use these good-looking new shoes?"

The man faintly smiled and said, "When the war is over and I return home, I plan to wear them then." He had a small bag made of a dirty cotton-like material, and a string of the bag was tied to the right side of his belt. The bag was less than half filled with dry crushed grains and three strands of a half-dried scallion. When he was hungry, he boiled water in his helmet and mixed the crushed grains and scallions and ate them. He was asked why he had been left behind and caught. He said, "Ttapo, ttapo" (artillery guns). According to the interpreter, the artillery attacks by UN Forces and the ROK Army were so fierce that many of his comrades were killed and the rest ran away, but he got lost and was left behind. "Will you fight again if you have another chance?" the interpreter asked.

His appearance while he said, "No more fighting; no more war, please," his hands and arms shaking and his face anxious and agonized, is difficult to forget even now.

He explained, "Please listen; I have been drafted or forced to fight in three major wars; first, to defend our country against Japanese invasion as a soldier of the Guomindang under the leadership of Chiang Kai-shek; then the Communist Revolutionary War; and now the Korean War, the latter two under the leadership of Mao Tse-tung. I want to go home in peace and be a farmer to help my father, but I have never had a chance to help my father on the farm and settle." I gave him a pack of Lucky Strikes, an American cigarette; a Hershey's chocolate candy bar; a small pack of saltines; and a cool soda. His eyes were welled with tears, and he said, "Shi-e, Shi-e" (Thank you, thank you). The interpreter lit a cigarette for him. He inhaled the smoke deeply and exhaled thick smoke through both nostrils. He grabbed the chocolate bar and saltines from my hands and gobbled them down, saying, "Ding-ho, Ding-ho; Shi-e, Shi-e" (Very good, very good; thank you, thank you). He told us he had starved for almost two days because he could not find water to cook his grains. He then asked, "What will happen to me now? I don't wish to be returned to North Korea."

The interpreter said to him, "You are our prisoner of war. You will be soon transferred to the UN Prisoner's Camp on Jeju Island." He appeared so relieved. This prisoner of war had spent his most productive years as a soldier. His participation in the Korean War was certainly not voluntary, although the Communist China regime claimed these soldiers were volunteers in order to support and defend the North Korean comrades who were chased by ROK Military and UN Forces to the Sino-Korean border. It appeared that he did not volunteer to join either the so-called People's Volunteer Army or the Korean People's Army.

# A Young Soldier with Acute Appendicitis

Late one evening, a nineteen-year-old soldier was brought on a stretcher by battalion medics to our medical station. He appeared acutely ill and dehydrated. He had chills, fever, and severe abdominal pain, with a recent episode of nausea and vomiting. The pertinent findings were severe tenderness in the right lower abdomen with rebound tenderness. These clinical features were consistent with acute appendicitis. I recalled a brilliant lecture on the subject by Professor Kim Ja-Hoon at the medical school and a superb demonstration by a master surgeon—Professor Chang, a professor of surgery, performing an appendectomy—on a young male at Gospel Hospital in Busan. The surgical facilities were in a large tent, where Professor Chang performed not only appendectomies and cholecystectomies but also many other major surgical procedures, such as subtotal gastrectomy, colectomy, and even partial lobectomy of the lungs. From time to time, I scrubbd with Professor Chang to assist him during surgical operations. It was indeed my unforgettable privilege and honor to be under his tutelage.

I ordered the young soldier to be transferred immediately to Division Headquarters or a nearby ROK Army MASH. Soon a staff sergeant came into my tent and advised me that because of frequent barrage of Chinese artillery attacks, most of the bridges were destroyed. The regiment commanding officer, colonel Yoo issued a strict order to avoid transporting injured or sick soldiers to the rear. In my judgment, the soldier with acute appendicitis had to be transferred for an immediate surgical treatment. I visited the regiment commanding officer's tent. He was already in bed, wearing pajamas. We sat down on chairs. I advised him that this young soldier must be transferred as soon as possible. He said it shouldn't be done. I respectfully advised him that it was a serious violation for me to perform an open-abdominal surgical operation at our medical station. The ROK military medical manual clearly stated that such an operation was forbidden at a regimental medical station, such as ours. Suddenly he became very angry and stood up, looking down at me with his piercing eyes, which made me feel chills. He said, " Lieutenant, obviously you are not a real military officer in combat, are you? In the military, one must make the impossible possible. Do you wish for me to pump real military spirit into your soul?" That likely meant a physical punishment, which was not uncommon in the ROK Army culture in those days.

I returned to the medical station in dismay. In order to save the young soldier's life, I decided to perform the surgery for acute appendicitis. I had never performed this surgery by myself, though I had assisted Professor Chang during such a surgical operation when I was a fourth-year medical student. I quietly went over and over again a surgical manual that described the appendectomy procedure.

The tent's medical treatment room was cleared, and the patient was laid on a clean stretcher supported by two green wooden medical supply boxes. For the maximum exposure of the operating field of his abdomen, four medics stood on both sides of the stretcher. Each medic held one burning candle in both hands. We were forbidden to turn the light bulb on in order to avoid the enemy's artillery attack, With the patient under ether anesthesia (as that's all we had), a local anesthetic solution was injected into the right lower quadrant of the abdomen. Before opening the abdomen, I experienced sudden anxiety at the thought of the possibility that he did not have appendicitis. If the patient were in a MASH or the medical company in the Division Headquarters, the doctors would have taken X-ray images to look for findings that might suggest appendicitis. But it was too late. I had no choice but to act depending on my clinical impression. When I reached the appendix, I found that it was indeed markedly swollen to the size of my thumb and was red. There was no perforation or pus. It took me more than two hours to complete the surgery. For a qualified general surgeon, it should take about forty minutes or less if there are no complications. It was already midnight, and I virtually passed out on my bunker bed until I was awakened by bright sunlight beaming through a small, round paper window. I found myself in dirty fatigues with both of my boots still on. I instantly jumped out of the bed and rushed to the operating room tent.

To my dismay, the operating room was empty. When I turned around to look for the patient, the smiling master sergeant stood at attention and saluted at me. I asked him, "Sergeant, where is he? What's happened to him?"

He said so delightfully and proudly, "Sir, he woke up early and walked down to the stream in the valley."

"What?"

I ran down the valley to find the patient in a squatting position, watching a small stream while holding an IV bottle in his raised left hand. I was amazed, and I screamed at him, "Hey, you there—stay put and don't move!"

Two medics soon arrived with a stretcher. As he was being carried to the tent, I asked him how he felt. "Fine, sir," he replied.

"Don't you have pain?"

"A little bit, sir."

"Did you pass gas?"

"Yes sir, quite a few times."

I said to myself, "It is good to be young and strong." If he had not been young and strong, he might not have survived the surgery, which was performed by a doctor who had never performed an appendectomy, without appropriate facilities, and without qualified operating room personnel. I felt that the events that had taken place since the previous evening were miracles. And I was overjoyed to be a physician serving in the ROK Army and to have saved someone's precious son who was serving his country.

The soldier was transferred in an ambulance to the division headquarters medical company. Having experienced these unbelievable events, though, I feared facing the consequences of arguing with the regimental commanding officer the night before and violating the rules regarding the prohibition of surgical procedures in the regimental medical station. My conscience was clear, however. I had never felt such pleasure and pride at being a healer. Had my parents known of this incredible deed that saved the life of a young soldier, they would have felt thrilled and proud of their son.

In the afternoon, Staff Sergeant Lee walked into my tent and saluted me longer than the usual period and said, "Sir, everybody in the regimental headquarters heard about your successful surgical operation under the candlelight last night and are ecstatic. They said they didn't realize that they had a great doctor in the regiment and shared their pride—as we do, sir." Then I heard that many soldiers in the combat battalion at the front were excited by the good news about their comrade. The truth of the matter was that I'd had no choice but to do what I had to do. Even then it was clear in my mind that a very sick patient came before my concern about possible consequences for violating military rules. In my heart, I profoundly thanked Professor Chang, who taught me and showed me the appendectomy procedure while he was humming gospel songs in his operating room tent in Busan. He was a genuine Christian and observed Christian life every day.

I received a phone call from a liaison officer of the regimental commanding officer's office. He said, "The colonel is very pleased and wants to have dinner with you this evening." I was pleasantly surprised. He offered a delicious meal prepared by the head chef of the regiment headquarters and drinks, including Budweiser beer, which I had not drank for a long time. He proposed *geunbae* ("cheers" in Korean). We drank a glass of Seagram's whiskey, and then he said, "I heard you performed a successful surgical operation under very difficult conditions and saved a young soldier's life. It's like a miracle! It was very good indeed for our regiment's morale, pride, and reputation. Thank you, Lieutenant." Then we had another drink of whisky. I couldn't believe that the day prior we were so distant, but now we were sharing drinks and eating dinner together just as if we were good friends. Then I asked him if I would receive any punitive blame or criticism from the commanding general of the division. He said, " Don't worry, Lieutenant. When I talk to him about your splendid work to save the soldier's life, he will be very pleased. The commanding general is an intellectual who was a college graduate and a doctor's son." My anxiety was considerably relieved. After that we had had a close friendly relationship until I was released from military service.

# Peace Conference in Panmunjom

We heard that the peace negotiation between UN forces and ROK Army officials and Communist forces, including both North Korea and Communist China, was coming to an end, and an optimistic air was prevalent on both sides of the front line. We knew the fighting may end in the near future. After many debates and negotiations, on July 27, 1953, both sides agreed to an armistice without a permanent peace treaty. In order to gain more ground before the armistice, there were fierce fights along the front line, particularly in the central zone, called the Iron Triangle, where our entire division was ordered to be relocated. In order to enforce and defend the areas gained by the ROK Army and United Nations forces, particularly American infantry divisions, we were mobilized from the northeast front to the central front area.

How cruel this war was; we witnessed a young soldier seriously wounded below a nearby small bridge by the enemy's artillery shelling on the morning of July 27, the day of the truce, which should have been effective at noon. Shrapnel slashed the twenty-year-old soldier's left chest wall and lungs. He died while being transferred to the division headquarters medical company station.

# Return to Northeastern Front near the DMZ and a US MASH

I n early August, the Seventh Infantry Division soldiers returned to the original northeastern front, which was below the demilitarized zone (DMZ) and north of Yanggu, in Gangwon Province. Our pace of daily activities was no longer as hectic, as we were in active and fierce combat in the central area of the frontline. I was still in charge of the same medical company in the headquarters of the same infantry regiment.

**Two US medical personnel, the author, and ROK Army medical officer Captain Kim in a US MASH.**

I had visited a nearby US Forty-Fifth mobile army surgical hospital (MASH) located about forty minutes away from my medical company station. I enjoyed immensely the visit to the MASH to meet with young and friendly American army doctors, nurses, and medics. Most of these young doctors with the ranks of first lieutenant and captain had been drafted to serve in this unwanted war in Korea. Back home, they had been in residency training at teaching hospitals when they were called up. I liked their sense of humor in the dining room, living quarters, and operating room. I learned English conversation and their friendly manners during social occasions in officers' clubs and dining rooms. I was fortunate to be associated with these young doctors and senior surgeons in operating rooms. In particular, I became friendly with a young doctor named Donald Weeks Jr. III, who had just finished a straight internship of surgery and was to advance to surgical residency training at the prestigious New York Hospital in New York City, my dream city. What made him even more homesick than others was that he'd had to leave his beloved wife after only three months of marriage. He was always friendly and kind; we were on a first-name basis. My first American name, a nickname, was proposed by some of these doctors at a small gathering one evening at an officers' club. Because my Korean name was Woo-yoon, Donald said, "How about William—Bill?" The others unanimously agreed and supported Donald. They enjoyed calling me Bill from then on. It was always such a treat when I was invited for a lunch or a rare dinner with the medical staff, which included not only doctors but also surgeons, nurses, and other officers in the MASH, and I learned their manners in social gatherings. The meals they served were always particularly delicious—quite a change from our own. Donald was quite interested in our Korean way of life. On occasion, we used to visit Seoul when he was off duty on weekends. He met my father at a party at which he was served traditional Korean food and presented with pleasant entertainment, including dancing and original Korean music. He was very interested in the traditional wedding ceremony, in which he was invited to participate as my friend's best man.

**Lt. Donald Weeks Jr., MD, and the author, Seoul, Korea, 1954.**

*Part 3*

# Leave of Absence from ROK Army and My Post-Graduate Medical Education and Training in the United States of America

# To Come to the United States of America

O ne evening, I was unexpectedly invited to the tent of the regiment commanding officer, Colonel Yoo, for dinner. This was a very unusual treat from the commanding officer. It turned out that I was the only one invited. Ever since my successful appendectomy on the young soldier, he respected me and was kind and friendly. I enjoyed eating a specially prepared delicious meal and drinking cans of Budweiser beer. He showed me a special notification to division commanding generals from ROK president Syngman Rhee, stating that "those young soldiers who have opportunities to study in advanced countries ought to be encouraged to obtain a scholarship in advanced countries. They have my permission for a temporary leave from active military duty. I expect your full cooperation on this matter." Colonel Yoo looked straight at me and said, "Lieutenant, this is your lifetime opportunity. I will help you with whatever I can." I was deeply touched and humbly appreciative. Later I found out that President Rhee's message was mostly ignored by generals and colonels in combat areas. "When you get a scholarship, I assume you will have a lot of work to do. You may have to go to the headquarters of the ROK Army in Daegu and the US Embassy in Seoul. I will let you use my jeep. I will tell my driver, Sergeant Lee. Do not waste time, Lieutenant. You have been a good medical company commander, and I thank you." This was such an unusual kindness offered to me by the regimental commander. He offered his valued jeep to his subordinate for his personal use. I had known he enjoyed and loved his modified and comfortable jeep and he had never shared with anyone in the regiment.

When I visited the MASH the next day, Donald welcomed me to his tent with a smile. "Bill, you got an internship appointment from New York City Hospital," he said, and he shook my hand. "Congratulations." The letter was written by the superintendent of City Hospital of New York City, Dr. Herman Bauer, and it stated, "Dear Dr. Chey, you have been accepted for a rotating internship beginning September 1, 1954 … with a monthly stipend of $68.00 and free room and board in staff house in the hospital campus …" I was so excited, and I thanked Donald enormously; he appeared even more excited than I. That night, I was up without much sleep. The following morning, Donald came over to my medical company in a jeep driven by a US MASH driver. He knocked on my tent door and, smiling, showed me another letter and said, "This appears even better, Bill." The letter came from the Department of Surgery, Baylor College of Medicine, Houston, Texas. Frankly, I didn't know about Houston, Texas. Nor did I remember whether I had applied for an internship there. This was a letter of appointment for straight internship of surgery at Jefferson Davis Hospital, Baylor College of Medicine. The letter stated, "Dear Dr. Chey, My former colleague, Dr. John Howard recommended you highly. You are hereby appointed as Straight Internship of Surgery … Your monthly stipend is $9.00 with free room and board … Michael M. DeBakey, M.D., Professor of Medicine and Chairman."

I met with Dr. John Howard, then a US Army Major, twice briefly at the MASH in early August, but I did not discuss with him my desire to have postgraduate training in the United States, for I did not know him well. He was a distinguished-looking officer and directed the US Army Mobile Surgical Research Team in combat zones to save casualties with injured or ruptured arteries of the lower extremities, preventing amputations by transporting the casualties to MASH units by helicopter, which were first deployed during the Korean War. I found out later that Donald mentioned me to Dr. Howard, but he did not realize Dr. Howard wrote so promptly about me to his former boss, Dr. DeBakey, a legendary American surgeon in Houston, Texas. After returning home, I was told that he became a professor and chairman of departments of surgery in three different medical colleges, including Emory University in Atlanta, Hahnemann University in Philadelphia, and the Medical College of Toledo in Ohio. He was a nationally and internationally recognized distinguished surgeon, educator, and researcher. Some thirty years later, I had the honor of meeting with Dr. Howard at the annual meeting of the American Pancreatic Association in Chicago in 1980s.. He was by then an internationally known biliary-pancreatic surgeon. I thanked him for his kindness and effort in obtaining for me the internship in the prestigious Department of Surgery at Baylor College of Medicine.

After careful consideration of the two internship programs, I chose the rotation internship, which gave me opportunities to learn not only surgical discipline but also other specialties, including internal medicine. I wrote to Dr. DeBakey about my decision to start with a rotating internship and asked him whether I could start the surgical internship in his department the following July. He promptly wrote me back and mentioned, "Dear Dr. Chey, I always liked rotating internships. I look forward to seeing you on July 1, 1955. Good luck."

Back to the regiment headquarters, Colonel Yoo was very pleased and advised me to leave for Daegu in order to receive the permit for temporary leave from active duty at the Personnel Department of the ROK Army Headquarters. The driver, a staff sergeant, and I left early the next day from the regimental medical station. I enjoyed the smooth ride of the best jeep in the regiment. We saw civilian women workers scattered about doing what had traditionally been men's work in the farm fields of both sides of dusty roads. We could hardly find male workers, for most of the young farmers had been drafted to serve in the military. Nonetheless it was so good to see civilians. We passed the major cities, including Chuncheon, Seoul, and Daejeon. At early dusk, we entered the outskirts of Daegu, the provincial capital of North Gyeongsang Province, where the general headquarters of the ROK Army was situated. Uniformed soldiers and green military vehicles dominated the streets and sidewalks of the city, which used to be the regional commercial, higher education, and cultural center of southeastern Korea. We both rested and stayed in a small hotel near the army headquarters.

The next morning, I submitted the application form for the permit to be released from active duty in the ROK Army. The application was accompanied by the approval of both the commanding officer of the Third Regiment and the commanding general Kim of the Seventh ROK Infantry Division. When I submitted the application, the major in charge of the reception section, who was wearing a well-pressed and clean uniform, advised me to return sometime in the afternoon. I purposely wore combat fatigues, dusty boots, and my metal helmet. There were several wooden benches in the room. I decided to sit on a bench and wait. A dozen soldiers, mostly junior officers, submitted similar brown envelopes holding documents to the major. Some of them handed over bulky extra envelopes which I suspected contained cash.

About noontime, the room was nearly empty; the major and I were the only two remaining. The major approached me and said, "Lieutenant, go out and have something to eat and come back." I could not ask why most of the others seemed to have their applications sealed with an official stamp and left but mine had been left unstamped. I was too intimidated to ask the embarrassing question to the major. Instead I gently explained, "Sir, I came directly from the front line, and I have to return to my infantry regiment as soon as I have the document with your seal." After he took a deep puff of his cigarette and stared at me, he returned to his desk, stamped my document loudly, and handed it to me without making direct eye contact with me. I knew my staying in the room throughout the morning made him uncomfortable.

We returned to my medical company late at night. It was hard and sad to return home to Seoul the next day, leaving the company comrades who had shared with me good times, sad times, and times of incredibly hard work over the past year. When they were discharged from active duty, many of them would return to finish their high school or college education. I felt honored to have participated in this cruel war to defend my motherland. It was, and even now is, unacceptable for South Korea to be run over by North Korean savages.

# Leaving Home for the United States

Having obtained my passport and Visa to the United States from the Embassy of the United States of America in Seoul in mid-August of 1954, I was overwhelmed with feelings of excitement about coming to the United States—a dream that I had had, like so many Koreans, since I was a middle school student. But I was also feeling painful sadness because I had to leave home and my close family, with whom I had shared so many difficult times, so much happiness, and so much sadness in overcoming the oppression and insults of the Japanese and enduring the tragic and cruel war against North Korean Invasion. Along with my caring and loving parents, I had six siblings: four brothers and two sisters. The youngest one, Ok-Hee, was a beautiful, lovely, and cute sister, but we did not have time to get to know each other well.

On the afternoon of August 24, my family and I had a heartbreaking farewell in front of the entrance to Northwest Airlines at Seoul International Airport. There was no modern terminal or bus to the plane then. As I climbed the ladder to the four-propeller plane, it was hard for me to see them off at the entrance. My father handed me a brown envelope full of many American dollars—mostly one-hundred-dollar bills. I took only one fifty-dollar bill and put the envelope in his inside jacket pocket and quickly entered the plane. I could not possibly take his hard-earned money, which he must have saved for a long time. From now on I would earn my own wage.

As I looked down, the plane was already leaving the southern end of the Korean Peninsula, where I had been born twenty three years before. I felt so sad that I sobbed. Now I was really leaving my homeland, now a war-ridden and impoverished country. Hardworking Koreans didn't deserve atrocities, corruption, poverty, or the injustice of being second-class citizens exploited by foreign forces. I considered that if the king or emperor's court or the government worked hard for the people without selfish motives and corruption, the country could not be ridiculed, insulted, oppressed, and exploited. Koreans in general are hardworking and value education for their children. I know no one in Korea who would want to return to the humiliating past.

Soon, the plane landed at Haneda International Airport in Tokyo, Japan.

My youngest uncle, Gyu-Bok, was waiting for me in the airport. I was so glad to see him for a long time. After graduating from Waseda University, a prestigious university in Tokyo during World War II, he remained in Tokyo after the war and achieved the fourth degree of black belt in Judo. He was the proud captain of the judo team at the university. He also taught judo at an American military base near Tokyo. This generated an additional income, although most Japanese people were not financially well off in those days. He lived in a nice Japanese home in a residential area of Tokyo. One elderly couple lived with the uncle, and they appeared to take care of him like their son. Both were so courteous, friendly, and polite every time I met them, morning or evening. I wondered how such nice people could have possibly started such a cruel and terrible war, and why so many Japanese people who lived in the small town where we once lived in Korea behaved so arrogantly and discourteously toward Koreans and treated us like second-class citizens. My uncle told me in later years when I visited him that the Suzuki family treated him like their son, and as he spoke, he was in a nostalgic mood, with tears in his eyes.

Although my uncle had always dressed clean and well before wartime, he now dressed in wrinkled trousers and an unpressed shirt and jacket, reflecting the hard times the people in Japan were experiencing during the postwar era. When we walked the streets downtown, we still witnessed disabled veterans wearing old, dirty uniforms standing on the street corners. They sang sad songs and asked for money. War is a terrible event for any nation. Once a country starts a war, the country must win. If they lose, they must face sad and painful misery—particularly a proud country like Japan.

# Landing on United States Soil

On August 26, my plane landed at Hawaii International Airport. One young Korean man introduced himself at the terminal as Kim and offered me lodging in his home. Mr. Kim and his widowed mother were very kind hosts. He was a University of Hawaii graduate, and his mother appeared to be over sixty years old. Her husband had passed away many years earlier, when she was still quite young. Many teenage Korean women born to poor rural families in Korea used to marry old Korean migrants in Hawaii by picture interview before World War II. These men worked hard on pineapple plantations to earn low wages. By the time they could afford to invite potential brides from Korea, they were quite old. I remember, as a young boy, young teenage women leaving for Hawaii or Japan as chosen brides though they had never met their prospective grooms.

Mr. Kim kept us busy on sightseeing tours of these beautiful tropical islands using his Chevrolet passenger car for two days. I and two other Korean students were so excited to enjoy the pleasant weather and this beautiful paradise where only a few hours of sleep was enough until we left the island. In retrospect, the reason for sleeplessness was probably attributable to jet lag.

# New York City and City Hospital

The plane landed on the runway of then New York (now John F. Kennedy) International Airport about noon. I decided to stop by the office of the consulate general of the Republic of Korea by taxi in Manhattan. The driver was a friendly African American gentleman and asked me, "Where are you from?" He said, "My friend has just returned from Korea. He is an army sergeant." He was familiar with the location of the consulate's office. The highways and a magnificent bridge from Long Island to Manhattan were very impressive—well built, very wide, and clean. Many vehicles were moving in ordinary fashion, following the traffic rules with courtesy. I felt this was a part of the symbol of a powerful country, the USA.

The consulate general's office was in an ordinary residential house in upper Manhattan. One office worker showed me the direction to the city hospital on a map of New York City. It was in the southern end of a small, slender island between Manhattan and Queens called Welfare Island, which made me think of an island populated with poor people in New York City.

Interestingly, there was no bridge connecting the island from either Manhattan or Queens. The two boroughs were connected by Queensboro Bridge, which had on it both a four-lane street and two trolley car tracks. I asked the taxi driver, "How do we get to the island?" He explained that there are large elevators in the middle portion of the bridge that bring visitors, hospital employees, and vehicles— including ambulances bringing patients to the hospitals—to the four large city hospitals and their grounds on the island. The island had four large hospitals managed by the city government of New York, including City Hospital of New York for acute patient care, Gold Memorial Hospital and Bird S. Coler Memorial Hospital, both for patients with chronic diseases, and Metropolitan Hospital for acute patient care. The latter three hospitals had more than one thousand beds each. It was an interesting experience to enter a huge elevator that carried the taxi car, which descended ever slowly down to the island. A shuttle bus then carried me and my luggage to the hospital.

City Hospital was a complex of old stone-built buildings with a total bed capacity of over nine hundred for acutely ill patients, patients with tuberculosis in isolated wards, and a small emergency room. The hospital was a teaching hospital affiliated with New York Medical College. The house staff quarters and staff dining rooms were located on the southern end of the hospital campus, which was at the southern end of the island. There was a well-maintained courtyard between the hospital buildings and the buildings for house staff quarters and dining rooms. I was assigned to the room in the very end of the south wing, which was a well-furnished dormitory room. Through the window, I could see the East River, the beautiful light-blue United Nations building, and the downtown skyline of Manhattan that I used to admire in pictures only. I could not believe myself that only one month before I had been living in a bunker or a tent in the combat zone of the northeastern front line in war-torn South Korea.

I reported my arrival to the superintendent's office at the hospital. Dr. Herman Bauer was pleased to see me and welcomed me. At the dining room, I was joined by two Korean doctors from Seoul, Dr. N. G. Cheung, a surgical resident, and J. J. Kim, a female intern who had been one of my classmates at the wartime combined medical school in Busan. It was so good to see her again. Dr. Kim had started her internship in July, as all the new interns did. I chose my favored meal from the menu, and the waitress was delighted to serve me spaghetti with meatballs. Most of the interns and residents were from foreign countries, including Mexico, Guatemala, Cuba, Santo Domingo, Japan, South Korea, Spain, West Germany, Austria, France, Italy, Greece, Turkey, Iraq, Iran, India, the Philippines, and Taiwan. They all came to this country with new dreams and new hopes, as I did. They worked hard and were eager to learn.

**Interns and residents at City Hospital, New York City, 1954.**

# Life at City Hospital

The hospital had all the major departments found in other hospitals, including Internal Medicine and the major surgical specialties. I had the opportunity of rotating through various departments of the major specialties, including internal medicine, general surgery, pediatrics, and obstetrics and gynecology. After completing the rotating internship, I planned to have a straight internship in Surgery at Baylor College of Medicine, Jefferson Davis Hospital, in Houston, Texas, the following year. I started my rotating internship on the medical floor. Our daily work started at seven thirty in the morning, and we reviewed the charts of patients assigned to me and new patents I received overnight. There were two rows of beds lined against two opposing walls, with windows in one of the two. The thirty beds were almost always completely occupied by patients who were mostly from Manhattan's impoverished areas. What I enjoyed the most during the morning rounds was visiting each patient in bed with a team of interns, residents, attending physicians, nurses, and a social worker. The workers of different disciplines worked together for the individual patients and met their needs, which included not only their medical problems but also their individual psycho-socio-economic status. Sometimes, however, the work was quite demanding. Interns had to work twenty-four-hour shifts.

While rotating through obstetrics and gynecology, I had to cover both the maternity ward and the gynecology ward. Starting about six o'clock in the late afternoon one Friday, I admitted twelve patients by myself, which required careful history and physical examination, including pelvic examination and catheterization of the urinary bladder for urine collection. Then urinalysis for sugar and protein levels and microscopic examination of urine for each new patient was performed in the small laboratory attached to the ward. After midnight, I was called to the maternity ward twice to deliver newborn babies. In the dawn, when I was about to lie down on my soft bed in the dormitory, the telephone rang to let me know that another young woman with vaginal bleeding had just arrived. By that time, the ward was completely and fully occupied with patients. Even portable beds temporarily placed between regular beds were filled. It was bright Saturday morning by then, about time for breakfast.

As I sat on a chair in the dining room before a cup of coffee was served, I was paged again. Father Cunningham, sitting across the table, was looking fresh and smiling. "You look like you had a rough night, Dr. O'Shay." (He always called me O'Shay, which cheered me up.)

"Yes, Father, I have."

A nurse in an operating room said on the phone that I was scheduled to assist Dr. O'Neal and Dr. Fusco, a chief resident in General Surgery, in Operating Room B. A dirty look from the attending doctor was readily noticeable on my arrival, although I had never met him before. The intern assigned for this work had become ill overnight. The patient for the surgery was a thirty-nine-year-old African American female with weight of 290 pounds and a height of five feet five inches who was suspected to have acute cholecystitis and gallstone disease. My job was to stand to the side of Dr. O'Neal to hold a spreader with my two hands, keeping her thick upper abdominal wall open wide. In the middle of surgery, Dr. O'Neal looked at me and asked, "Doctor, did you have breakfast this morning? Pull harder."

I answered, "No sir, not this morning. I didn't have time." He looked at me again and said nothing until the operation was completed.

I was exhausted and slept until late afternoon, when an intern from Japan, Dr. Kinoshita, knocked on the door and woke me up. It was already five thirty, and we had dinner together. After dinner, I sat alone on the bank of the island near my dormitory for a while, watching the waves of the East River hitting the shore and small ships passing by. It was hard working twenty-four-hour shifts, and I was still tired, but whenever I faced hard work and stressful conditions, I reminded myself of the hardship I had endured during my incredibly harsh combat experience on the hill near Heartbreak Ridge on the day of my arrival on the front line in the Korean combat zone. I knew that if I could stay up and work almost two sleepless days there, I could survive here. Besides, I was learning every day, no matter how hard I worked.

The attending physicians were mostly well-qualified physicians in private practice who had clinical faculty appointments at New York Medical College, New York University School of Medicine, and Mount Sinai Hospital in New York City. Each team of attending physicians rotated throughout the year and conducted teaching rounds with us that were quite instructive, and I enjoyed them. Weekly clinical conferences were prepared by house staff to present their cases for problem solving as well as interesting or instructive cases for mutual learning. Some attending physicians were exceptionally outstanding clinicians with a wealth of medical knowledge and were motivators with enthusiasm for teaching and professional career counselling for house staff.

So often, monthly clinical–pathological conferences made us feel humbled when the pathologists unraveled the real causes of death. One fifty-four-year-old female patient with massive rectal bleeding had suffered cardiac arrest. Her death occurred one day after admission. The autopsy revealed a large and deep ulceration and extensive inflammation in the terminal ileum, with fresh and old blood clots in the ulcer. The ulcer was found in a segment of the terminal ileum about four inches long, which was inflamed and moderately narrowed. The pathologist mentioned that the finding was consistent with terminal ileitis as reported in the *Journal of the American Medical Association* in 1932 by Dr. Burrill Crohn and associates at Mount Sinai Hospital, New York City, but I did not know this disease existed. None of my peers had seen or heard about it. Nevertheless, I was embarrassed, as others did.

I wanted to learn more about medical sciences, particularly internal medicine, by attending conferences or regularly scheduled lecture series held at the New York Academy of Medicine and other institutions in the city whenever my time allowed. Here I found many eminent professors and faculty members from the leading academic institutions in the country, such as Columbia University, Cornell University, New York University, and Mount Sinai Hospital. By attending these lectures and conferences, I enriched my medical knowledge. All speakers at the academy wore black ties and suits, and they were impressive and appeared dignified. In order to attend the academy meetings, I had to walk or take a bus to the bridge elevator, ride a trolley car over the bridge to Manhattan, take the subway to the station near the academy, and then walk to the academy building near Fifth Avenue and One Hundredth Street. I usually sat in a back-row seat. I always found myself the only Asian in the auditorium, and I never saw anyone from City Hospital there. This was an unforgettable and rewarding experience which inspired me to become a physician with a scholarly career.

After the daily hard work—sometimes twenty-four hours of continuous work—when I returned to my room late at night and lay down on the bed, the view out my window of the picturesque Manhattan skyline in the clear night sky, decorated with such a variety of beautiful colors, soothed my fatigue. It was such a delight to see the blinking red light on the top of the Empire State Building every night—an iconic symbol of the great New York City. It was also refreshing in the morning to standing on the bank of the island and enjoy watching Manhattan and East River Drive, with the quiet waves of the East River tapping the bank.

**Friends in City Hospital, Manhattan, and the East River, New York, 1955.**

# Home Care Visit and a Friendly Parrot

One early afternoon, I was scheduled to visit a patient at his home who had recently been discharged from the hospital. A city ambulance was already waiting for me in front of the hospital. I sat to the side of a rather chubby middle-aged female nurse who was rather untalkative. The ambulance entered the slow-moving elevator that carried the car to the busy Queensboro Bridge leading to Manhattan. I asked the driver, "Where is Harlem?"

The driver, Tom, said, "We will get you there, Doc." The nurse kept still quiet.

The car stopped in front of an old red brick apartment building. The nurse said he was on the third floor. I said to her, "I know where he is. Are you coming?"

Pointing at her right knee with her right index finger, she said, "I have a bad knee."

I entered the building through the entrance door, which was a halfway open. There was about a sixty-year-old skinny man sitting on a doorstep inside, smoking a cigarette. He looked at me and said, "He is in there."

"Where?"

"Third floor."

The nearby elevator was out of order. As I climbed up the stairs to reach the third floor, the hallway was dark, and there were no lightbulbs in the ceiling or on the hallway wall. With a flashlight on, I looked for room 316. One lightbulb in the ceiling was covered with wire mesh, but it wasn't on. Suddenly, in the dark, I heard, "Hello, my name is George." I turned around and searched for someone talking to me. By this time I was scared, but I moved one step forward. Then I heard again, "Hello." I felt as if my hair was rising stiffly on my scalp. The friendly voice had come from a parrot in a wire cage hanging from the ceiling above my head—a lonesome bird! Right in that vicinity, I found room 316.

I gently knocked on the door. After a few more knocks, I heard a faint voice say, " Come in." In the room, I found the real George sitting in an old, soft brown chair, breathing hard. The room was littered with papers and prescription bottles. His lungs were severely congested, and he was dyspneic. Both of his legs were markedly swollen. The patient had a long history of diabetes mellitus, hypertension, and arteriosclerotic heart disease with congestive heart failure; he needed immediate inpatient care. I called his only son, but he declined to come to see his father. The patient was admitted to City Hospital in the late afternoon.

# "Doctor, I am not crazy; help me please."

A twenty-nine-year-old African American woman was admitted to our medical floor from the emergency room with a diagnosis of hypertension and hysteria. The patient was accompanied with three thick volumes of copied medical charts from three major teaching hospitals in Manhattan. Her diagnoses included hypertension, severe headache of unknown cause, psychoneurosis, hysteria, and more. When I initially interviewed her, she appeared quite depressed and said, "They tell me that I am a crazy woman, but I know I am not crazy, Doc." I told her that I believed her and asked her to tell me all about her problems. During the previous three years, she had had countless emergency room visits because of the sudden onset of severe splitting headaches, shakiness, and extreme nervousness that was so intense it made her scream. By the time she reached the emergency room and saw a doctor on these occasions, the symptoms were almost gone. Occasionally doctors found high blood pressure, but other doctors could not document it because they checked her blood pressure after her headaches stopped, while she was waiting for a doctor or nurse in the emergency rooms.

I felt that her mysterious and challenging condition ought to be carefully observed and evaluated in a setting other than a hospital emergency room. I had the opportunity to study her condition in an inpatient setting, such as ours at City Hospital. I hoped to observe the entire daily course of her illness in the medical ward. I requested that the nursing staff contact me if symptoms presented, whether I was on call or not. The patient remained asymptomatic for one week after her admission. She even asked when she could be discharged. The telephone rang at two o'clock one night and woke me up. The nurse apologetically said, " Dr. Chey, I know you are not on call, but you instructed us to call you for this particular patient if she is in trouble with a severe headache even if you are not on call. I am sorry." I immediately jumped out of the bed and rushed to the hospital through the courtyard. As I ran up the three flights of stairs to the medical floor, I could hear her screams. Her forehead was covered with sweat, and she was trembling. She was pulling at her hair because of a severe pounding headache.

I quickly checked her pulse, which was strong and was over 150 beats per minute. Her blood pressure was above 300 mmHg. I was just about to call a senior medical resident on call, but I soon found her agony gradually becoming less and less severe. Her blood pressure declined to 200 mmHg in ten minutes and gradually reached about 120 mmHg in one hour. She no longer had a headache at that point and became calm and appeared to be somewhat embarrassed. She said, "Thank you, Dr. Chey. You are here. Otherwise, no one would have believed me."

I wrote a long note in the chart about her interesting clinical event, which I had never seen or heard of before. I felt I was fortunate to have witnessed all of the clinical features she described to me during our initial meeting. Certainly she was not hysterical but had a real unexplained clinical condition. I then recalled a presentation by Dr. Goldberg from Columbia University College of Physicians and Surgeons at the New York Academy of Medicine some months before. He had described clinical features of patients with pheochromocytoma of the adrenal glands who exhibited episodic severe hypertension and headache. I made a proposal in my note that in our differential diagnosis, we should include pheochromocytoma.

The next morning, when I returned to the medical floor, three colleagues, including another intern, an assistant resident, and the chief resident, were reading my note in the chart with considerable interest, and one expressed a skeptical remark: "Never heard of it." Then I overheard the intern say, "When Bill approaches the patient's bed, watch out. Her blood pressure may shoot up. He is coming." Another giggled.

In the late morning, the attending physician started to go over the new patients. The chief resident brought his attention to the senior attending physician about my interesting observation that I had made the night before. He intensely listened to the presentation of the resident, who expressed skepticism about pheochromocytoma. The attending physician read my note while listening to his presentation. The attending physician said, "I agree with Dr. Chey. Pheochromocytoma [a tumor of the adrenal glands] should be considered in differential diagnosis." I was thrilled. The attending physician was Dr. Lester Tuchman from Mount Sinai Hospital, clinical professor of internal medicine at Columbia University, a senior medical attending physician, and an editor of the *Journal of Mount Sinai Hospital*. This distinguished-looking doctor, about sixty years old, said, "Although I have not seen one personally, this clinical entity was recently cited in the medical literature."

As he ended his remark, there was a loud scream from the corner of the floor, complaining of severe headache. Indeed it came from my patient. The chief resident asked me to go and check her blood pressure. I suggested someone else check her blood pressure since some were skeptical about my impression. Dr. Tuchman volunteered to go over to her bedside and checked the pressure. He found it to be as high as 290 mmHg, which steadily declined to normal in twenty minutes. He saw her trembling and sweating, the sweating being particularly prominent on her forehead. He was very pleased that I had made such an exciting and important observation. He suggested I should contact Dr. Goldberg at P and S, a nickname of the College of Physicians and Surgeons at Columbia-Presbyterian Medical Center about the patient and said, "He should be very pleased."

I explained to the patient about her condition. I told her she was not a hysterical woman; nor did she have anxiety neurosis. When she heard my explanation for her symptoms, she grasped my hands with hers and had tears in her eyes. She said once more, "You mean I am not a crazy woman." I shook my head. "Thank you, thank you; you are the only doctor who listens to me with sincerity, respect, and interest. Even my boyfriend didn't believe me; he was disgusted and left me. God bless you, Dr. Chey." For further diagnostic workup and management, I felt she needed an expert consultation and treatment. I asked her, Ms. Smith, for her permission to contact Dr. Goldberg at Columbia-Presbyterian Hospital. She was overjoyed that she might be seen by a famous doctor at the prestigious hospital, a leading world-class medical institution.

When I called, Dr. Goldberg answered, "Yes, Dr. Chey." I was overwhelmed by his kind response. He listened to my brief presentation and agreed, "I would be delighted to have her transferred to my service for further evaluation." The next day, she was transferred by ambulance to the Presbyterian hospital on the west side of Upper Manhattan. Before she left the hospital, I told her that I would be there if she had to be operated on. She said, "You promise?" I nodded.

A week later, I received a phone call from Dr. Goldberg's office notifying me of the date and time of the surgical operation. I was excited. I was, however, heavily concerned that the surgical exploration might fail to find the tumor. The imaging studies and blood measurements of catecholamines at Presbyterian Hospital strongly suggested a flying saucer–like tumor sitting on the left adrenal gland. The professor had concurred with my initial diagnosis and decided to go ahead with the surgery, but that still did not relieve my anxiety.

On the day of the surgical operation, I caught a taxi on Lexington Avenue and Fifty-Eighth Street and asked the driver to take me to Presbyterian Hospital. By mistake he took me somewhere in the Bronx. It was almost eight o'clock when we arrived, the time for the operation to start at the correct hospital, which was about forty minutes away. My heart was pounding and anxious. On my arrival at the correct hospital, two uniformed security guards approached the car in a hurry and asked, "Are you Dr. Chey? Please come with us, sir." I was escorted to the operating room via a rapidly climbing elevator. In the operating room, everybody appeared relieved. I met Dr. Goldberg in a mask, and the operation was started. Later I was told that Ms. Smith refused to be anesthetized until I arrived. She said, " Dr. Chey promised me he would be here. Please let me wait for him a little longer." Both professors of anesthesiology and surgery honored her request and were patiently waiting for my arrival. I was very impressed that the two distinguished gentlemen respected her sincere request even though she came from a humble, low socioeconomic environment.

The operation found that she did indeed have a one-and-a-half-inch tan-colored flying saucer–like tumor sitting on her right adrenal gland instead of the left adrenal gland. After the careful and skillful removal of the tumor, she had an uneventful recovery. She no longer experienced episodic high blood pressure and terrible headaches for more than five years while I was periodically in contact with her. I again was overjoyed to be a healer who solved the mysteries of challenging medical problems, leading to comfort and healing for suffering patients. When Dr. Tuchman found out about the outcome of Ms. Smith's surgery, he was so pleased.

Back at City Hospital, the team of attending physicians was succeeded by another team of attending physicians, and they resumed the teaching service, including daily rounds and weekly clinical conferences. I presented, during the regular bedside rounds, a new fifty-one-year-old Caucasian male with a recent history of increasing jaundice, anorexia, weight loss, and dark to black stools that contained blood. He did not complain of severe abdominal pain. The endoscopy, which examines the esophagus, stomach, and duodenum, was not available in 1955. The chief attending physician examined the patient personally and asked me, "What is your diagnosis, doctor?"

"Dr. Marks, I listed three pathological conditions in differential diagnosis. First, ulcerated cancer in the ampulla of Vater; second, cancer of the head of the pancreas; and third, ulcerated cancer of the duodenum." He insinuated doubts regarding my clinical impression of probable cancer of the ampulla. He apparently felt that the diagnosis was too fancy for an intern from a foreign medical school.

In the attending team, there was a superb clinician from Mount Sinai Hospital. He gently and tactfully stated, "It seems to me that Dr. Chey's impression of an ulcerated ampullary carcinoma is more likely because of a recent development of obstructive jaundice with melena but without significant weight loss or the typical severe upper abdominal pain radiating to the back as occurs in patients with cancer of the pancreas. I was so relieved and grateful to Dr. Morris Steinberg, who supported me. The diagnosis was confirmed by the surgeons who operated on the patient, and our early diagnosis led to a successful surgical removal of the tumor to cure this malignant disease. This is the joy of being a thinking physician. I was always looking forward to making rounds with Dr. Steinberg and discussing our problem cases. He was also a graduate of the Columbia University College of Physicians and Surgeons and an attending physician at Mount Sinai Hospital. After that I respected Dr. Steinberg, who was another mentor in my early career at City Hospital. He used to call me and invite me to his office near Madison Avenue for lunch. He showed me how to perform fluoroscopic examinations of the chest and abdomen, and barium meal studies to examine the esophagus, stomach, and small intestine. Apparently, in those days, it was not uncommon for general internists to practice limited radiological studies at their offices.

My medical knowledge was enriched further by attending the meetings at the New York Academy of Medicine. Some of the outstanding speakers in my field of internal medicine whom I remember were Doctors Alexander Gutman, Arthur Masters, Burrill Crohn, Asher Winkelstein, Thomas Almy, Marvin Sleisenger, Henry Janowitz, and Paul Klemperer. I felt that I needed to study harder and move on to further graduate training. Attending the meetings held at the New York Academy of Medicine had already paid off for me. I also began to like internal medicine more than other specialties including surgical specialties. There was no doubt in my mind that internal medicine specialties demand more intellectual challenges, and I enjoyed studying physiology and pathophysiology of internal organs. I wrote to Dr. DeBakey, the legendary surgeon of our time, at Baylor College of Medicine in Houston, Texas, and let him know about my decision to pursue an academic career in internal medicine. The graceful Dr. DeBakey wrote me back immediately, wishing me the best of luck and giving me his best wishes. After one year of rotating internship, I was advanced to become an assistant resident in internal medicine at City Hospital.

Both Doctors Steinberg and Tuchman extended kindness and friendship from time to time, which I treasured. They separately used to invite me to their offices at noontime on Saturdays. I enjoyed visiting their beautiful offices on either Park Avenue or Madison Avenue while they were still seeing their friendly private patients. After office hours, they invited me to upscale restaurants for lunch in the neighborhood. On these occasions, I had opportunities to enjoy a variety of meals, such as French, Italian, and American cuisine, and delicious Kosher sandwiches in Jewish delicatessens. Sometimes they invited me to a concert or a Broadway show. It turned out that Dr. Tuchman's wife, Barbara, was a famous writer who won a Pulitzer Prize for her famous novel *The Guns of August*, and the wife of Dr. Steinberg was Evelyn Sachs, an opera and concert singer. I was overwhelmed by their kindness, friendship, and thoughtfulness. I could offer them very little.

One Saturday at his office, Dr. Tuchman mentioned that I should consider a special fellowship in pathology for one year at the Mount Sinai Hospital Department of Pathology under the tutelage of Professors Paul Klemperer and Sadao Otani, who were faculty members of Columbia University. Both of them had received PhDs from the University of Berlin under the guidance of Professor Karl Albert Ludwig Aschoff, one of the foremost pathologists in the early part of the twenty century. Dr. Tuchman winked at me and said, "You will like it and will enjoy the year enriching your medical knowledge further." Many bright young doctors in clinical residency training programs in various specialties, including internal medicine, spent one year in the pathology department in those days. I found out that even legendary gastroenterologist Dr. Burrill Crohn spent one year in the same department many years earlier. He was the senior author of the original article on a specific inflammatory small bowel disease that he and his colleagues at Mount Sinai Hospital published in the *Journal of American Medical Association* in 1932. Subsequently, this specific disease involving both the small bowel and large intestine (colon) was named after Dr. Burrill Crohn as Crohn's disease, which is universally recognized today.

Dr. Tuchman said, "If you agree with my suggestion, I will strongly recommend you for the fellowship, which will provide you a scholarship fund to get by."

I answered, "Thank you, Dr. Tuchman. I would be honored to accept the fellowship appointment."

Then he said, "The specialty of internal medicine is exciting, challenging, and rewarding, but we don't starve." I have always remembered this remark throughout my career. I was told that the fellowship fund allowed me to have a monthly stipend of fifty dollars with free laundry. I had to pay twenty dollars monthly for my dormitory room, leaving me only thirty dollars for spending, which included daily meals. I found out that the same compensation applied to the entire house staff, including chief residents of the major clinical departments at Mount Sinai Hospital. I realized that this was a significant cut in the stipend and benefits provided by City Hospital, which I enjoyed.

One of my friends at a US MASH during the Korean War, Donald Weeks Jr. III, had returned from Korea and resumed his first-year assistant residency in surgery at New York Hospital, the major teaching hospital of Cornell University College of Medicine. New York Hospital is on the east side of Manhattan in New York City and is one of the most magnificent and beautiful medical centers in the world. When I told him about Mount Sinai's compensation for my fellowship, he smiled and giggled, stating, "That's about right. You and I are in the same boat, Bill. All the highly competitive teaching hospitals don't pay well." His situation was harder than mine because he had to take care of his wife and an adorable baby daughter. Donald completed his seven years of training at New York Hospital. He was a chief resident when he finished the training with two specialty board certifications, including general surgery and chest surgery. He returned to his hometown in Florida and enjoyed a very successful surgical practice there. At the time of his retirement, he was the director of the Orlando Regional Health Care System in Florida. I owe him so much for his kindness, help and guidance, which started during the Korean War and lasted through the earlier days of my career in the United States.

94

# Mount Sinai Hospital in New York City

The large general hospital complex was built in Upper Manhattan, across Fifth Avenue from Central Park It had about a one-thousand-bed capacity, with superb clinical and teaching facilities and research laboratories. A nationally and internationally well-known pathologist, Dr. Hans Popper was appointed as the new chairman of the Department of Pathology when I started fellowship training in July, 1956. Dr. Popper was instrumental in establishing the Mount Sinai School of Medicine in 1963. Dr. Sadao Otani, an eminent morphological pathologist, and other outstanding faculty members, participated in our training activities. We met new and existing residents and fellows—twelve in total. Except for five career residents in pathology, the remaining seven were, like myself, newcomers from various clinical disciplines during their training, which included internal medicine, radiology, general surgery, pediatrics, and obstetrics and gynecology. They were graduates from highly competitive American medical schools, including Yale University School of Medicine and Columbia University College of Physicians and Surgeons. They were extremely competitive professionally and eager to show themselves how much they knew and how smart they were.

My daily activity started in the early morning, with autopsy examinations of patients who had died from highly significant and complicated medical problems. It was so much fun to review sometimes as many as two or three volumes of carefully prepared inpatient charts before each examination started. The performance of each autopsy case was supervised closely by the chief resident or a junior faculty member. Also they participated in the dissection and examination of the main pathological organs or tissues and taught us the art of dissection. I appreciated it very much. It took three hours or longer to complete the examination. Young enthusiastic resident physicians who took care of the patients often visited the autopsy room to find out the autopsy result firsthand. At noontime, there was a regularly scheduled surgical pathology conference supervised by Dr. Otani. So many clinicians—mainly surgeons and gastroenterologists, including the legendary Dr. Crohn—and some radiologists walked over to the laboratory to find out the morphological diagnosis expressed by Dr. Otani. To get to the pathology laboratory, they walked through the long walkway from the clinical buildings (about one block) to the laboratory building. They came every day. I was overwhelmed by the wealth of so many varieties of pathology that I saw in such a short first three months. For example, there were at least one or two bowel specimens with Crohn's disease, whereas I saw only one case in two years in the previous large city hospital just before I came to Mount Sinai.

In the afternoon, starting at four o'clock, a daily autopsy conference was held in the pathology amphitheater. The conference was usually conducted by either Dr. Hans Popper or Dr. Sadao Otani. First, the resident who took care of the patient presented a brief clinical history and features and other diagnostic findings.

This was followed by a junior pathology resident performing the autopsy and describing the pathological findings. Then discussion was extended to clinical attending physicians, who shared their clinical views. Finally, either Dr. Popper or Dr. Otani made their comments, and the meeting was adjourned. One last conference of the week was conducted by Dr. Popper on Saturday morning, starting at ten o'clock and running until noon. In the conference, every autopsy case had to be presented to all members of the department by a first-year resident or fellow in pathology, including myself, who performed autopsies. To present the case, each one had to prepare the autopsy findings for weeks under the supervision and instruction of a junior faculty member. Before the presentation, one had to be comfortable explaining the cause of death that correlated with the clinical features. Not infrequently, Dr. Popper was not convinced of the correlation. Then one had to extend research further until the boss was convinced. During one case I presented initially, I could not convince either Dr. Popper or Dr. Otani. Both giants could not accept "essential" pulmonary hypertension as the cause of the patient's death. Both claimed "essential" means one doesn't know the real cause and told me to search harder.

The patient was a twenty-six-year-old female who died with a clinical diagnosis of essential pulmonary hypertension with frequent episodes of syncope and chest pain. One month prior to her death, the patient was presented and discussed at medical grand rounds, and the chairman of the Department of Medicine and senior cardiologists agreed with the diagnosis. Previously, she was investigated extensively by an eminent cardiopulmonary research group at Mount Sinai. They concluded the most likely cause of death was essential pulmonary hypertension causing syncope. After several weeks of extensive histochemical studies of the lungs, pulmonary artery, and heart, I, early Saturday morning, discovered numerous small arterial blood vessels with inflammation and necrosis, which were mostly embedded in peripheral parts of the lungs. I called the junior faculty member who had supervised me for months on this investigation, and when he saw the findings under the microscope, he was more surprised and pleased than I was. Then we found that many of these blood vessels were plugged by small thrombi. The finding was consistent with periarteritis nodosa, mainly involving the lungs.

This could explain why she had pulmonary hypertension, because numerous tiny arterial blood vessels in the lungs were partially or completely obstructed, meaning that the fresh and oxygenated blood could not pass through the lungs. The finding convinced both of us that the patient certainly did not have essential pulmonary hypertension. When I presented once more at the Saturday meeting, both Dr. Popper and Dr. Otani were convinced by my presentation. They were very pleased, and Dr. Popper congratulated me. It was such a gratifying experience. First, I was so thrilled and felt honored when I saw that both professors were so pleased; second, I earned self-confidence in seeking answers regarding an unknown by working hard with reasonable logic; third, I learned about a disease I had never been taught about or heard of; and finally, research was very fun. These were invaluable lessons I learned from these two great mentors. I cherished these valuable lessons, which remained with me throughout my entire professional career, and shared them with many of my former students and colleagues.

In addition, there were many learning opportunities on the campus of this great institution. For example, there were gastrointestinal physiology lectures given by Dr. Franklyn Hollander, a well-recognized gastrointestinal physiologist, at GI Physiology Research Laboratory; weekly gastroenterology conferences conducted by Dr. Henry Janowitz, which were also attended from time to time by the Cornell Medical College / New York Hospital GI group, headed by Dr. Marvin Sleisenger; a combined radiology and pathology conference and clinical pathological conference conducted by Dr. Popper of the Department of Pathology; and Dr. Hans Popper's hepatology course.

I also had an opportunity to write a scientific paper together with a medical resident, Dr. James Bernstein. Jim, a Harvard Medical School graduate, came to see me to find out whether or not I would be interested in critically evaluating patients with small bowel tumors that were reported in the Mount Sinai Record Room and the Pathology Department. It was a nice clinicopathological project. We documented 104 cases with histologically proven small bowel tumors, including cancer. The paper was published in the *Journal of Mount Sinai Hospital*. Dr. Lester Tuchman, the editor of the journal, was very pleased. I finally realized I was in the right place at the right time for my professional career development. I became more and more interested in pursuing academic medicine in internal medicine and returned to my alma mater in Seoul, Korea, when I finished my training in clinical and research medicine in this great country.

# Life at Mount Sinai

Mount Sinai Hospital, a world-class medical institution, in addition to the small monthly stipend they paid to each house staff member and other hardworking young doctors, such as fellows in pathology, offered free meals for everybody at nine o'clock at night. All kinds of free fresh food items, including warm meals, sandwiches, desserts, beverages, and coffee, were piled up on a long, large table in the huge hospital cafeteria. Many young doctors dined together with their families, including their children and their loved ones. These nine o'clock meals saved many of us from hunger. Those who lived in the house staff dormitories made additional white uniforms that had two large inside pockets that could hold many foods and beverages that were brought to the dormitory and were kept on individual dormitory floors in secondhand refrigerators that we purchased from a nearby junk store in Harlem. Sometimes the rattling noise from the refrigerators was irritating, but it kept the food and drink fresh for the next few days. Initially this was hard for me to adjust to—especially eating cold sandwiches every day, which gave me indigestion.

Hans Popper, MD, PhD, Professor and Chair, Department of Pathology,
Mount Sinai Hospital, New York, 1956.

I decided to discuss the issue of the very low stipend with Dr. Popper, although none of my colleagues would think of discussing this with "the boss." I made an appointment with him, although I was quite uncomfortable while thinking about the meeting for a week. In my earlier days at Mount Sinai, he gave me the impression of a typical caricature of a strict and dignified European professor. He rarely smiled when he was with us.

The appointment day finally arrived. His secretary escorted me to his room. He said, "Sit down, Doctor Chey. How was your work today? What can I do for you?"

I replied, " Sir, I need your advice and help, if possible. Since I came to Mount Sinai, I have been having dyspepsia [indigestion]. Because of my limited resources, I have been eating mainly cold sandwiches, which I am not used to."

He appeared somewhat amused, but he seemed to try hard to hide his feelings. "Let me see what I can do for you. I will recommend you for a special scholarship fund from a foundation." Within a week, I indeed received a letter from Dr. Howard Rusk that stated, " Dear Doctor Chey, Dr. Hans Popper recommended you for a special scholarship fund for your fellowship training in pathology at Mount Sinai Hospital. I am pleased to let you know that the Board of American- Korean Foundation approved a scholarship fund of $1,000.00 … Sincerely, Howard Rusk, M.D., a Professor, and Chairman, Department of Physical Medicine and Rehabilitation, New York University School of Medicine and Chairman, Board of Trustees, American Korean Foundation." In the letter, he asked whether I wanted to receive a monthly check for twelve months or a lump sum for the total amount. My answer was quick and simple. A check for $1,000 arrived shortly. I was so grateful to Dr. Popper and Dr. Rusk, who made my life at Mount Sinai more pleasant and enjoyable.

# A Midnight Phone Call and a Beautiful Young Nurse

In early spring of 1957, I was awakened by a midnight phone call from someone in a hospital in Washington, DC. A doctor called and informed me that my brother-in-law, Mr. Kim, had been operated on by him, and he was in coma. The doctor mentioned that Mr. Kim developed "an acute intestinal obstruction after having a heavy meal." He had arrived in Washington, DC, two days earlier from Seoul, Korea. I was told by my father a few weeks earlier that he was an official of the Ministry of Foreign Affairs of the Republic of Korea and had recently been invited by the Department of State of the United States as an observer for a period of six months. He had been married to my sister, Sang-ok, for only three months before he came to the States, and he was a graduate of Seoul National University, studying political science. I had not met him until I left Korea three years before.

I rushed by train to Washington, DC, early in the morning. In the hospital, I was surprised to find my brother-in-law, Kim Yong-chun, in an isolation room. Everybody entering the room had to wear a white gown and mask. He was indeed in a coma. He was a good-looking, tall Asian male in bed with a nasogastric tube in his nose for suction of stomach juices. Reviewing the chart, I saw that he had had an exploratory laparotomy that had revealed diffuse peritonitis and a small bowel obstruction. Because the patient was from Korea, they made a presumptive diagnosis of tuberculous peritonitis with extensive adhesions. However, there was no convincing X-ray evidence of tuberculosis in the chest when I reviewed the film. The tissue biopsies of the peritoneum were also negative for tuberculosis. The nurses, however, were hesitant to work around him because of the diagnosis of TB, although the majority of the nursing staff were nuns in a Catholic hospital. Anticipating possible difficulty with nursing coverage for the isolation room over the coming weekend, the hospital requested a local newspaper advertisement stating, "Seeking a volunteer nurse for an Asian male patient for the weekend …" One Asian nurse responded to the advertisement and came to the hospital on Saturday morning. When I entered the isolation room, a young Asian female nurse with a mask covering most of her face was already caring for Yong-Chun. I felt so relieved. She was already making eye contact with him, and he was responding to her gestures. I said, "Good morning," and she answered me back, "Good morning, Doctor," in perfect English. Yong-Chun was very pleased to see her every time she entered the room, but unfortunately she could not speak Korean. For him, this was the first time he had seen an Asian nurse in this hospital. When she removed her mask, I found her a delightful, attractive, and beautiful young lady whose name was Fan K. Tang. She and her family had immigrated to the States from China by way of Taiwan when she was a young teen. I asked her whether she had time to have a coffee with me. We went to the hospital cafeteria. I thanked her very much for taking care of Yong-Chun for the weekend.

She thought there must be a reason for the advertisement to recruit a nurse for an Asian patient in an isolation room, but she did not realize that the nurses in the hospital were so afraid of a TB patient. She said she would be glad to take care of him on Sunday also. I was deeply touched by her kindness, sympathy, and compassion in a situation where I was alone and felt helpless and very concerned about Yong-Chun's critical medical condition. The next day, we met again in the isolation room. We had lunch together. She was a charming person to be with. She told me that she had been accepted by a Catholic nursing school in Boston with a scholarship and had graduated last year. This was her first month in Washington, DC, working in another hospital. Her family—including her mother, two older sisters, and one younger brother—lived in Forest Hill, Long Island, New York. Although it was a short period, her presence, sympathy, and help meant a lot to me at this time of crisis in my life. I felt so sorry for my dear sister and her gravely ill husband's family and my family—including my mother and father in Seoul, who were unaware of Yong-Chun's grave medical condition.

I was quite disturbed, however, by the fact that the attending doctors of Yong-Chun could not come up with a definitive diagnosis in five days since the surgical operation. It was an unexpected and incredibly traumatic experience for a young man to have an ileostomy for a bowel obstruction, and he was absolutely bewildered to be facing such a totally unexpected and disastrous situation in a foreign country, even with my presence and Fan's kind support and care, though it was only one short weekend. Moreover, I was very disappointed that no representative from the ROK Embassy visited Yong-Chun, who was a midlevel official diplomat. Nor was there any contact from the US State Department. I visited the office that dealt with Far Eastern affairs. The person in charge of this section was Mrs. Pearce, a kind and soft-spoken middle-aged lady. I informed her of Yong-Chun's current critical condition. I pointed out to her that he had been invited to the States by this department as an observer. In my opinion, he was being treated by doctors in a community hospital for a very serious medical condition without a definitive diagnosis. Ms. Pearce was very kind, apologetic, and sympathetic.

I asked whether he could be transferred to either Walter Reed Army Hospital or Bethesda Naval Medical Center. I emphasized that his grave condition be taken care of by highly qualified specialists in a hospital with better facilities and a more qualified team of experts. Ms. Pearce sighed and suggested contacting the Korean Embassy. Only a presidents, kings, cabinet members, or high-ranking generals of foreign countries could be admitted to these two hospitals. But if a Korean ambassador recommended a need for special care, he might be considered for transfer. I made an appointment with Dr. Y. C. Young, a physician who was the ROK ambassador to the United States, who had received his medical education in the United States. When I explained the serious condition of Yong-Chun, I saw no sympathy or empathy in his expression—not even once. He said, "Only President Rhee or cabinet members or ambassadors may be considered for care in these prestigious hospitals." I was very disappointed and disenchanted at his attitude, considering that he once was a practicing physician. Without financial resources, I was at a complete loss and was desperate.

A remotely possible consideration was a transfer to Mount Sinai Hospital in New York City for further evaluation and care. I visited Ms. Pearce again. I informed her that my visit to the Korean ambassador was a big disappointment. She was very sympathetic, and she didn't appear to know what to do. I told her that I was considering having Mr. Kim transferred to Mount Sinai Hospital if possible. Before I mentioned my difficult financial problems, Ms. Pearce interrupted me with her bright eyes open wide and asked, "Dr. Chey, is it possible to transfer him to Mount Sinai?"

I said, "Yes. I have already contacted Dr. John Uhr, a chief resident of internal medicine at Mount Sinai Hospital, and I was assured by Dr. Uhr that his team will take care of him."

She gasped for air and said, "This is great news, Dr. Chey. The State Department will take care of all the medical and transportation expenses for Mr. Kim."

I was almost shocked by the totally unexpected generous offer. In hindsight, I think Ms. Pearce must have felt helpless and embarrassed by her inability to help the desperately ill young Korean diplomat whom they had invited.

Within a few days, Yong-Chun was transferred to Mount Sinai Hospital via a comfortable ambulance. I accompanied him all the way to the hospital in New York City. I found that Yong-Chun was the oldest son of a well-respected family in Seoul and had been selected as the top candidate to come to the US State Department as an observer in hopes of pursuing his career as a diplomat. He was so happy to marry my sister, Sang-Ok, whom he adored and described as a beautiful, kind, and devoted wife. They were so happy together. He had missed her so much already.

As he arrived at Mount Sinai, he was thoroughly evaluated and treated by one of the best teams of bright interns, residents, and outstanding attending staff. An exploratory laparotomy was repeated by a team of surgeons, and they invited Professor Sadao Otani into the operating room for his valued opinion regarding the pathological finding. Dr. Otani was a recognized top-notch morphological pathologist in the city. They confirmed the abdominal findings described by the surgeons in Washington, DC. The abdominal cavity again showed extensive inflammation and fibrosis without any signs of cancer or tuberculosis. Numerous biopsy specimens were obtained, but they showed no cancer cells or tuberculosis. Careful X-ray examinations of the stomach and remaining small intestine were carried out twice using barium meals by the most experienced senior radiologist, and they failed to show a tumor or inflammation. Even Dr. Crohn agreed with the results of the radiological examination. The only consistent finding was segmental narrowing of the small bowel resulting from extensive adhesions, which caused intermittent bowel blockage. Dr. Otani spent many hours with the tissue slides, but he could not come up with any recognizable specific pathology. The recurrent bowel obstructions and steady deterioration of his general condition ended his life two months after his arrival at Mount Sinai. I was dissuaded by Dr. Otani to be present in the autopsy room. Although a small cancer of the pancreas was suspected by the majority, they found a small, flat cancer instead, smaller than a half inch, with a shallow ulcer in the back wall of the very upper part of the stomach. In 1957, without the endoscopic help we have today, a small tumor like this was almost impossible to be suspected or found. Undoubtedly, Yong-Chun had had this condition for quite a while before he married my sister. Indeed it was a tragic fate.

Fan had been very concerned about my stressful situation in a new country without family or any other support. Within a month after Yong-Chun moved to Mount Sinai, she decided to move to the New York City area and wished to offer me any possible support or help. I was so deeply touched by her warm heart and kindness, which Yong-Chun recognized and deeply appreciated. One evening just before the cafeteria was opened for the free meal at nine o'clock, a beautiful Fan was waiting for me in the hallway, smiling and holding a large bag full of what appeared to be food. This was a totally unexpected surprise. She had never been at Mount Sinai. She said she had gotten a new job in New Jersey, just across the river, and she giggled. She would start work in a week as a registered nurse at Newark Beth Israel Hospital in New Jersey. We walked to my room in the pathology laboratories. Dr. Masugi, a faculty member of Tokyo University, Tokyo, Japan was still working. He joined us in enjoying a feast of genuine, delicious Chinese dishes she had purchased from a restaurant in Chinatown near Wall Street, quite distant from One Hundredth and Fifth Avenue, near Central Park. Dr. Masugi was so pleased to meet with Fan. He didn't know she was a Chinese woman. The time was soon approaching midnight. I escorted her to a taxi waiting on the Fifth Avenue exit of the hospital. I accompanied her to her mother's home in Forest Hill, Queens. It was such a memorable time we had spent together. I returned by subway to the hospital alone, with a feeling of emptiness.

# Fan K. Tang's Family

Fan invited me to her mother's home the following Sunday. This was my first experience in meeting with a Chinese family, and I was somewhat nervous, particularly since they were Fan's family. They all welcomed me as I entered their living room, which was beautifully decorated. Fan had a graceful mother who was in her sixties; two older sisters, May and Nan; a younger brother, James; a brother-in-law, William Chang, the husband of May; and William and May's two little daughters, Dallas and Mei Mei. Except for her mother, they spoke English like any other Americans. They were very friendly and hospitable, and they made me feel at ease. Fan's mother's English vocabulary was somewhat limited, but I soon found out that she could speak Japanese well. We both could easily communicate in Japanese, which I had not used for more than ten years. She had lived in Japan to study agricultural science for two years during her high school years. She was a kind and friendly lady. Soon I was served a delicious home-cooked Chinese meal. After the dinner, I found that Bill Chang, a Chinese man who had been born in Hawaii, was a newspaper reporter; May, his wife, was a part-time accountant. Nan was a certified dietician working at New York Hospital, and James was a geologist.

Her father had passed away only five years prior from a digestive ailment, in a university hospital in Tokyo, Japan. His name was Tang Un-Bo, and he was one of the most decorated Republic of China Army generals for the defense of China against the Imperial Japanese Army invasion in Shanghai in World War II. He was a brilliant general and was only one of a handful of young Chinese natives who were selected to enter and had military education at the Imperial Japanese Military Academy, which was highly competitive and difficult to enter even for the many hardworking and ambitious young Japanese students in the early 1900s. I was told that some of Japanese students who failed to pass the entrance examination for three consecutive years committed suicide in disgrace, profound disappointment, and embarrassment. So many Japanese students wanted to become honorable cadet of the prestigious academy for the Emperor of Japan. When I was invited to Beijing and Shanghai in 1981, I was surprised to find that many Chinese people, even high school students on the street, still remembered General Tang as one of their national heroes. In the time I had known Fan, she had not mentioned her famous father. She has always been a modest and humble person.

After a pleasant visit with her family, I thanked her mother and the remaining family members for the lovely evening, and we walked to the subway station. Fan asked what I thought of her mother and family. I told her that she had a beautiful family and a wonderful mother. She said "Thank you, Bill," and she appeared to be pleased. "I wish I can meet with your family someday."

Fan was a kind, caring, and warm-hearted young lady who had been so often with me at the time when I needed someone whom I could talk to and feel comfort with. She knew how concerned I was about Yong-Chun, whose condition was steadily deteriorating. I was very worried about my family, as well as his family in Seoul. No doubt both families were happy and proud of Yong-Chun and Sang-Ok, who had married only three months before he was invited to the US government as a young diplomat. They did not realize how grave Yong-Chun's illness was. My lovely and beautiful sister was brought up in a warm, caring, and protective family, just as if a beautiful flower blossomed in a warm and well-cultivated nursery. I was so worried that soon their dreams and hopes would be shattered when Yong-Chun's life ended. Recognizing his own serious situation, he said to me on several occasions, "Please convey my sincere message to my family and Sang-Ok that she remarry if I die. I will be very happy for her." He did not realize, however, that his wife was already pregnant. Neither did I. How sad they must have been to receive their loved one at Seoul Airport in a wooden box filled with his remaining ashes. He had left the same airport with high hopes only three months earlier.

It was already June 1957, and my training at Mount Sinai was about to end. The past year had been an unforgettable and rewarding year, and I had gotten an incredible break in my professional career. I had the honor of being mentored by two great pathologists, Drs. Hans Popper and Sadao Otani, and I worked with very best young career pathology residents, future physician-scientists who spent time in pathology as a part of their training program in medicine and other clinical disciplines, and eminent visiting fellows, such as Dr. Yozo Masugi, a pathologist from the prestigious Tokyo University Faculty of Medicine. I was also inspired by great clinicians, teachers, and scientists, such as Drs. Lester Tuchman, Burrill Crohn, Alexander Gutman, Henry Janowitz, and Franklyn Hollander. This rich experience allowed many of us who came from clinical disciplines to enrich our knowledge of pathological anatomy directly correlating with clinical medicine and pathophysiology of so many diseases, and I also had daily interactions with brilliant and hardworking young American coworkers. In addition, I had an opportunity to prepare a scientific manuscript as a co-author with James Bernstein, MD, a medical resident, a Harvard Medical School graduate. The article was published in *Journal of Mount Sinai Hospital*, titled "Small Bowel Tumors: A Clinical Study of 109 Cases." This one year of rich experiences helped me to pave my career as an academic clinician and physician–scientist.

# Hepatology Fellowship

Dr. Hans Popper advised me to consider a clinical/research fellowship in hepatology for the coming year. I appreciated his appropriate advice. Among several programs in the country, I chose Dr. Carroll M. Leevy's program at Seton Hall University College of Medicine and Dentistry, Jersey City, New Jersey (the name of which was later changed to "Medical University of New Jersey, Newark, New Jersey"). This was one of Dr. Popper's suggestions also.

At the end of June 1957, I moved to a gorgeous marble-walled building on the premises of Jersey City Medical Center, which was a separate tower from the hospital complex. My bedroom was larger than any at the previous two hospitals and was built in a pleasant style. In the beautiful dining room, meals were served by friendly waiters, as at New York City Hospital. We ate three meals together with house staff and faculty members. Additional amenities were a swimming pool in one lower level, and in another lower level there was a billiards room, a card room, and a large room for gymnastic equipment.

**Dr. Carroll Leevy, professor of medicine and chief of hepatology,
Seton Hall University School of Medicine and Dentistry, Jersey City, New Jersey, 1958.**

Dr. Leevy, professor of medicine and director of hepatology, was a rising star in academic hepatology and was the only African American academic hepatologist with national and international recognition. He was in charge of both the male and female medical floors. He treated and investigated patients with various liver diseases. He oversaw clinical research facilities, including a hepatic vein catheterization laboratory, to study the circulatory function of the liver, such as portal hypertension in patients with cirrhosis, and biochemistry laboratories. Having spent one year in Dr. Popper's pathology department, I was ready to further study liver pathology among Dr. Leevy's inpatient population with liver diseases and contribute to his program. I learned a wealth about clinical hepatology under the tutelage of Dr. Leevy and his team of clinical faculty, and I learned investigative methodologies including hepatic vein catheterization and skills that led to the investigation of blood ammonia levels in patients with cirrhosis of the liver. We found that patients with advanced liver diseases, such as severe cirrhosis of the liver, who exhibited sensorial changes and confusion had high blood levels of ammonia, which was corroborated by the reports of other colleagues in world scientific literature.

Our work was chosen for presentation at the annual meeting of the American Association for Liver Diseases at Duke Hotel, in Chicago, Illinois. In spite of rehearsing so many times with Dr. Leevy, I rehearsed again the night before the day of my presentation. This was my first presentation at this well-recognized national and international meeting. Moreover, the front-row seats were occupied mostly by nationally and internationally renowned hepatologists and professors. I was probably the first young Asian selected for the presentation at this annual meeting. It was a nerve-racking experience to see eminent professors such as Sheila Sherlock, from London; Gerald Klatskin, from Yale; Leon Schiff, from the University of Cincinnati; and Charles Davidson, from Harvard, who were known to ask sharp and sometimes difficult questions. Both Dr. Leevy and Dr. Popper were also in the front row. Both of them sat there holding their arms crossed on their chests. When I finished my presentation, I heard a loud round of applause from the audience, and I saw both Dr. Popper and Dr. Leevy looking at each other and smiling. When I came down from the podium, Dr. Popper came to my seat and shook my hand and said, "Congratulations, Bill." For the first time, he had used my first name.

Dr. Leevy also praised me and said, "You presented very well, Bill," and he smiled at me. I called Fan on the phone as soon as I had a chance to get into a nearby phone booth. Luckily she answered, and I told her, "Fan, I did it."

She responded, "I am so thrilled. I am very proud of you and love you. That's wonderful, darling." Being with her in a nearby city where she worked, my life was emotionally settled and secure. This was another reason I decided to stay in Jersey City.

Dr. Leevy was a superb clinician and teacher whose patients trusted him, respected him, and adored him. I benefited from these fine qualities of his professionalism. One Saturday afternoon, he called me on the phone and said, "Bill, I have an urgent out-of-town consultation. Would you like to come with me?" I hopped in his Oldsmobile sedan waiting for me in front of the staff house entrance. I asked him, "Where is the patient?"

"There is a thirty-four-year-old female with deep jaundice in a coma in a small town near Trenton."

When we entered the house, an exhausted husband led us to their bedroom. The patient was indeed deeply jaundiced and nonresponsive. Four small children were in the room, crying and sobbing. A visiting nurse had already started an intravenous infusion of glucose, as requested by her family physician. Dr. Leevy, after his thorough assessment of the patient's condition, comforted her husband and children and told her children, "Your mom will be okay soon." Then he turned to her husband and said, "She has an unusually severe hepatitis. She should recover soon."

The husband appeared very relieved and shook Dr. Leevy's hand and said, "God bless you." Then Dr. Leevy handed him a prescription.

On the way home, I asked him, "Do you really believe she will recover that soon?

He said, "I had to say something to comfort them. Yeah, I have seen some patients in similar conditions regain consciousness after several days of coma." Then he grinned at me.

"Do you think there is any use for tetracycline for her condition?" I asked. "It may do some good. The drug has been used for hepatitis, and more importantly, her husband might be more satisfied and comforted when I prescribe medicine for her."

Two days later, the following Tuesday morning, I hesitatingly called her husband. He immediately answered the phone and said, " Oh, Dr. Chey, sir, my wife, Nancy, woke up last evening. You and Dr. Leevy are miracle workers." I rushed into Dr. Leevy's office and told him, "Nancy woke up last evening." His two big eyes were open and bright, and he laughed in his typical high-pitched way. I asked him, "Did you really believe she would recover so soon?"

He said, "Well, Doctor, miracles do happen in medicine."

I was very impressed with Dr. Leevy's handling of this crisis with a desperate family surrounding an unconscious patient. His performance was indeed a combination of both the art of medicine and medical science. Dr. Leevy was an excellent physician and scientist, a prolific writer, and an orator. He taught me how to write scientific manuscripts and how to prepare speeches. It was my privilege and honor to be under his tutelage.

My hepatology fellowship was about to end in the summer of 1958. I explained and discussed my future professional goals to my closest friend and confidant, Fan. She was always willing to listen and participate in the discussion when I needed her. I had felt such comfort whenever I was with her. I explained my desire to teach, research, and take care of sick patients in a highly respected teaching institution. I told her that I might have to pursue my plan for further education and training in a reputable university. She said, "It sounds wonderful. Where do you plan to go and start? I am proud of you. I like a man with high ambitions and hopes for many years ahead." I told her that meant I would have to move to another city, such as Boston or Philadelphia. She said, "I have no problem following you and supporting you however I can." I was deeply grateful for her kindness and support.

# University of Pennsylvania Graduate School of Medicine

I was very excited in looking into the graduate program offered at the University of Pennsylvania Graduate School of Medicine in Philadelphia, Pennsylvania. The program offered a ten-month review course of general internal medicine and gastroenterology combined with basic sciences, including human anatomy, biochemistry, and physiology. The course was offered by faculty members and headed by a legendary world-renowned gastroenterologist, Dr. Henry Bockus, professor of medicine and chairman of the Department of Medicine. The eminent clinical and basic science faculty members participated in and contributed to the course. The teaching institutions for the course were Graduate Hospital, Philadelphia General Hospital, the Hospital of the University of Pennsylvania, and the School of Medicine. After completing the course, the graduate would be qualified to become a candidate for advanced-degree work, including work toward becoming a master of gastroenterology (MSc in gastroenterology) or a doctor of medical science (DSc) if the candidate graduate was academically qualified based on the scores of the final examination. I felt as if the program was designed just for my needs, considering the inadequate medical education I had received during the harsh and cruel war in Korea and my one year of military service in combat zones. Indeed, I did need such a well-structured refresher and review course. Furthermore, I would have an opportunity to work in a research laboratory toward an advanced degree, such as a DSc in Medicine. This degree was valued highly in academic institutions in Korea when I returned home.

My plan was to move to Philadelphia in early August to settle in a small apartment near the university campus and seek a part-time job at night and on weekends for the coming ten months while taking courses at the graduate school. I thought that the money I saved during the fellowship and my earnings from these extra hours might be sufficient for me to get by on for ten months. I discussed the plan with Fan in late July while having dinner at the medical center. Fan was delighted to hear my plan and said she, too, would like to move to Philadelphia to be near me. She said, "Your ambition is admirable and exciting." Fortunately she soon found a nursing position at Graduate Hospital, starting in the first week of September. I found a small apartment in a row house. She found a studio apartment six houses away from mine.

The graduate class comprised twenty-three coeds: three females and twenty male physicians. The majority of them were from abroad, sponsored by their own home institutions. They had come from areas including Thailand, the Philippines, Turkey, Santo Domingo, and Argentina. Six American and Canadian doctors took the course, and two of them were taking it as a part of their senior residency training in medicine. The rest of the American doctors and Canadian doctors had come for a refresher course after years of medical practice. One notable physician taking the course was a forty-six-year-old physician, a graduate of the University of Pennsylvania Medical School, Dr. James Myers, who had spent ten years in Nigeria as a missionary doctor. He was a friendly gentleman who possessed good leadership qualities. He was elected as the president of the class. All the faculty members were excellent lecturers and highly seasoned clinicians. The professors in basic sciences were friendly, and their lectures were comprehensive. Above all, Professor Henry Bockus was an outstanding clinician, teacher, and orator. He was a tall, distinguished-looking gentleman with silvery hair. I still admire and cherish his oratory lectures. He expressed his interest in having me as his graduate student for an advanced degree if I qualified.

In order to qualify as a candidate for an advanced degree, I had to study very hard for the final examination of the course to earn a high average score from both the clinical and basic science courses. It became harder and harder for me to support myself as the coursework progressed. I had to work in emergency rooms of community hospitals in the city from early evening to midnight and on weekends. The unlicensed physician's wage was very low, but somehow I had to get through the coming school year. I had to eat and pay rent. Recognizing the hardship that I had to endure, Fan frequently prepared food in the evenings or left fast food on the small dining table in my apartment; these were such welcome treats, which I enjoyed before she left for her own work in the evening. I was grateful for her thoughtful deeds every day. In Seoul, no one knew the hardship I endured every day; nor were they aware that there was someone pushing me to achieve my goal—a young, pure, warm-hearted, and beautiful woman who so happened to be Chinese. I was more determined than ever that I must obtain a DSc degree from the prestigious University of Pennsylvania for myself as well as for her, no matter what. Indeed, I fell in love with her.

During the last week of June, I was notified by the dean's office of the graduate school that I had qualified as a candidate for the advanced-degree work. I was so excited. I said to myself, "So I may be able to bring a degree of doctorate of science in medicine home and to my alma mater, Seoul University, in Korea."

That night was almost silent, and it was near midnight when I drove to Graduate Hospital and waited for Fan in front of the entrance door. A little after midnight, she came out and spotted the car. As she entered the car, I told her that I had been accepted. She was thrilled, and with tears running from both of her eyes, she kissed me on my cheek. Then she said, "Let's go and celebrate."

I said, "This late?"

We drove to Chinatown. The lights were still on in our favorite small restaurant. The owner looked at us while cleaning the floor. He opened the locked door and told us they had just closed. "Is there a special occasion this late?" he asked.

I said, "Yes, very special."

He said, "I was about to turn the light off, but you are our good customers and friends. I will cook a special meal for you."

We both immensely enjoyed his home-cooked meal. After we ate, we divided the leftovers between us, and they fed us for the next two days. Since then, we visited his restaurant every weekend with our entire family until we moved to Rochester, New York, in 1971.

# Fellowship in Gastroenterology and Advanced Degrees

Fan asked me where I planned to do my thesis work. I told her that I must find a qualified mentor with a research laboratory or laboratories and adequate research support. Then I had to submit a proposal for the work to the graduate school. A committee would evaluate my proposal with the support of a qualified senior faculty member. Also I had to seek a combined clinical and research program suited to achieve my academic goal. I planned to have interviews for the fellowship in the institutions in Philadelphia in which I would like to settle until the degree work was completed, at which point I hoped to secure an academic position in the institution in which my research work would continue. I let Fan know for the first time about my dream—an American dream. She looked at me intensely and hugged me, quietly saying, "I am so proud of you, darling." If I could obtain a fellowship position with pay, I would propose marriage.

For the fellowship position, I was interviewed by four competitive gastroenterology division directors in Philadelphia, including one from the Hospital of the University of Pennsylvania. They were willing to accept me as a fellow and would be glad to sponsor and support my degree work combined with clinical fellowship training. The first three institutions offered a stipend of $4,500 per year. I was content with the financial offer. This was the highest stipend that I would have ever earned. The last interview was arranged with Dr. Harry Shay, a professor of medicine, director of the gastroenterology division, and director of the Samuel Fels Research Institute at Temple University Medical Center. He gave me a tour of the gastroenterology clinic and the clinical research facilities, including the X-ray room; the biochemistry laboratory, which was run by well-qualified technicians supervised by a senior biochemist; and laboratories for physiological research using experimental animals, led by Dr. Simon Komarov, who originally emigrated from St. Petersburg, Russia, and who was one of the pupils of the legendary Professor Ivan Pavlov. In my opinion, Dr. Shay had the program best suited to what I needed for both clinical and research gastroenterology training. I was very excited.

We went to his office, and he said he would be delighted to support and sponsor my degree work. I expressed my enthusiasm and gratitude for the fellowship. He was pleased to have me as a fellow for the coming fiscal year. Although I surmised that the stipend would be the same as the other three institutions offered, he did not mention the stipend. When I hesitantly asked about the stipend, Dr. Shay offered substantially less, $3,000 per year, but I accepted it because I had asked for the job and because my work would be carried out in the best research environment, organized by well-recognized researchers in the field. His program was already well known nationally and internationally. Some outstanding academic gastroenterologists passed through the program before I started, such as Dr. Basil Hirschowitz, the developer of the modern fiberoptic gastrointestinal endoscope, professor and director of the University of Alabama Division of Gastroenterology, and a recipient of the prestigious Julius Friedenberg Award from the American Gastroenterological Association; and Professor I. N. Marks in Cape Town, who was the founder of modern gastroenterology in South Africa. I phoned Fan at her office and let her know my decision. She was thrilled. She said, "Congratulations. I am very proud of you, darling. I love you. We will get together soon for celebration."

# Marriage Proposal

I t was already the last week of May, 1959. I had known Fan for over two years. On the day I saw her for the first time in Washington, DC, I had a special feeling I had never experienced before. Since then our affectionate feelings had been mutual, and we were inseparable. My agony and serious concern, however, related to whether or not my parents would accept her as a daughter-in-law, as she happened to be Chinese. In the world where I came from, most of the people were still uncomfortable about international marriage. I felt immense guilt toward my parents, who had brought me up in incredibly harsh and difficult environments under Japanese oppression and during cruel war in Korea. I knew they dreamed that when their son returned to South Korea, he would marry someone who was not only well educated but had also been brought up in a respected family in their society.

Fan is a daughter of an eminent Chinese family in modern Chinese history. She is beautiful, attractive, bright, honest, kind, and compassionate, and she has a strong will and handles difficult situations with a calm disposition. And in these early days, she was willing to venture along the life of a man whose dream was to pursue his career in academic medicine rather than a lucrative private practice. At the age of twenty-five, she was appointed as a supervisor of the Nursing Department at Graduate Hospital, the University of Pennsylvania. She was the only nurse of Asian origin at the hospital. I was so proud of her. I found it ironic that when I was invited to Chinese universities as a visiting professor many years later, I met several Chinese people with our same family name in sidewalk cafés, restaurants, and hospitals in Beijing, Shanghai, Xi'an, Chongqing, Chengdu, Tianjin, and even in Taipei, Taiwan. It is quite possible, as is the case with many other Koreans, that our ancestors migrated from the Chinese mainland to the Korean Peninsula centuries ago. In spite of the concerns I knew my family might have at home, I decided to propose marriage, because I couldn't think of anyone who could come between us. I wanted a good and happy family. Fan would be a good mother and wife. We could raise an ideal and loving family together in a secure environment, which was another dream of my life.

One Saturday afternoon, while walking on the bank of the Schuylkill River in Philadelphia, I humbly asked Fan to marry me. Fan looked at me so affectionately and said, "Thank you, and yes, Bill. This is the best thing that could ever happen to me in my entire life." Then she hugged me and sobbed, with tears welling in both her eyes. It was a wonderful Saturday afternoon that remained in my heart for a long time. I had always felt sorry for her, because I suspected she was a neglected third daughter in a country with male dominance, as was prolific in Asian culture at the time. A boy was desired as the first or second baby. Fan's parents were likely quite disappointed when they found the third newborn baby was again a girl. This type of unfairness was unfortunately pervasive until the early part of our generation. Indeed, this was the case in her family culture. I felt so sorry for her, and this made me love her more than ever. To celebrate our important event, we went to Fischer's Seafood Restaurant near Temple University Medical Center. Then we spent a wonderful evening together.

At the end of the evening, we discussed how to break the news to my parents and Fan's family—particularly her mother. On my side of the family, both parents were very disappointed, and my father, in particular, was so depressed that he stayed home for several days without attending meetings in the office. Not unexpectedly, her mother opposed it also, because she felt that, in general, Korean males and Japanese males were chauvinists. Nonetheless, we, two independent and highly intelligent people, looked at each other in the shade under a roadside tree near Fan's mother's home, and I asked her, "Are you sure you will marry me?" Fan nodded with tears in her eyes. I said, "Let's go," and we went ahead with a quiet civil wedding. I bought a wedding ring made of white platinum and adorned with small diamonds. When we went to her mother's home, her mother gracefully approved our marriage. Her entire family congratulated us, and we were invited to an elaborate restaurant for a celebration in Chinatown. Fan's elder sister, May, said, "Well, we have a doctor in our family now. Welcome, Dr. Chey, Geoun Bai" ("a drink for celebration" in Chinese). Everybody (except for the children) drank Chinese wine, and we enjoyed many Chinese dishes. Everybody liked the wedding ring that I had purchased with the money I had earned and saved from moonlighting in the emergency rooms of local private hospitals. My difficult problem was that I had to keep this news from the Korean community in Philadelphia until it was the appropriate time to let my parents and family know. It was an agonizing time keeping this secret news from not only my family but also my friends, particularly the Korean ones. I did not want to hurt them. I hadn't seen them since 1954. It indeed caused me heartache. We rented a two-room apartment near the university campus; the location made it convenient for Fan to commute to the hospital. We were so happy, but we had to remain silent and without support from my family.

Soon after our marriage, Fan became pregnant. We both were very happy and thrilled. We shared this delightful and special news with Fan's family in New York City. Her mother and her remaining family were so happy to hear the news and sincerely congratulated us. It was indeed an unforgettable day. Now we had to go out and hunt for another apartment to accommodate our new baby. We found a spacious apartment with a kitchen, a master bedroom, and a small room for the newborn baby in an apartment complex near a small park in the Germantown area of Philadelphia. This area, with less traffic than the city center, was clean, quiet, and pleasant. I liked the small park, where I and the baby could play someday. On May 13, 1960, our first new baby boy, Billy, was born at Pennsylvania Hospital. He was a beautiful, good-looking, and healthy baby with black hair that looked striking among the many newborn babies in the maternity room. Both Fan and I were ecstatic and happy to have such a beautiful, delightful, and good-natured baby boy.

*Part 4*

My Further Post-Graduate Training,
Advanced Academic Degrees,
Temple University Medical Center,
Late Dr. Harry Shay, Academic Physician,
U.S. Citizenship, My Family,
Philadelphia Medical Community,
Invitations Abroad, My Seoul Visit
in 14 Years and American Dream

# Combined Fellowship Training in Gastroenterology

My fellowship training started on June 1, 1959. Throughout the following three months, I worked in the Clinical Gastrointestinal Research Laboratories at Fels Research Institute, Temple University Medical Center. I started to work with Dr. David Sun, an assistant professor of medicine in gastroenterology who was investigating serum pancreatic enzymes and exocrine pancreatic secretory function in patients with acute and chronic pancreatitis. His work had already been well recognized by peers. We investigated both pancreatic juices and blood levels of pancreatic enzymes, both amylase and lipase, before and after intravenous injection of secretin. In order to collect pancreatic juices that were as pure as possible from the human duodenum, the patient swallowed a soft and flexible double-lumen rubber tube (Dreiling tube) to reach the empty stomach. Using a fluoroscopic screen, the position of the tube in the stomach was confirmed, and then the tip of the tube was advanced through the outlet of the stomach to position the tube in the duodenum. Then both stomach and duodenal juices were collected separately by constant suction for about two hours.

The juices were analyzed chemically to determine whether the pancreatic juice was abnormal, consistent with pancreatitis or even cancer of the pancreas in some cases. The juice collected from the stomach was analyzed (by gastric analysis) to determine whether or not the stomach produced an excessive amount of hydrochloric acid or no acid. In either situation, there is a clinically significant implication. These tests are still very useful in some clinical circumstances today, although they are labor intensive and expensive. In performing these tests, I was excited to watch the increasing volume of clear pancreatic juice from the duodenum, a sign of increased production of pancreatic juice, after intravenous injection of a gastrointestinal hormone called secretin, indicating that the pancreas was stimulated by this hormone to produce pancreatic juice. It was intellectually stimulating and rewarding to be able to evaluate functional aspects of the pancreas, which is a deeply seated organ in the upper abdomen that cannot be felt or palpated with hands from the abdominal surface.

After that time, research on secretin's actions on digestive organs—not only the pancreas but also the stomach and intestines—was one of my main research interests throughout my professional career. This important hormone, secretin, was originally discovered by two eminent physiologists, professors Bayliss and Starling, in London, England, in 1902. They successfully found canine small intestinal mucosal extracts that stimulated a copious flow of clear pancreatic juice into the duodenum in anesthetized dogs. It was indeed an exciting year for those researching gastrointestinal physiology, including professor Ivan Pavlov, a Nobel laureate, in Russia. The humoral substance in the canine intestinal mucosal extracts that stimulated the production of pancreatic juice was indeed secretin, a peptide, as discovered by professors Mutt and Jorpes in Stockholm, Sweden, in the 1960s.

I enjoyed my clinical training with other gastroenterology fellows both at inpatient and outpatient services and facilities. Faculty members in clinical gastroenterology services, including Drs. Harry Shay, Stanley Lorber, and Phillip Bralow, were superb clinician teachers. I am indebted to their devotion and enthusiasm, as well as their sharing of their clinical experience, knowledge, and wisdom.

It had always been satisfying and rewarding to work in general internal medicine when I could help patients with unexplained symptoms and clinical features by detecting as yet unknown medical conditions that might explain patients' clinical problems. There was a patient in a medical ward, a thirty-four-year-old white married female, who had been followed by doctors in both the general medical clinic and the hematology clinic in the medical center for more than five years for unexplained iron deficiency, anemia, bleeding tendency, and weight loss. A senior medical student assigned to the patient brought my urgent attention to her while I was being consulted regarding another patient on the same floor. He was quite disturbed and worried because after he gave an injection of vitamin $B_{12}$, as ordered by a medical resident, her injection site became markedly swollen, warm, and red.

In reviewing her chart with the student, I saw that in addition to the clinical features that she had had for years, she had had foul-smelling diarrhea off and on for years, strongly suggestive of a malabsorptive condition, which might explain her bleeding tendency as being due to probable vitamin K malabsorption and deficiency, her iron deficiency and anemia as being due to malabsorption of iron, and her weight loss as being due to malabsorption of fat. We made a presumptive diagnosis of a malabsorption syndrome, and a more definitive diagnosis was made by a small-bowel X-ray study showing a sprue pattern, and a small-bowel mucosal biopsy taken by way of a biopsy capsule, which showed histopathological findings consistent with a gluten-sensitive enteropathy or, in other words, a non-tropical sprue, or adult celiac disease. The student was very relieved and gratified because the bleeding and swelling of the arm stopped after injection of vitamin K, which indicated the presence of vitamin K deficiency. He was so excited to find that the patient had a malabsorption syndrome, as that would also explain the anemia, the bleeding tendency, the impaired small-intestinal absorption of fat, the weight loss, and the diarrhea. These clinical features are consistent with adult celiac disease. This clinical condition was not that well known in the early 1960s, even in some university teaching hospitals.

I told him that a more specific and decisive diagnosis could be made by way of therapeutic response to a gluten-free diet. Indeed, when the patient began the new diet, her diarrhea ceased and she began to feel better and stronger. Within a month, her pale-looking cheeks turned pinkish. It was a gratifying experience to watch a young student so excited and motivated to follow his patient closely and diligently. I was delighted to help him to prepare the presentation of this interesting case at the weekly medical conference (professors' rounds) in the presence of Dr. Thomas Durant, professor and chairman of the Department of Medicine. In fact, this patient was the first patient with diagnostically proven gluten-sensitive enteropathy at Temple University Hospital. Two new patients with this condition were later found in the same year, 1962.

During my clinical training in gastroenterology, because of my fascination with gastrointestinal hormones—including secretin and cholecystokinin, which stimulate the production of pancreatic fluid rich in digestive enzymes and contract the gallbladder to evacuate dark bile, and gastrin, which stimulates the acid production of the stomach—I continued participating in testing pancreatic function in patients with pancreatic diseases, such as pancreatitis and cancer of the pancreas, using a gastroduodenal tube (Dreiling tube) and other diagnostic methods I was encouraged to employ by Dr. Shay. Using these tests, I had the honor of participating in the diagnostic workup and care of a legendary professional basketball player, a superstar of the NBA, Mr. Wilt Chamberlain, for an unexplained abdominal ailment that was successfully treated by our team at Temple University Hospital. He returned to continue his pivotal role as the star player of the Philadelphia 76ers in the 1960s.

Dr. Harry Shay, professor of medicine, chief of gastroenterology,
and director, Samuel Fels Research Institute, and the author, Temple
University Medical Center, Philadelphia, Pennsylvania, 1962.

One morning, while performing a secretin test using a Dreiling tube on a fifty-two-year-old white female patient with a clinical impression of cancer of the pancreas, we found an unusually large amount of highly acidic fluid obtained not only from the stomach but also from the duodenum. Her stomach was putting out an enormous amount of acid juice—more than a half liter (500 cc) of clear, water-like fluid per hour for four consecutive hours. (Production is normally less than 100 cc per hour.) This amount of acid juice was more than five times the normal amount produced in healthy persons.

Dr. Shay saw, looking over my shoulder, many tubes of stomach juice that had been collected, and he said, "You know what I think she has, Bill?"

I looked up at him and answered, "Zollinger-Ellison syndrome?"

He said, "I have never seen a patient putting out this much acid juice." We were so excited, because neither one of us had seen a patient with this clinical syndrome. Subsequently, she was found to have large ulcers in both the stomach and duodenum, and a special cancer of the pancreas. Sadly, the cancer had already spread to the liver and tissues near the pancreas. In fact, this was the first proven case of Zollinger-Ellison syndrome at Temple University Hospital until 1963. We published the exciting observation we made on this patient in a scientific journal. This clinical syndrome was originally discovered early 1950s by two legendary American surgeons, Drs. Robert Zollinger and Erwin Ellison at Ohio State University Medical Center, Columbus, Ohio. They published their historical landmark work in a prestigious American surgical journal, *Annals of Surgery*, in 1955.

At that time, they, for the first time in medical history, proposed that a humoral substance, like gastrin, is produced in certain tumors of the pancreas and travels through the circulating blood to reach the stomach to stimulate the production of massive amounts of highly acidic juice, causing ulcers in not only the stomach but also the upper part of the small intestine. Subsequently, researchers in this field discovered that the humoral substance in the pancreatic cancer tissue proposed by Zollinger and Ellison was indeed gastrin, which had been known to stimulate production of acid in the stomach since the turn of the twentieth century. Gastrin is an important hormone for acid digestion of food in humans as well as other mammals.

This was such an exciting time for those, including myself, interested in gastrointestinal hormone research. Certain tumors of the pancreas might produce excessive amounts of other known or yet unknown humoral substances or hormones, such as secretin or vasoactive intestinal peptide (VIP), which have been shown to produce severe diarrhea by stimulating either excessive production of fluid in the small intestine or the pancreas in later years. In this era, an exciting time for those of us involved in gut hormone research, it was my honor indeed to personally know Dr. Zollinger. He was indeed a kind and brilliant surgeon, scientist, and educator in the history of American medicine whom we admired and were proud of.

The discovery of this exciting clinical syndrome associated with a hormone possibly produced by tumors opened a new era in the science of gastroenterology. This led to the knowledge that when gastrointestinal hormones—such as gastrin, vasoactive intestinal peptide (VIP), or secretin—are excessively produced in a tumor of a digestive organ, it can cause certain clinical and pathological conditions, such as ulcers in the stomach and upper intestine or excessive watery diarrhea. I became very interested in developing a career that would allow me to research gastrointestinal hormones in normal and abnormal clinical conditions. The tests evaluating exocrine pancreatic secretion (function) using secretin and cholecystokinin as stimulating hormones led me to investigate exocrine pancreatic secretion in many patients with pancreatitis, cancer, and diabetes mellitus. A proposal based on this work was submitted to the committee for advanced degrees at the University of Pennsylvania Graduate School of Medicine, a master of medical science in gastroenterology was approved. The degree was honored in the spring of 1962. As a result of this thesis, we were able to publish two separate articles in two prestigious medical journals: *Annals of Internal Medicine* and the *Journal of the American Medical Association*. Dr. Shay was very pleased, and it was nice to have compliments from the boss from time to time.

# Professor Harry Shay as a
# Mentor and Guardian

After joining his gastroenterology program at Temple University Medical Center in 1959, I learned about the program director, Dr. Shay's personal life and professional career. He was born in South Philadelphia. Unfortunately, his father passed away during his childhood. He was brought up by a widowed but strong-willed mother who worked hard day and night. The young Harry was an extremely bright and hardworking student who eventually entered Central High School, a highly competitive school in Philadelphia. He was then accepted to the University of Pennsylvania, including its School of Medicine, in the 1920s. After years of service for the University of Pennsylvania as a junior faculty member, he decided to open a private practice in a small office housed in a basement on Broad Street in Philadelphia.

One day, an old male patient walked in for a consultation. He mentioned to young Harry his "indigestion," which had been treated by a professor at the university clinic, but without a satisfactory relief of symptoms. Harry expressed his disagreement with the professor's theory regarding indigestion and his treatment. The patient told Harry that the professor was Harry's teacher and Harry shouldn't be critical of him. The patient responded to Harry's treatment, and Harry became the patient's lifetime physician and friend. Their bond became stronger as time passed by. The name of this patient was Samuel Fels, a self-made multimillionaire. He built and owned the Fels Soap Company in Philadelphia in the early twentieth century. With Mr. Fels's support, Dr. Shay was appointed as a professor of internal medicine and director of Samuel Fels Research Institute at the Temple University School of Medicine. Then he established the Division of Gastroenterology at Temple University Medical Center. The division offered not only a clinical fellowship program but also a strong research program at Fels Research Institute, an envy of the academic gastroenterology community in Philadelphia. He was a kind and caring clinician, teacher, and scientist in the area of gastrointestinal medicine. Here I learned an admirable part of American culture: when a hardworking physician helps his or her patients, the patients appreciate the help and offer or return their gratitude, such as in the case of Mr. Samuel Fels. He and Dr. Shay had a warm lifelong relationship. After Dr. Shay established a research institute in the 1940s as the director of the institute, Dr. Shay was richly endowed by the Fels Foundation for his lifetime, and the research program was generously supported also. This was indeed his American dream, which anyone could be proud of. When I joined as a member of the institute, he was an innovative physician and scientist, and he guided me to become an academic gastroenterologist throughout my career.

On one afternoon in 1972, he called me into his office and asked me what my future plan was. I told him that after the training was finished here and I earned my advanced degrees, I planned to return to my alma mater, one of the two best medical schools in Korea, Seoul University School of Medicine, to teach and research. He asked, "Do you think you can continue what you are doing here? I am concerned that your dream may not come to reality in Korea, considering the present political and socioeconomic conditions there. You should think about your academic career. You have a family now."

I responded, "I do appreciate your thoughtful concerns over my future and my family. May I come back and continue this discussion in the near future, sir?"

He said, "Any time when you are ready." I discussed with Fan that evening Dr. Shay's kind concern about our future. She said whatever I decided for my professional career, she would support me. She was willing to go to Korea with me if my future was more promising in Korea. My thought was that I had just started to enjoy teaching and researching under a wonderful mentor's guidance, and he would provide me with a desirable academic environment. I needed at least three years to complete my thesis work for my doctorate of medical sciences at the University of Pennsylvania and in order to become an independent researcher. I wished to undertake several years of hard work, funded by an organization such as the National Institutes of Health.

More importantly, in order to accomplish my plan, I needed to have a passport issued by the US Immigration and Naturalization Authority that would allow me to stay in the United States. As I thought over my situation, I realized that the right thing to do was follow Dr. Shay's advice. A few days later, when I met with Dr. Shay in his office, I again thanked him for his kindness and thoughtfulness regarding my professional career and family. He was very pleased to hear my decision to continue academic work under his tutelage and as a junior faculty member. I pointed out to him that this was only possible if my passport could be extended so I could stay longer in the United States. He looked at me and said, "This might be a tough challenge to deal with. We need a smart lawyer specializing in immigration and naturalization, and the strong support of Temple University." Very fortunately, the hired lawyer, Mr. Isidor Ostroff, esq., mentioned that he would try to renew my passport annually until I was qualified to obtain a green card for permanent resident status. I was very grateful to Dr. Shay and the Temple University Administration. My passport was indeed extended for one more year, covering the year of 1973. I was delighted.

Late one Sunday afternoon, after he and Mrs. Shay had a nice dinner including lobsters at Bookbinder's Restaurant, Dr. Shay had severe upper right abdominal pain. He was found to have numerous cholesterol stones in his gallbladder. To our total dismay, a simple cholecystectomy led to a severe heart attack in the recovery room, from which he never recovered. He was only sixty-three years old. We were so saddened by this unexpected tragedy, and I, for one, felt like a helpless orphan on the street. In this crisis of my career, both Dr. Robert Bucher, dean of the medical school, and Dr. Stanley Lorber, provisional chief of gastroenterology, were very supportive of me and my research program and clinical activities at the university hospital.

# Golden Years for Academic Medicine and Physician Scientists

My research work was progressing well, and my team was quite productive. It was a golden day for young, productive faculty everywhere in the United States of America. Funding agencies, such as the National Institutes of Health, were reasonably generous for research academic institutions. Every spring, annual scientific meetings for young medical researchers (young Turks) were held in the auditoriums of big hotels and civic centers in Atlantic City, New Jersey, along the long and broad boardwalk, for several days. Countless meetings were simultaneously held. Many of us felt that it was the greatest academic event in medical sciences in the world. Indeed it was. The young researchers came from all over the country, representing institutions from Boston, New York, Philadelphia, Chicago, Rochester, Minnesota, San Francisco, Los Angeles, San Diego, St. Louis, Dallas, and elsewhere. In the breaks between the meetings, many went out to the boardwalk to enjoy sunshine and meet with friends and former colleagues.

# Two Graceful and Kind Professors at a National Meeting in Atlantic City, NJ.

One of our scientific abstracts was chosen for an oral presentation at a morning session in an auditorium at the Hotel Ritz-Carlton. The selection committee chose our abstract because we made a novel observation that pure secretin, a hormone that had been known to stimulate pancreatic juice production, also delayed emptying of liquid from the stomach in humans. In the early morning, I went down to a huge restaurant of the hotel where I was staying. A smiling young waiter in a clean white and dark blue uniform seated me at a small table located in a corner. I was somewhat nervous about the presentation, thinking that someone might ask a challenging question after my presentation. There were so many young and old physician scientists and professors from leading university medical schools and teaching hospitals in the country, and even foreign countries. Somebody tapped me gently on my right shoulder. I turned to find it was Dr. Thomas Durant, professor of medicine and chairman of the Department of Medicine at Temple University Medical Center.

Tom was always a gentleman. He had grown up in the Midwest and was a graduate of University of Michigan Medical School. He smiled and said softly, "Good morning, Bill. Would you like to join us? Dr. Wood and I are about to have breakfast there." He pointing with his right index finger toward a distant corner of the restaurant. I could barely recognize in the distance a silver-haired distinguished gentleman whom I had seen from time to time when I was a graduate student. At the medical grand rounds held in the hospital of the University of Pennsylvania years ago, he used to sit in a chair on the podium. While walking to the table, Tom said, "I read your abstract. It is a beautiful work. Congratulations." I was very gratified.

It came time to meet with Dr. Wood. He smiled and extended his right hand to shake my hand. After we both sat, Tom didn't waste time. "Bill will present his paper this morning."

Dr. Frances Wood was a graceful and dignified-looking gentleman. He was the chairman of the Department of Medicine at the University of Pennsylvania. He too said, "Congratulations, Bill."

I responded, "Thank you, Dr. Wood." Here I was, sitting with two giants in internal medicine in the country, but I felt warmness and kindness, and both made me feel a part of them. It had always been my pleasure and honor to be a member of Tom's department. He had always made me feel at home. I still remember and cherish his kindness, his warm friendship, and his gifted clinical skills and teaching. In the yearbook of our graduating class, called *Skull*, below the picture of Dr. Durant was the caption "Speaks softly but carries a golden cane."

My presentation went very well. For the first time, I shared the new information that secretin, the hormone known to stimulate pancreatic secretion, was also found to influence stomach motion and acid production, which excited many workers in the audience. I had such a rewarding feeling when my peers and audience accepted my presentation with enthusiasm and respect. This was the fun part of being an academic physician or physician scientist who was involved in active and meaningful research. Meanwhile, I continued to serve and teach as a clinical gastroenterologist at the hospital and gastroenterology clinic, which satisfied me as a faculty member of the university. In this working environment, one must have institutional and departmental support and well-trained and cooperative team members in the research laboratories. I was fortunate to have research fellows and technicians who worked hard and well as a team.

In 1965, I was promoted to assistant professor of medicine. My thesis work for my doctorate of medical sciences at the University of Pennsylvania had been in progress, although the pace had been somewhat tardy because of Dr. Shay's unexpected death and the burdens of clinical teaching activities. The objective of my research was to investigate the role of the pancreas in gastric acid secretion. I was very fortunate to have learned the operative surgical techniques in animals and the experimental physiology of digestive organs from Dr. Simon Komarov to study pancreatic secretion and gastric secretion in chronic canine models. Dr. Komarov was then, in 1967, the last surviving pupil of the famous Russian professor of physiology Ivan Pavlov, a Nobel laureate at St. Petersburg before the Russian Revolution. What we found was that pancreatic juice is essential in the regulation of gastric acid secretion in dogs. In later years, my colleagues and I found that secretin was one of the hormones that controls stomach acid production after ingestion of a meal. I defended my thesis successfully in front of the thesis evaluation committee, and my long-awaited doctor of medical sciences degree (DSc) was honored in May 1966. I sincerely thanked my wife, Fan, who had encouraged and supported me for all those difficult years. Another unforgettable event in the same year was that I was able to become a permanent resident of the United States. I was so grateful to the late Dr. Shay, who initiated the monumental task in cooperation with the Temple University administration on my behalf. I was and am deeply indebted.

# My Family in the 1960s

All three of us, Fan, Billy, and I, were happy. Our son, a beautiful and delightful baby boy, Billy, grew up fast. By the spring of 1963, he was my playmate. In the late afternoons and early evenings, we often played in the nearby small park, and he enjoyed swinging, laughing, and giggling. Fan again became pregnant, and she delivered a cute new baby girl, Donna, on Labor Day. Donna was such a good-natured baby. I was always looking forward to seeing her and hugging her. We then realized we had a house that could accommodate us comfortably. This time, we looked for a house with three bedrooms.

Fan and I (the author) in the front yard of our first house, Roslyn, Pennsylvania, spring 1966.

Luckily, we found a beautiful three-bedroom house in Roslyn, Pennsylvania, a suburb of Philadelphia about thirty minutes away from the medical center. The split-level house had three bedrooms, a large living room, a dining area, a kitchen, and a two-car garage. The house was surrounded by a finely manicured yard with shrubs. Our neighbors were friendly and had children of Billy's age or older. Billy often had to look up at them while he followed them. The neighbors were typical middle-class Caucasian workers and their families.

We felt comfortable in the community, and the neighbors accepted us as a part of them. From time to time, when I was doing yardwork on Saturdays, male neighbors would walk over to my yard to say hello and find out what I was doing. We would sit in the yard and chat. One afternoon, while mowing the backyard, I found the rim of a metal garbage can that was buried in the ground. The metal caused my mower to make a clicking noise when the machine passed over the area. I decided to dig up the large metal garbage can full of waste materials. I thought it would take most of my afternoon time to dig the heavy can out. Before I began to dig, two male neighbors walked over and asked me, "What are you doing, Bill?" One said he thought I was mowing the yard. "You need help, Bill," one of them said when they saw what I was doing. Soon the two guys came back with big shovels and joined me in digging out the heavy can. George, one of the two, giggled and said the previous owner had had one dog and one cat. The other neighbor, John, said he would bring a pickup truck and get rid of the heavy can. While he was gone, we filled the empty hole with dirt and covered the area with turf. Afterward we all sat on our picnic table in my backyard and drank beer with snacks. Then two other guys joined us. All five of us got to know each other and had a wonderful time under the shining early-summer sun. I and Fan were happy and grateful that, for the first time, we lived in a small, friendly suburban American town, which we had always wanted to live in.

**Fan and children, 1970.** *From left:* **Laura, Bill, Richard, and Donna.**

We had two more beautiful children, Richard and Laura, by December 1965. We were so happy together. It was such a delightful family—six of us in total. We used to go to Chinatown on Saturday afternoons and enjoy delicious meals in our favorite restaurant. On one Saturday, when we drove through Chinatown for the first time, Billy, looking through a half-down window in the back, said, "Look! Chinese, Chinese! Dad?" Then I realized that our children, Asian descendants, were color blind, as they were accustomed to our Caucasian community. Bill had grown up and played only with white neighborhood kids and Caucasian children in kindergarten. He did not realize he was an Asian boy. I told him, "When we go home, we will look at ourselves in our long wall mirror, okay?"

Fan was a totally devoted mother, and our children were brought up with her unconditional love. The children loved her and worshipped her. Every day, I felt so deeply sorry that I could not spend enough time with our lovely children, who were invaluable jewels in our lives. We enjoyed playing in the nearby park and visiting the Philadelphia Zoo. They loved to sit on the back of a hippo made of brass.

**Children on a brass hippo's back in the Philadelphia Zoo, 1970.** *From left:* **Bill, Donna, Richard, and Laura.**

# Fishing with Billy, reminding of me of My Father in My Childhood

Whenever we could, Billy and I went fishing in a nearby small lake or reservoir. We both had fun trolling in a small motorboat and catching fish. I enjoyed seeing Bill get excited at the moment he caught a fish that jumped and splashed in the water. It reminded me of myself and my father during my childhood. When I was an elementary school student, early on Saturday afternoons, my father and I used to walk on a narrow three-mile-long path across a plain from home to reach a river, a tributary of the Nakdong River in southeastern Korea. At the bank, he rented a rowing wooden boat, and we fished with fishing rods. It was such fun to catch the fish, which splashed out of the water after taking the bait, which was usually earthworms. I caught them in our backyard using a small shovel in the early morning. Then father rowed to move the boat to a wider area of the river to net fish. When he threw the net from his left shoulder, left upper arm, and right hand, the net fully expanded in the air to cover as wide an area as possible, and many small lead weights attached to the lower end of the net brought the net to the bottom of the river. After a while, when he pulled the net slowly, many fish the size of my palm or larger were caught in the net's walls. Many of them shook their bodies vigorously to escape from the net.

During sunset, with carpets of crimson and red-colored clouds in the western sky, when the golden-red sun was approaching the horizon, the beautiful scales of the fish reflected shining rainbow colors that I was unable to forget for a long time.

We harvested twenty-two fish in total from the netting on one outing. When we returned home, it was already dark. I was tired and hungry, but my father started to work in the kitchen with helpers. They cleaned the fish and scraped their scales off with knives, and the fillets were cooked in boiling water with herbs and a special hot bean sauce. The aroma was irresistible. Then father prepared thin raw fillets for sashimi, and hot spicy sauce. He called his favorite coworker, Mr. Kim, at his home. We all had delightful feasts, and both father and Mr. Kim enjoyed Korean rice wine, cooked fish, and sashimi. It was indeed a wonderful evening.

# Academic Clinical Physician, Physician Scientist, and the Future of Our Family

T he academic clinical physicians in teaching hospitals were mostly talented clinician teachers. Physician scientists combine both clinical teaching activities and productive research activities in either clinical investigation facilities or bench laboratory research settings. I, as a physician scientist, and my research colleagues had been steadily productive in the investigation of physiology and pathophysiology of the pancreas and gastrointestinal tract in relation to gastrointestinal hormones. The investigations involving these hormones had become exciting because, using newer technological methodologies available since the early 1960s, the chemical structures of gut hormones—such as secretin, gastrin, and cholecystokinin—could now be determined so that biologically active synthetic substances could be produced in relatively large quantities. For example, to obtain one milligram of over 90 percent pure secretin from pigs' intestines, the intestines of more than one thousand pigs is needed. Thus, obtaining an adequate amount of biologically active secretin is labor-intensive and very expensive. It was such welcome news when, in 1969, synthetic secretin became available through the efforts of Professor Mikros Bodandzky, a former professor of biochemistry at Case Western University, and his associates in Squib Research Laboratories in New Jersey. Thus, pure synthetic hormones could now be used for research in animals as well as humans in normal and diseased states. We investigated the biological actions of pure and synthetic secretin and cholecystokinin in animal models as well as humans. Our work drew national and international attention and recognition.

In May of 1966, I was promoted to associate professor of medicine with tenure and director of gastrointestinal research laboratories. I was thrilled. This promotion meant to me that the chief of gastroenterology, Dr. Stanly Lorber; the chair of the Department of Medicine, Dr. Thomas Durant; and the dean of the medical school, Dr. Robert Bucher, recognized my progress in academic activities and contributions at Temple University Medical Center. I was very gratified. I hoped that someday I could be promoted to professor of medicine—a dream that I'd had ever since I started my career in both academic clinical medicine and as a physician scientist. Fan was so happy to hear the news that evening. We celebrated together with our children by having a delicious dinner at a well-known restaurant in the city. Our children were growing up and had rapacious appetites. Billy enjoyed the meal so much that he told the waiter, "Give my compliments to the chef." Billy was a six-year-old elementary school student. We were a very happy family.

Because of my heavy involvement in research and my busy work in the hospital, we searched for a house closer to the medical center. Luckily we found a beautiful contemporary house for sale just outside of Philadelphia city limits, along the southeastern border. It took only fifteen minutes by car to get from there to the medical center. The house included four bedrooms and a magnificent living room and dining area with a high ceiling, picture windows, and a large den. It was located only a three- to five-minute walk away from Curtis Arboretum and had a pond with ducks, a wide creek across the front yard, a big yard with a flower garden in the backyard, and a long driveway. More conveniently and importantly, the house was positioned equidistant from the local elementary school, middle school, and high school. They were all within walking distance, so there was no need for our children to ride school buses to attend their schools. Fan and I were very happy to have found this beautiful house in an ideal location for all of us. The children were also very happy. We felt that this was the home where our children would grow happily until they were ready for college education. We had such wonderful times at home, in the friendly neighborhood, and in the park after dinner. I hoped and wished to cherish such a wonderful livelihood for a long time in suburban Philadelphia.

There were five medical schools in the City of Brotherly Love, Philadelphia, in the 1960s, including the University of Pennsylvania School of Medicine, Temple University Medical School, Jefferson Medical College, Hahnemann Medical College, and the Women's Medical College of Philadelphia. We had the Philadelphia Gut Club organized by senior academic gastroenterologists from the five medical schools and their affiliated hospitals in the city. The Gut Club was a professional organization for academic and clinical gastroenterologists and fellows training in gastroenterology that promoted research and education in the field of gastrointestinal medicine. Only a few major cities in the country had such professional organizations. The quarterly scientific and educational meetings of the Gut Club were held at an alternating host medical institution or nearby reputable pharmaceutical industry building. The research work performed by fellows and faculty was presented at the meeting and discussed by the audiences, who were from these institutions. It was always nice to hear the opinions of members from other institutions and to constructively exchange views and suggestions. Rarely could young faculty members have so many resourceful audiences from so many medical schools and pharmaceutical firms in the area. It was also a delight to have social occasions after the meetings, which gave fellows and junior faculty members opportunities to interact with faculty and fellows from other institutions. This was indeed a unique aspect of the Philadelphia gastroenterology community. I always enjoyed presenting my research work at the meetings and valued criticism and constructive suggestions from my former teachers in the University of Pennsylvania medical community.

Although I was deeply concerned about our future as a family, I was hesitant to open discussion with Fan for some time. I had had a heartrending struggle by myself with sleepless nights regarding possibly returning to my former home country, South Korea, where my parents wished for us to be with them and contribute to the country as a senior faculty member at a leading university medical center in my former hometown, Seoul. I had to painfully think about my dear and aging parents, whom I had promised I would be their good and beloved son. But now I had a Chinese American wife and four lovely children who had been born free in this great country, and both their parents loved them very much. After lengthy and serious discussions, Fan and I agreed that our children's roots were in this country and their future was here. I felt it would have been selfish and cruel to ask my family to resettle in South Korea, which they were not familiar with. We also felt strongly that our dream, an American dream, would be accomplished here, in the United States of America. Of course we realized that we had a long road of hardship ahead of us, just as all immigrants experience. My guilt toward my beloved father and mother from breaking the promise that I made to return to Korea will remain in my heart for my lifetime. One contribution that I was able to make for my former country was to train young physician scientists from Korea in my research laboratory for their futures in Korea. That was the least I could do.

# Invitations Abroad: Tokyo, Japan

In December, 1968, I received an unexpected invitation letter from Tokyo, Japan. Dr. Sakida Takao, director of the National Cancer Center in Tokyo, was inviting me as a visiting professor to the prestigious institution in Japan. I was thrilled and honored to visit Tokyo again after fifteen years. At this time, I was invited to deliver a lecture titled "Neuro-Hormonal Regulation of Pancreatic Secretion," which had resulted from our hard work in gastrointestinal hormone research. The lecture was received by the audience with high enthusiasm. I was wondering in my mind who had recognized our work and recommended this welcome invitation. Moreover, I was pleasantly surprised that a Japanese institution was inviting a Korean physician scientist when the wound of historical hostility between the two countries had not healed yet. Then I remembered a Japanese doctor who had a fellowship in biochemistry at the University of Pennsylvania School of Medicine, my alma mater, in the early 1960s. His name was Takeuchi Tadashi, and he was a graduate of Tokyo University Faculty of Medicine, the most prestigious medical school in Japan. We had met a few times in an auditorium of the medical school. He must have recommended me for the visiting professorship. My lecture was well received by faculty, fellows, and students at the cancer center. I still can't forget the warm hospitality in the evening that I received during their traditional dinner party, including elegant and unique traditional Japanese entertainment.

After the dinner party, Dr. Takeuchi invited me to his favorite hangout in Ginza, the entertainment capital of Asia, and we shared sake and enjoyed our true friendship, which lasts even now. We both cherished our mutual warm memories when we meet on special occasions. We still exchange cards each New Year. The following day, I was scheduled to visit the University of Kyoto Faculty of Medicine in Kyoto, one of the most prestigious universities in Japan. Unfortunately, the visit was cancelled because of a student riot instigated by an extreme left wing student group during Japan's politically turbulent time. A few years later, I was invited again to Kyoto University and delivered my lecture in Japanese, which surprised many senior faculty members who had been entertained by beautiful and highly professional geisha ladies at a party the previous evening. They thought I didn't understand their conversations with the geisha, which were sometimes inappropriate. One geisha had responded politely with smile to one professor, saying, "Professor shouldn't make such a joke." Everybody laughed.

I also had the pleasure of visiting my uncle and his family in Tokyo. For the first time, I met my aunt and their two sons, who are my cousins, Ken and Seiji. I could communicate with them easily with my Japanese vocabulary. My aunt was such a delightful and kind young lady born in a Japanese family, and the two cousins were in their teens. They were so delighted to meet with me. My cousins were deeply touched to find a cousin from the United States who had been invited to a well-known Japanese medical institution as a visiting professor. I sensed that they might have felt lonely without any cousins or relatives in Japan. Ken said, "Now we know we, too, have cousins in South Korea and the United States of America." I had a wonderful time with my uncle's entire family. I enjoyed staying in their beautiful home in suburban Tokyo for one night. They had a beautiful garden that had a gorgeous pond with many large, colorful koi swimming around in the pond. The length of the koi ranged from one foot to one and a half feet. They were so friendly and swam toward me on the bank often to nip at my fingers just above the water surface. I told my uncle, "You have so many friendly pets in the pond. I envy you, Uncle." He said proudly, "It takes time to become acquainted with them."

At night we visited Ginza again, and we enjoyed a wonderful dinner and shows together.

# My First Visit to South Korea in Fourteen Years and a Memorable Family Reunion

Realizing that I was originally from Korea, Dr. Sakida kindly arranged my Tokyo trip to include a visit to Seoul, South Korea. This visit meant so much to me. I returned home after fifteen years. On the airplane, so many things passed through my mind: my parents, brothers, and sisters; the humiliating colonial time; the cruel war caused by the communist North Korean army invasion of South Korea; my escape from North Korean army, fierce fights against soldiers of North Korean army and Chinese communist army near Heartbreak Ridge, at the northeastern front line and central combat zone; and my own family in the United States, including my lovely wife, Fan, and my children, Bill, Donna, Richard, and Laura. When the plane descended to the runway of Seoul International Airport, I was surprised and was proud of the modern magnificent airport in Seoul, which was like the international airport in Tokyo.

In the arrivals area, I was welcomed by my entire Chey family, from my father and mother to my grown-up baby sister, Ok-hee who was now a college student. Time had passed so quickly in fifteen years. We were so glad to see each other. Everybody became emotional and had tears welling in their eyes. I hugged everybody and sobbed. Fifteen years had passed since I saw them off in the small Seoul Airport, which had no modern terminals. As I looked at the Seoul streets from the car, I was thrilled to see that the city had completely recovered from the war-torn city that I remembered and had become a proud modern and bustling city. It was so good to return to our old home where we spent good times and hard times together during the tumultuous years of the early 1950s. My older brother and my sister in-law used to live with us in the house after their marriage, and my younger brothers and sisters lived under the same roof. But it was hard to forget the three months of terror, fear, and hard life under North Korean communist oppression in the summer of 1950. I stood for a while in the courtyard reminiscing about August 11, 1950—the day I had returned home on a late dark evening, having escaping from the North Korean volunteer army.

My younger brother Jim tapped my shoulder and said, "Let's go inside the house to celebrate." For the first time in fifteen years, the entire family sat together surrounding the dining table and enjoyed delicious home-cooked meals of more than ten different dishes, which reminded me of good times we had before the war started nineteen years prior. I had been a twenty-year-old medical school student, and my parents had been about fifty years old. They had been healthy and active. My father worked as the chairman of the board of an educational foundation. I was pleased to meet with two of my sisters-in-law, wives of my two younger brothers, James and Woo-shik, who were young, attractive ladies. It was such a happy and pleasant evening. I wished my entire family in Philadelphia were there with us, and I began to miss them.

**Chey Family in Seoul, 1979. The adults sitting on chairs are (*from left*) Woo-kyeung (my younger brother), Woo-jik (my older brother), Father, Mother, the author, and Woo-shik (my youngest brother). The rest are the author's sister, Sang-ok, and the author's sisters-in-law, nephews, and nieces.**

The next day, I visited my alma mater, Seoul University College of Medicine, and the university hospital, and paid respects to my favorite professor of medicine—Dr. Han Shim-suk, who became the dean of the medical school—and several former classmates. In the evening, I was invited to dinner by Dean Han. The restaurant we went to happened to be his favorite place. My classmates and some members of the Department of Medicine joined us. We all enjoyed the dinner and the entertainment afterward. The following morning, I delivered a lecture for students and faculty titled "The Frontiers of Research in Neuro-hormonal Regulation of the Stomach and Pancreas." The lecture was well received. My lectures were extended to two more medical schools in Seoul over the subsequent two days: Yon-Sei University College of Medicine, the oldest in Korea, and the Catholic University of Korea College of Medicine. I spent the remaining days with my family on my father's ranch and small farm in a Seoul suburb. Father loved to cultivate strawberries, tomatoes, watermelons, golden yellow melons, and sweet potatoes. He also had a hobby of maintaining twelve beehives to harvest honey. He had prepared the farm for his coming retirement in the near future. The melons and strawberries were so fresh and sweet—so different from the ones we found in the supermarkets back at home in the United States.

The following day, part of my family, including Father, Mother, me, and my brother Jim, traveled on an express train to Busan, the second-largest city, in order to briefly visit my older brother's family and my grandparents' cemetery plots. I had grown up in Busan proper until I attended kindergarten. The chauffeur of my elder brother, Woo-jik, drove us to a mansion surrounded by beautiful gardens with old pine trees and stone statues. Among my brothers and sisters, he and I had been closest during my childhood. His three sons and daughter were all grown up, having become adults. My sister-in-law was so glad to see me. We were entertained by a delicious dinner, and the evening passed quickly. My brother was a successful business executive and the chief executive officer of a life insurance company. During Japanese colonialism, he was drafted as a hard laborer and spent time in a labor camp in a big Japanese Navy shipyard in Yokosuka, Japan. We shed many tears during those hostile years because of my brother suffering in the camp.

The next day, we all went to Gijang, a small city forty minutes by car from Busan, where my father, my elder brother, I, Sang-ok, and Jim were born. By train, it used to take about one hour and a half from Busan. Our grandparents' cemetery plots were located on the sunny side of a small hill covered by beautifully manicured grass and pine trees. We had a brief ritual ceremony that included deep bows on knees in front of the two plots.

We returned to Seoul the next day. Now I had to face the reality of a sad time, as all of us were soon to be separated again. The entire family came to the airport the following morning to say farewell. Mother was in tears again, and she asked, "When can we see you again?"

I answered, "Sooner than you realize, Mother. You and Father will have to come to visit with the family in the United States to see your new grandchildren and daughter-in-law."

Mother said, "I hope that dream comes true soon."

"It will soon, Mother."

The warm tears flowed down my cheeks as I saw them off at the check-in point. The plane lifted from the runway and entered the blue sky.

The trip to Korea overwhelmed me with the joy of seeing my family, particularly my mother, father, brothers, and sisters, as well as my professors from Seoul University, Yonsei University, and Catholic University, who were so proud of me. As I looked down through the window, the plane was already leaving the Korean Peninsula. I knew that down on the ground, millions of honest and hardworking Koreans like me were struggling to live every day. For centuries they had suffered because of foreign invaders, selfish and incompetent kings, and corrupt governments. The majority of the people there could not have the good and secure lives they deserved. I felt sad, and I sobbed as I saw the southern end of Korea from the sky. Why do so many innocent people have to suffer? I prayed for a better future for them under the present political system led by President Park Jung-Hi, who was a sincere patriot and capable statesman. The plane soon landed at Haneda International Airport in Tokyo.

# Returning Home to Philadelphia

The plane arrived at Philadelphia International Airport in the late afternoon on June 20, 1969. It was so good to return home and reunite with my entire family after such a long time. We all hugged each other. Even our little baby daughter Laura clapped her hands and opened her arms to hug me. Then I felt at home more dearly. We were all together again.

My research team at the medical center had made steady progress both in clinical research as well as experimental animal research since I left for the trip. The manuscripts prepared from our hard work were accepted for publication by reputable peer-reviewed journals, such as *Gastroenterology* and the *American Journal of Physiology*. It gave me such pleasure and gratification when peers recognized our hard work. It had been announced by the dean of the medical school that our beloved and respected chairman of the Department of Medicine, Dr. Thomas Durant, was retiring, and a search committee had been looking for a suitable candidate for the chair. This news was a shock to me. He was a gentle and highly respected academic physician, and we all felt comfortable seeing him at medical conferences or at bedside rounds. With him around, many of us felt warm and comfortable.

# Invitation to a Nobel Symposium, 1970

In the later part of 1969, we were invited to participate in a Nobel symposium titled "Frontiers in Gastrointestinal Hormone Research," which was to be held in Stockholm, Sweden, in July 1970. This special symposium was organized by a Nobel symposium committee and funded by the Nobel Foundation. I and Dr. Lorber were very pleased and honored to accept the invitation. We were the only group invited from the Philadelphia area. The organizing committee considered us eminent researchers in our fields. Our gastrointestinal hormone research work was recognized by peers nationally and internationally. We were quite grateful.

This was my first trip to a foreign country as a US citizen, and I was able to proudly show my US passport to the officials when I was passing through customs at Stockholm International Airport. During the following two days, this historic meeting was held in a conference hall of the prestigious University of Stockholm Karolinska Institutet. Thirty-five scientists had been invited to participate in this historic symposium, and many other scientists attended to discuss the presentations of participants. They came from not only Scandinavian countries but also from other countries, including Great Britain, Scotland, Ireland, Germany, France, Italy, the United States, Canada, Poland, Australia, Japan, and China. I met with many eminent scientists in the auditorium whom I knew through their scientific publications. Fifteen participants were from the United States. I was one of them, and I was the only Asian American—a fact I was proud of. Among the participants, we had distinguished scientists who could be considered as future potential Nobel laureates, such as Doctors Solomon Berson and Rosalyn Yalow, who were from the United States; Professors Eric Jorpes, Viktor Mutt, and Bent Uvnas, from the Karolinska Institutet; and Andrew Ivy, the original discoverer of cholecystokinin, from the United States.

My presentation was entitled "Effect of Secretin and Cholecystokinin on Gastric Emptying and Gastric Secretion in Man," which was preceded by the presentation of my coworker Dr. Stanley Lorber, who presented our work entitled "Secretin and Cholecystokinin on Gastric Motility." The two presentations were well received by the distinguished audience. Besides us being one of the groups who demonstrated the primary actions of secretin and cholecystokinin on pancreatic secretion and contraction of the gallbladder, respectively, we had also found that they influence the functions of the stomach. Our observation garnered considerable international attention in the field. It was such a gratifying experience for us when the world experts recognized our work. We also appreciated the organizing committee's warm hospitality, which included an evening banquet and invitations to individual professors' villas in suburban Stockholm and their homes in the city. It was a rewarding experience for me when I was able to personally converse with Professor Erik Jorpes and hear his wisdom as a scholar and scientist who, with his colleague Professor Viktor Mutt, was a pioneer biochemist of gastrointestinal hormones. They had purified the intestinal hormone secretin, which was my favored hormone for research for years to come. I used to test his purified secretin for human pancreatic secretion. I was astonished to hear from Professor Jorpes that to obtain one milligram of pure secretin, they needed one thousand hogs' small intestines.

# Changing Trends in Academic Medicine

Back at home, as our beloved leader, Dr. Thomas Durant, retired as the chair of the Department of Medicine, the medical school searched for a new chair who would emphasize more research and was capable of recruiting more research-oriented faculty whose research work was funded by competitive funding sources, such as the National Institutes of Health and the National Science Foundation. Dr. Sol Sherry, a former vice chair of the Department of Medicine at Washington University School of Medicine, St. Louis, was chosen as the new chair. This new chair began to recruit new faculty who met certain qualifications. The new recruitments brought not only young talented academic physicians and researchers to the institution for the advancement of medical sciences but also research funds that would financially enrich the department and the medical school. My research laboratory was supported by one NIH research fund and by Fels Research Institute at Temple University Medical Center. However, I was not happy from time to time when some of us who were original Department of Medicine members felt estranged by the new chairman. He was adapting to a trend in those days that was pervasive in highly competitive academic institutions in the country. The academic Department of Medicine and other disciplines, including surgical specialties, were encouraged to run more like a business. In those days, fellow faculty members with professional strength in clinical practice and teaching began to feel insecure about their professional careers in academic institutions. I always felt that a good department of medicine in an academic institution should have a well-balanced faculty that includes both talented members who combine both research and clinical work, and those who have talents in clinical work and teaching, with limited time spent in clinical research.

My professional goal has always been the pursuit of research combined with clinical activities, because I wanted to be a clinical investigator (physician scientist) who combined research and patient care. To continue meaningful research, one must have research funds awarded from highly competitive funding sources, such as the National Institutes of Health or the National Science Foundation. I worked hard and was productive enough to compete with my peers in the country. Many of these physician scientists and clinician scientists spend their valuable time meeting deadlines for submission of grant applications, publications, or critical reviews of manuscripts requested by peer-reviewed scientific journals. Thus the words "publish or perish" come frequently to their minds in learning institutions. In addition, I had to serve as a member of the Study Section of Surgery and Bioengineering at the National Institutes of Health and as a member of the FDA that evaluated applications for clinical usage of new gastrointestinal drugs. Each member of these committees spent enormous amounts of time and effort to review each application. Although it was an additional heavy burden to bear, it was indeed my honor to serve the government.

*Part 5*

# University of Rochester School of Medicine and Dentistry, and Medical Community in Rochester

# Invitation to the University of Rochester Medical Community

For some time in the late 1960s, my friend and esteemed colleague William Faloon, a professor of medicine at the University of Rochester, advised me to take a visit to Rochester, New York. Apparently the university had been looking for a qualified senior faculty member in gastroenterology to organize a digestive disease unit in one of the teaching hospitals. After visiting three teaching hospitals in the fall of 1970, I became very interested in an offer made by Genesee Hospital, one of the oldest teaching hospitals of the university. The physician-in-chief, Dr. Alvin L. Ureles, a physician trained at Harvard and Beth Israel Hospital, was a very kind and friendly gentleman and was eager to explain to me the hospital's plan to establish a first-rate gastroenterology program with adequate research funds and facilities for both clinical and research programs. His enthusiasm for the project was contagious This was my last visit in the late afternoon before I planned to leave by plane for Philadelphia, but because of his persuasion and my interest, I agreed to stay overnight to continue further discussions.

Dr. Alvin L. Ureles, physician-in-chief and professor of medicine, Genesee Hospital and University of Rochester, School of Medicine and Dentistry, in the 1970s.

At breakfast the next morning at a nearby hotel, I asked him, "You are interested in continuing the discussion, but why me?"

He smiled and said, "Bill, we have been looking for an academic physician who can develop a digestive disease center which can achieve excellence in both clinical services and research programs for the university. We would like you to seriously consider establishing and directing a digestive disease center that will be an integral part of the University of Rochester Digestive Program." Then he suggested I meet with Dr. Lawrence Young, the chair of the Department of Medicine and physician-in-chief at Strong Memorial Hospital, the flagship of the university teaching hospitals.

I told Dr. Ureles that I wasn't looking for a job but that his plan was quite inviting and attractive. However, I did express my interest in a possible new position. I had been wishing to have an academic digestive disease program combining both clinical services—including both inpatient and outpatient facilities in the same location of the hospital—and research facilities for both clinical and experimental investigations. At Temple University, even if the Fels research foundation provided me with more research funds, I could not have the well-organized program that Rochester offered.

I expressed to Dr. Ureles my desire to have a special medical floor for digestive disease patients who were being treated and managed by physicians, nursing staff, and technicians who were well trained in this specialty. Dr. Ureles said, "Bill, we can meet your demands. A specialty floor for patients with gastrointestinal diseases is needed for expert and efficient care for referral patients with complicated and difficult problems." The university and the hospital had just recruited an eminent general surgeon as the new surgeon-in-chief, Dr. Rene Menguy, a former professor of surgery and chair of the Department of Surgery at the University of Chicago. I had known of Dr. Menguy for his excellent investigative and clinical work for years. In his earlier career, he was trained at the Mayo Clinic and received a PhD in surgery from the University of Minnesota School of Medicine. Dr. Ureles said, "Here you can combine both medical and surgical patients with a variety of digestive diseases with the support of Dr. Menguy's strong surgical team." There was enthusiasm in the air that Genesee Hospital was determined to develop a strong gastroenterology program.

Dr. Young, a tall, soft-spoken, and kind gentleman, and the chair of the Department of Medicine at the medical center, was very pleased to see me at his large, spacious office. It seemed he had been looking forward to meeting and speaking with me further that morning. He confirmed Dr. Ureles's plan at Genesee Hospital, and he expressed his desire that I would develop an independent university gastroenterology fellowship program like the fellowship training program at Strong Memorial Hospital. He offered a position of a full professorship in medicine and directorship of Isaac Gordon Center for Digestive Diseases and Nutrition at Genesee Hospital, and a position of physician at Strong Memorial Hospital.

I asked Drs. Young and Ureles whether I could return for a second visit in two weeks, and they agreed and welcomed me. This was a totally unexpected and unbelievable event. I was excited because what might happen with me in Rochester could be a dream—the American dream that I had had for a long time. First, I could build a gastroenterology center; second, I could continue to practice clinical gastroenterology as a good physician and healer; third, I could have enough research space, facilities, and sound financial support; and fourth, I could be promoted to a full professorship. There were times when I was concerned about whether or not I could ever be promoted to a full professorship, because of my minority status. I felt that if I could develop the program as I negotiated with the university and the hospital, this would be my dream—the American dream I'd had ever since I started my career as a gastrointestinal physician. The University of Rochester School of Medicine and Dentistry is a very good medical school—one of the top-tier medical schools in the country.

Returning home to our beautiful home in Wyncote, Pennsylvania, I explained the situation to and discussed it with my dear Fan. She was very excited at the proposal made by the University of Rochester and Genesee Hospital. She felt that I should accept the offer and we should move to Rochester, New York, for my career and for the family. Rochester was a beautiful, clean, and quiet city. People there were friendly and generous. Moreover, the city was a university town. Besides Strong Memorial Hospital as a university hospital, there were five teaching hospitals including Genesee Hospital, Rochester General Hospital, Highland Hospital, St. Mary's Hospital, and Monroe Community Hospital, which admitted patients with chronic diseases. Each hospital had a full-time faculty appointed by the University of Rochester. They seemed to have a friendly and comradely working relationship.

The next morning, I met with Dr. Stanley Lorber in his office at Temple University Hospital and explained my visit to Rochester. He seemed to be quite concerned about my possible move. Stanley said he wanted to have a meeting with me and Dr. Sol Sherry, the new chair of the Department of Medicine, in order to discuss my potential move to Rochester. At the meeting, Dr. Sherry was very friendly and said he would propose a full professorship and co-chairship of the Gastroenterology Division at Temple University Medical Center. There was another reason why Dr. Sherry was quite concerned; he knew I was entitled to bring my research grant, funded by the National Institutes of Health, to the University of Rochester. Moreover, a very important antisecretin serum that my research laboratory produced would no longer be available to a group of endocrinology faculty in his department for joint research with my team.

In two weeks, I made the second visit to Rochester. Upon my arrival at Rochester Airport at noon, I found Dr. Alvin Ureles at the terminal to welcome me back. He was delighted to see me again. We had lunch together in his office, and we went over the blueprint of the Clinical Gastroenterology Center. The hospital emptied one entire floor of the West Building for the development of the Isaac Gordon Center for Digestive Diseases and Nutrition, which was contiguous, only two doors away, to the inpatient floor for patients with digestive diseases and liver diseases. The name was chosen in honor of the late Mr. Isaac Gordon, a philanthropist and a successful real estate developer in the greater Rochester area who generously donated funds that made it possible to undertake this dream program. On the floor, we would build a waiting room, endoscopy facilities, a fluoroscopy room, outpatient facilities, faculty offices, a conference room with a library, and bench research facilities on both ends of the floor. In addition, we were offered experimental animal facilities on the campus off of the hospital buildings. For research I was assured by both Dr. Urelese and the hospital administrators that sufficient seeding funds would be provided through the Isaac Gordon Foundation and hospital resources. Thus, I could perform both clinical and research work at the same location with sufficient budget and research funds. Moreover, an outstanding surgeon, Dr. Menguy, and my clinical team, in collaboration with my staff, would be able to provide the Rochester community and Upstate New York with the best service possible.

This might be a very demanding job offer, but the job could fulfill my dream of becoming a clinician-healer and a meaningful and productive researcher as a physician scientist and the promotion to a professor of medicine with a substantial increase in my salary at a reputable university. More importantly, I had a beautiful family who would live in Rochester, New York—a clean, friendly, and stable community. My children were born free and deserved to live in the community like Rochester. Moreover, my dear friend Al Urelese was such a wonderful person to work with. He welcomed me, helped me, and mentored me until I retired from the university in the year 2000. He was a World War II veteran who had been a medical officer, and he served in Korea for a short awhile in 1946 before he retired from the US Army. We still cherish our long-lasting friendship. With the strong support of my wife, Fan, I decided to accept the position as the director of the Isaac Gordon Center for Digestive Diseases and Nutrition at Genesee Hospital and the University of Rochester School of Medicine and Dentistry, and professor of medicine and physician at Strong Memorial Hospital.

# Moving to Rochester, New York

It was sad for us to leave Philadelphia, where we lived for eleven years. I had finished my graduate work at the University of Pennsylvania to receive two advanced degrees: an MSc in gastroenterology and a DSc in internal medicine. I was honored to have become a US citizen. Moreover, my precious four children, William D., Donna, Richard, and Laura, had been born in Philadelphia. We had to leave our beautiful home in a Philadelphia suburb and many good friends and close neighbors, but my wife, Fan, and I looked forward to having a new life with new hope and a better future in Rochester, a kind and friendly city where I wished to live and bring up our children. As we arrived in Rochester on July 4, 1971, we found that some of my research team from Philadelphia were already in Rochester, including Jack Hendrix, an experienced research technician and a research fellow; Dr. M. Yoshmori, from Japan; a second-year fellow in gastroenterology, Dr. Jorge Gutierrez; and their families. I was so grateful for their agreeing to move to Rochester, New York, and start a new program with me. My family settled in a comfortable home with four bedrooms in Penfield, a suburb of Rochester. My four children made new friends in the neighborhood and enrolled in elementary and middle schools in Penfield. They were happy together in the new environment with the unconditional support and love of their mother.

William Y. Chey, MD, MSc, DSc, Director of the Isaac Gordon Center for Digestive Diseases and Nutrition at the Genesee Hospital and professor of medicine at the University of Rochester School of Medicine and Dentistry, September 1971.

# The Isaac Gordon Center for Digestive Diseases and Nutrition

I was overjoyed and overwhelmed the first time I had the opportunity and responsibility to work hard and realize my dream of being a physician and educator with compassion, sympathy, and empathy as well as a physician scientist who could perform meaningful and productive research: a dream of my lifetime—an American Dream. The construction of all the new clinical facilities was completed in one month, including an inpatient floor for patients with digestive diseases and liver diseases, which was contiguous with the floor for outpatient services, endoscopy procedure rooms and recovery area, a fluoroscopy room combined with endoscopic procedures, examination rooms for outpatients, faculty offices, conference rooms, a library, and research laboratories. The number of inpatient consultations and referrals from the community and surrounding counties, as well as the number of endoscopic procedures, had steadily increased. The inpatient floor for digestive diseases or disorders and liver diseases was also filled. It was so gratifying that the patients requiring special and complicated care for digestive diseases and disorders were efficiently being treated by nursing staff skilled and experienced in digestive illnesses. Soon it became a busy referral center for digestive and liver diseases in Upstate New York. I was also gratified to receive some of my former patients in Philadelphia with malabsorption syndrome, inflammatory bowel disease, and other digestive disorders.

When the patients on the GI floor needed surgical treatment, after surgical procedures, they returned to the same beds to continue care with the same nurses and both surgical and medical teams of doctors. We were so fortunate and privileged to work with a prominent academic surgeon with superb clinical and surgical skills and high professionalism. We were always content with our mutual respect for the patients and their referring physicians. One physician in general practice in a small town, about one hundred miles away from Rochester, said to me on the phone, "Dr. Menguy, a professor, phoned me to let me know that the cholecystectomy for his patient went very well and that she will return home in a few days. I was very pleased." It was unusual for a senior faculty member at another teaching hospital to extend such a courtesy call to a referring physician. Good communication and mutual respect between consultants and referring physicians are essential for good patient care.

Our weekly conference for digestive and liver diseases was well attended by residents, students, fellows, and trainees in gastroenterology, and faculty, including attending gastroenterologists, surgeons, general physicians, pathologists, and radiologists. The clinical program became a popular elective in gastroenterology for medical residents among teaching hospitals. The clinical fellows were recruited nationally after having completed their formal residency training in internal medicine at teaching hospitals. The fellowship program for clinical gastroenterology, as one of the two programs of the University of Rochester Medical Center, was thus successfully started with high-caliber fellows whom we selected, and we were proud of them.

**The Isaac Gordon Center Members** (*from right of front row*): **Dr. Choon Kyu Kim, Dr. David Hamilton, Dr. Ashok Shah, Ms. Erika Bader, Dr. William Y. Chey, Dr. Chul Hee Yu, and others in the 1970s.**

# Accomplishments at the Isaac Gordon Center

From a nucleus of only six members, the center had grown to a forty-member group specializing in gastrointestinal fields and serving not only Upstate New York but also New York City and its environs, and other states, including Massachusetts, Connecticut, Pennsylvania, Maryland, the District of Columbia, Virginia, North Carolina, Texas, Florida, Oklahoma, Ohio, New Mexico, California, Illinois, and Michigan. The center's training program, which included both clinical and research fellowships, helped over fifty physicians and scientists to become competent specialists in gastroenterology throughout the United States. Many foreign scientists for research fellowship from China, Japan, South Korea, Poland, Scotland, Nigeria, and Kenya enjoyed working with our research team and returned to their own countries after training.

The center's research programs had been supported by Genesee Hospital, US public health research grants, private donations from friends of the center, and funds from pharmaceutical industries. Over 250 scientific articles were published in peer-reviewed and competitive journals and textbooks, and more than 400 presentations were made at national and international scientific meetings. Two international symposia were organized by the center and held in Rochester, New York. The first symposium was held in 1974 and was titled "Recent Advances in Gastrointestinal Hormone Research." This was also the first symposium held in the United States. The second symposium was held in 1983 and was titled "International Symposium on Functional Disorders of the Digestive Tract." Many internationally and nationally eminent clinicians and physician scientists attended and participated in the symposia with high enthusiasm.

# Research and Our Signature Achievement

The research facilities consisted of a biochemistry and immunochemistry laboratory, an immunohistochemistry laboratory, an experimental animal research laboratory, and clinical research facilities. The major areas of our research were the development of highly specific and sensitive radioimmunoassay methods that measure gastrointestinal hormones in blood and tissues; the hormones, such as secretin, cholecystokinin, and gastrin, that regulate the secretory functions of the stomach and the pancreas; and motor function of digestive tract, including that in the esophagus, stomach, intestine, and colon, in humans and animals. The successful development of highly sensitive and potent radioimmunoassay for measurement of these hormones in the blood and tissue was essential in investigating the functions of digestive organs. We were in fierce competition to achieve this goal globally.

Our first goal was to develop a very sensitive and specific radioimmunoassay method to establish the genuine hormonal status of the first known gastrointestinal hormone, secretin, which was believed to be the hormone discovered in 1902 by the two legendary British physiologists Professors William Bayliss and S. Starling in London.

I feel I should present some further background information on secretin. At the turn of the twentieth century, it was well recognized by then well-known researchers—including Ivan Pavlov, a Nobel laureate, and his students in St. Petersburg, Russia—that hydrochloric acid produced in the stomach that enters the duodenum increases pancreatic juice production in dogs and other mammals. In 1902, the two British scientists, Bayliss and Starling, proposed that the increased production of pancreatic juice in dogs was mediated by a humoral substance produced by acid in the duodenum. They hypothesized that the humoral substance enters the bloodstream from the duodenum to reach the pancreas and stimulates production of highly alkaline pancreatic juice, which digests food particles in the upper small intestine and maintains the alkalinity of the upper small-intestinal lumen for digestion and the prevention of duodenal ulcers. Thus they proposed this humoral substance, secretin, to be a hormone. However, they did not isolate the hormone from intestinal tissue; nor were many subsequent researchers able to decisively determine the chemical structure of this hypothetical hormone, secretin, or the presence of such a hormonal substance in the bloodstream until years after 1970.

The successful isolation of a secretin-like substance from the small intestinal mucosal lining in hogs was made by Professors Eric Jorpes and Viktor Mutt in Stockholm, Sweden, in the 1960s, and they successfully determined its chemical structure in the 1960s. They found that secretin was a small peptide that exhibited a potent stimulating activity on the pancreas in dogs, humans, and other mammals. It was indeed my honor to test the potency of many batches of their pure secretin preparations in human volunteers in the late 1950s at Temple University Medical Center during my gastroenterology fellowship training. Almost ten years later, it was my pleasure and honor to meet with both Professors Eric Jorpes and Viktor Mutt in Stockholm in 1970 when we were invited to participate in a Nobel symposium titled "Frontiers in Gastrointestinal Hormone Research." Professor Jorpes in particular was so kind, and he treated me like his son. Further investigations on secretin were needed to identify and isolate such a substance in the blood and determine its biological, physiological, and pathological significance in normal and diseased states. It was our honor to decisively determine the hormonal status of the very first (hypothetical) known hormone, secretin, more than seventy years later in Rochester, New York.

# Successful Radioimmunoassay of Secretin

Success in the measurement of secretin in both tissue and blood, and investigations on its biological and physiological actions, depended on the development of a highly sensitive and specific radioimmunoassay method for measurement of immunoreactive secretin. We had to produce highly potent antisecretin serums in rabbits. After six years of hard work by our team of talented researchers led by Dr. Daniel Tai and Ta-min Chang at the Isaac Gordon Center, we succeeded in producing a very potent (very high-titer) antiserum that made it possible for us to develop a world's-best radioimmunoassay of secretin. This assay method proved secretin to be a circulating hormone, as proposed by Bayliss and Starling in 1902. It could measure consistently increased secretin levels in the blood after ingestion of a regular meal, which was believed to drive pancreatic juice production in mammals including humans, dogs, guinea pigs, and rats. Using our antisecretin serums, the work was reproduced and published by Doctors K. Shiratori and T. Takeuchi and their associates in Tokyo, Japan, and Doctors L. E. Hanssen and his coworkers in Oslo, Norway.

The Rochester team had proven further, for the first time in the world, that circulating secretin is the major hormone that drives production of meal-stimulated pancreatic juice rich in bicarbonate in dogs, because when active secretin was eliminated from the circulation by immunoneutralization with our powerful rabbit antisecretin serum, the meal-stimulated pancreatic juice production was shut off as much as 80 percent or more in conscious dogs. This exciting and important work was published in a highly competitive scientific journal, *Gastroenterology*, in 1978. Secretin is indeed a real hormone, as claimed by the two brilliant British physiologists Professors Bayliss and Starling in 1902.

When this result was presented at the Second International Symposium on Gastrointestinal Hormones in 1978, held in Beito, Norway, I received thunderous standing ovations from the entire audience. This was indeed our signature research work in gastrointestinal hormone research at the University of Rochester medical community, which was initiated at Genesee Hospital, in Rochester, New York, in 1971. This historical work, recognized by the world community of gastrointestinal hormone researchers, was cited in text books of gastrointestinal physiology and medicine and review articles relevant to gastrointestinal hormones.

# The First International Symposium on Gastrointestinal Hormone Research

In August 1973, we held an international symposium titled, "Recent Advances in Gastrointestinal Hormone Research" in Rochester, New York. In collaboration with Dr. Frank P. Brooks, professor of medicine and chief of gastroenterology at the University of Pennsylvania School of Medicine, we felt that it was timely to have such a meeting in the United States to update rather explosive advances made by world-class pioneers in the frontier of gastrointestinal hormone research. By then, in addition to the chemical structures of gastrin, cholecystokinin, and secretin being known, at least three more new gastrointestinal peptides were found to exist, including motilin, vasoactive intestinal peptide, and gastric inhibitory peptide; and their biological actions on the gastrointestinal organs, such as the stomach, pancreas, biliary tract, and intestines had been reported.

Over two hundred scientists and academic gastroenterologists attended the historical meeting held for two days at the beautiful Xerox Auditorium in downtown Rochester, New York. Fifty speakers participated in the meeting. Among those invited were the future Nobel Prize winner Dr. Rosalyn Yalow, known for development of radioimmunoassay for insulin at Bronx Veterans Hospital, who was a distinguished professor at Mount Sinai School of Medicine; Dr. Vincent du Vigneaud, a former Nobel Prize winner, professor of chemistry at Cornell University, and a graduate of the University of Rochester; Professor Morton I. Grossman of UCLA and the Veteran's Administration Center, Los Angeles, California; Professor of Histopathology A. C. E. Pearce of the University of London; Dr. Werner Creutzfeldt, a professor of medicine at the University of Gottingen, Gottingen, Germany; and Dr. Miklos Bodanszky, a professor of chemistry at Case Western University, Cleveland, Ohio.

During the two memorable days, many experts in the field presented their research work and discussed it with colleagues. They renewed their friendship and made new friends during intermission and during the lunch and dinner banquets. We all learned from the speakers' updated knowledge of known hormones and many new candidate hormones that were to be further explored. Our group presented and shared the current progress being made in the work relating to secretin—particularly the development of radioimmunoassay of secretin. Without a reliable, specific, and sensitive method that could measure secretin levels in the blood and tissues, meaningful research would not be possible. Whichever lucky group in the world could develop a powerful radioimmunoassay method for secretin research would be able to establish the genuine hormonal status of secretin and could investigate its hormonal roles in normal and certain diseased states in humans and other mammals. (Five years later, we established that secretin was and has been indeed a genuine gastrointestinal hormone. The work was published in

*Gastroenterology* and was presented at the second International Symposium on Gastrointestinal Hormones, held in Norway in 1978.)

The invitees and audience appreciated this timely meeting. Furthermore, Genesee Hospital, as well as the University of Rochester School of Medicine and Dentistry, was recognized for our gut hormone research nationally and internationally and was credited with the historical meeting. The social activities during intermissions between the meetings, luncheons, and evening banquet were well organized by my wife, Fan, and were appreciated by the audience and invited speakers and guests. This success was attributed to my wife, Fan, who, with the help of my office workers, had worked so hard to organize orderly, pleasant, and memorable occasions during the two full days of the symposium. The invited speakers and other dignitaries at the meeting were also invited to our new GI facilities. Many of them expressed their envy for the new center for digestive diseases and research. I was gratified, because the gastroenterology program at Genesee Hospital had been recognized nationally and internationally.

# The Joy of Being a Physician Healer

I would like to mention the reason why I wanted to become a physician a long time ago. When I was a little boy in a small rural town in South Korea, our family lost a beautiful two-year-old baby girl, one of my two sisters, who became suddenly ill with fever, a stiff neck, and convulsions. My parents felt helpless because there was no doctor in the town. It took one day to seek the help of a medical doctor in the provincial capital, but sadly it was too late. She died of acute meningitis. Five years later, my five-year-old brother was afflicted by a kidney disease, a nephrotic syndrome. The little brother, quite close to me, begged for help because he did not feel well and told us many times that he did not wish to die, but he died three months later. It was indeed a heart wrenching experience for the family. My father's everlasting wish then was to become a doctor, but he could not materialize his dream. My reason for pursuing a medical career had two main motives: one was our family tragedies, which led me to care for the sick, and the other was the fulfillment of my father's dream.

There is nothing that pleases me more or is more gratifying than when our patients feel well after our care, having suffered for so long previously. In the following sections, I have written down my memories of some of the many who appreciated our care immensely and whose satisfaction I appreciated. Each time I remember them, even decades later, I am still gratified and satisfied as a healer who practiced art and science in the care of suffering patients. So often, even though I have been retired for years, I miss them and remember them; remembering them is both a good time and a sad time.

*Case 1*

A fifty-two-year-old female patient accompanied by her sister, a registered nurse, and her devoted husband presented with symptoms of weight loss, anorexia, dyspepsia, and watery diarrhea. She had been treated elsewhere for intermittent episodes of diarrhea with a diagnosis of irritable bowel syndrome (IBS) for years. She recently had an exploratory laparotomy at the same hospital because of an abnormal CAT (computerized axial tomography) scan of the abdomen showing a mass in the pancreas. When she was surgically operated on, she was found to have a golf-ball-size mass in the head of her pancreas and several small masses in her liver. A biopsy of the tumor in the pancreas confirmed the clinical impression of a cancer of the pancreas, which apparently to have spread to the liver. The surgeon told her and the family that the tumors were inoperable and that she had about six months to live. Chemotherapy was recommended. The patient and her family were profoundly disappointed, for she had been treated at the same institution for IBS with diarrhea for years. Her sister, a nurse working in the same hospital, was very upset because she had believed her sister had IBS, as diagnosed by the physicians there, whom she had known for years.

At our GI center, we confirmed the abnormal CAT scan findings and measured her daily diarrheal stool volume. The stool was mostly plain liquid, and the total daily volume was as much as one and a half liters. In our research laboratory, we examined the biopsied tumor tissue using our immunochemical staining method with a specific antiserum to vasoactive intestinal peptide (VIP) that showed abundant numbers of VIP-producing cancer cells. VIP is a well-recognized diarrhea-producing hormone found in patients with diarrhea-producing tumors. The blood level of VIP was measured using a specific radioimmunoassay developed in our research laboratory and was found to be very high. Thus we were convinced that she had a VIP-producing cancer of the pancreas, which increased the level of VIP in the blood, causing massive watery diarrhea, dehydration, and weight loss. This condition is known as Verner-Morrison syndrome, Vipoma syndrome, or pancreatic cholera.

Although most patients with pancreatic cancers have one of the worst prognoses in spite of aggressive chemotherapy, radiation, and surgical treatment, some patients with the type of VIP-producing cancer this patient had have better prognoses and live longer than those with the more commonly known cancer of the pancreas if properly managed. Anticipating that my colleague, Dr. Menguy, might be excited to discuss this patient, I walked into his office to discuss her condition. On reviewing the CAT scan and the data of our other diagnostic studies, he became very excited. He enthusiastically agreed to perform another exploratory laparotomy and said he would try to surgically remove the tumor from the pancreas, the small tumors surrounding the primary tumor, and the small tumors in the liver. The patient and her family, including her husband and two daughters, were very pleased. My fellows in training were also very excited, because not all gastroenterologists personally experience the care of such an interesting case in their lifetime. On the day of surgery, Dr. Menguy and his team spent six hours completing a successful surgery to remove a part of the pancreas with the main tumor and the rest of the small tumors. The anxious family in the waiting room was updated on the progress of the surgery throughout the day. The patient recovered from the extensive operation without any complications.

The patient smiled at me when I saw her early the next morning. Her diarrhea ceased immediately after the surgery, and the high blood level of VIP also dropped and returned to normal in twenty-four hours, indicating that the cause of the diarrhea was indeed VIP, which had been produced by the cancer. She received a course of chemotherapy and tolerated it well. She steadily improved clinically with good appetite and gained fifteen pounds in the following three months. During the subsequent ten years, she traveled with family and enjoyed her life, although she needed two more less-extensive abdominal surgeries to remove smaller recurrent tumors. This patient, who was initially told she had six months to live, was so grateful to us for over one decade.

*Case 2*

A middle-aged woman came to see me at my office to ask for special consideration in helping her nineteen-year-old son who had suffered from severe ulcerative colitis for more than one year. The young patient was currently admitted to a pediatric floor. I advised her that I did not see adolescent patients in the pediatric service at the hospital. She begged me to see her son, who was scheduled for surgical removal of his entire colon for the severe colitis, which had failed to respond favorably to medical treatment. During the past six months, this was his third hospitalization for worsening colitis.

While I and a fellow in gastroenterology evaluated him at his bedside, we noticed he went to the bathroom twice for bowel movements. When we examined the toilet, we found bright red blood and mucus. He was already scheduled for surgery the following morning to have a total colectomy. In my mind, the only chance he might have for recovery from this serious condition without surgery was a new drug, infliximab, which had been approved recently by the FDA for treatment of Crohn's disease, including Crohn's colitis. Although the new drug had been tested only in patients with Crohn's disease, I thought that the new drug might be effective not only in Crohn's colitis but also in patients with ulcerative colitis, since the new drug suppressed inflammation of the colon and small intestine in patients with Crohn's disease. The parents felt painfully sad about their son, who was about to lose his precious colon the next morning, and I was also deeply disturbed and sympathetic. Realizing the difficulty I would experience in facing the surgeons, I searched for an exceptional way to help the young patient. I decided to try this new drug for him if possible.

In order to use this drug for him, I contacted a senior medical officer of a local health insurance company and explained why the drug might also work for ulcerative colitis. I emphasized to him that if the drug was effective, it may not only save his colon but also would be cost effective by precluding the need for surgery and possible unexpected postsurgical complications. He reluctantly agreed and approved the use of the drug as an exceptional case. The drug was administered starting in the early evening. The next morning at seven o'clock, when I saw him at his bedside, he was awake, and he smiled. During the night, he had had only three small bowel movements with dark blood in much smaller quantities than before. He said, "Dr. Chey, thank you, sir. I slept well and had less pain and cramps." The toilet showed no more fresh blood but only old blood in the puddle of mucous materials. My fellow and I were ecstatic. My fellow said, "This is a miracle, Dr. Chey."

I said, "This is the fun of being a thinking physician healer." The surgery was cancelled, and he continued infliximab treatment. At the end of one week, the colitis was found to be healing well when we examined his rectum and lower sigmoid colon with a short colonoscope. In subsequent follow-ups over three months, the patient had no recurrence of bloody diarrhea. His mother was very pleased and grateful.

This is an example that shows a physician sometimes goes the extra mile to help a desperately ill patient by applying his expert knowledge for a given medical problem and negotiating with the health care industry regarding a new drug, if possible, or whatever means are available. A physician should always be proud of being an advocate for patients; this is something I have always been proud of. It is the sacred deed of a physician to protect patients from harm.

*Case 3*

A fifty-eight-year-old male had had longstanding severe constipation, abdominal bloating and swelling, and severe anal pain. The history of his illness went back to 1950 (about thirty-five years prior), when he passed out on a local public high school playground while he was playing soccer. In the middle of the game, he had marked swelling and severe discomfort of the abdomen and increasing difficulty in breathing, which led to unconsciousness. An emergency exploratory laparotomy was performed at a local teaching hospital to find a markedly enlarged and ballooned colon without any mechanical obstruction of the colon or discernible disease. About a half of the colon was surgically removed, resulting in complete cessation of the symptoms. However, there were no regular follow-up visits after the surgery. Since then, he had gradually developed recurrent abdominal discomfort and bloating, along with episodic marked swelling of the abdomen associated with shortness of breath and racing heart, requiring cardiologists' attention. Equally significant was his severe constipation. He made numerous visits to several local physicians' offices, including a cardiology office. With his personal background history of being a holocaust victim who migrated to the United States alone at age of fifteen and having a hard, stressful life, doctors felt that he had an anxiety neurosis, a stress-associated bowel condition, irritable bowel syndrome (IBS).

By the time I was consulted in the mid-1980s, he had been extensively evaluated and treated by reputable specialists, including gastroenterologists and surgeons in Boston, Massachusetts. He continued to have severe constipation and pain in the anus. He was virtually incapacitated and profoundly depressed, although he had been a very successful businessman and generous philanthropist in the community. The evaluation at my office and review of recent barium enema X-ray films revealed a huge and elongated colon. I was amazed to find that even though half of the colon had been surgically removed more than three decades prior, the colon was still huge throughout. However, some areas of the colon were not as large as other parts of the colon. The colonoscopy showed no discernible disease, but the caliber of the colon was unusually large, and deep and painful anal fissures were found. That condition alone could cause severe spasm and pain of the anus and constipation. After thorough evaluation of his overall condition, I reached the conclusion that he had a severe motility disorder of the colon of unknown cause. Reviewing barium X-ray films further, we found again that a certain part of the colon was less dilated than other parts of the colon. Specifically, the left portion of the colon was less dilated than the rest of the colon. This finding gave me a feeling of possible hope that surgical removal of the entire colon might not be necessary. Rather, the surgical removal of the markedly dilated part of the colon might still relieve constipation, and even anal fissures might be eventually healed.

A surgical resection of the colon was imminent in order to relieve severe constipation and abdominal swelling, and I felt it might relieve the episodic chest discomfort and shortness of breath, which were due to a markedly distended colon that pushed the left side of the diaphragm upward. These changes could pressure the lungs and affect the heart, which might be tilted transiently. While total colectomy was usually recommended by most surgeons, I discussed the case with my colleague Dr. Rene Menguy. Although most of the large colon would be surgically removed, the left side of the colon could be saved and connected to the lower end of the small intestine. Dr. Menguy was always willing to discuss special circumstances regarding individual cases, like this one, and he agreed to perform an appropriate surgery for the benefit of the patient. In this particular case, it was possible the man might recover to become an active businessman again. Dr. Menguy agreed to save the left part of the colon. Both the patient and I were very pleased.

The author, William Konar (*center*), and Rene Menguy, MD, PhD, professor
of surgery and surgeon-in-chief at Genesee Hospital and the University of
Rochester School of Medicine and Dentistry, Rochester, New York.

After the surgery, his longstanding and agonizing constipation and other symptoms were virtually gone. The combined medical and surgical treatments made him feel like a new person. He no longer had depression. He resumed managing a productive business as well as philanthropic work, and he continued with these for many years. Then his remaining left colon became enlarged, and his constipation returned. Dr. Menguy performed a second surgery to remove the remaining colon, and the end of the patient's small intestine was connected to the rectum, the last part of the colon. After the surgery, although he was expected to have diarrhea every day, miraculously, he had only one or two formed stools per day.

Helping the sick, such as this patient, with compassion, sympathy, and empathy, no matter how hard and demanding it may be, is the mission of the sacred work of the physician healer. It was such a gratifying feeling when this man recovered from his agonizing and painful illness. He and I became a lifelong friends. We mutually cherished our friendship, and I was privileged and honored to be his physician and friend.

*Case 4*

A twenty-nine-year-old female teacher at a local elementary school had had chronic constipation for five years. She barely had one small, hard stool weekly in spite of being treated with daily laxatives prescribed by her physicians and over-the-counter drugs. She had crippling abdominal discomfort, including bloating, swelling, and pain when she could not have a bowel movement. Her additional problems were pelvic discomfort and frequent urination. As time passed by, her frequent urination became worse and she began to have incontinence, leaving her hesitant to sneeze or laugh hard, which resulted in the leakage of urine. More disturbingly, she could no longer continue her morning jogging because of urinary leakage. More troublesome also was the pelvic discomfort she felt during coitus and the postcoital period (dyspareunia), which discouraged her from having sexual intercourse.

On her first office visit, the patient was initially embarrassed and annoyed by my questions, because she came to see me as a gastroenterologist for constipation. I explained to her that a gastroenterologist or stomach specialist like myself must be a physician first, a keen clinical observer, and a good listener. I explained that I spend time evaluating a patient's overall medical problems that might be related to her present illness by asking about symptoms regarding urinary bladder disorders, gynecological symptoms, and even psychosocial problems. She began to understand my reasoning, and I began to earn her trust. Nevertheless, she consulted with an out-of-town gastroenterologist in a recognized clinic for a second opinion. She was told she had constipation-predominant irritable bowel syndrome (IBS-C).

When she returned to my office, a series of diagnostic studies including a barium meal X-ray of the small intestine and colon revealed abnormally slow transit of the colon, a markedly enlarged cecum that was four times the normal size. (Normally this first part of the colon looks like a pouch located in the right lower abdomen near the appendix. The cecum empties liquid stool from the small intestine into the rest of the colon.) The enlarged cecum descended into the pelvis when the patient was in a standing position. It appeared that the large cecum pressed against the urinary bladder and other pelvic organs.

Because the colon was so slow in evacuating the fecal materials and was resistant to conventional medications for severe constipation, the colon was surgically removed laparoscopically by Dr. Vincent Chang, one of the best general surgeons in the Rochester community. She had an uneventful recovery after the surgery, and the constipation was relieved. Even more significantly, her pelvic symptoms, particularly dyspareunia and the urinary bladder symptoms, virtually disappeared; she was able to resume her morning jogging and teaching at the school. She was subsequently married and had a newborn baby girl. My team of providers were overjoyed. The success in her care emphasizes again that we specialists with multiple procedure skills must be physicians first, with good bedside observation skills and careful listening, empathy, sympathy, and compassion. It had been my privilege to work with Dr. Chang for years. He had been trained by the legendary surgeon and my dear friend Professor Rene Menguy, whom I miss dearly.

The care of patients who were once seriously ill or in despair requires not only cutting-edge knowledge to establish an accurate diagnosis and design effective treatment for their illnesses but also the physician's assurance, comfort, understanding, patience, and compassion for the patients as well as their families. After five decades of my career as a physician healer, I still feel there is nothing that pleases me more than when my patients feel better. I still believe that being a physician is one of the most satisfying and rewarding professions.

University of Rochester Medical Center, Division of Gastroenterology and Hepatology members, 1993. Front row (*from left to right*): J Hsu, MD; A. Shah, MD; F. Ona, MD; W. Chey, MD, DSc.; F. Klipstein, MD; C. Kim; M. Brown, MD; G. Potter, MD. The remaining faculty and fellows are in the back rows.

# University of Rochester Medical Center, Strong Memorial Hospital Konar Center for Digestive and Liver Diseases

D r. Raphael Dolin, MD, chair of the University of Rochester Medical Center Department of Medicine, Strong Memorial Hospital, with the support of dean and professor of medicine Dr. Marshall Lichtman, discussed with me on several occasions in 1990 whether I would consider becoming the director of gastroenterology and hepatology at the medical center. It was indeed an honor. In fact, I needed a new challenge after my service at Genesee Hospital for twenty years. I thanked Dr. Dolin and accepted the offer. To my knowledge, I was the first one to become a division chief at the medical center, chosen from among the affiliated hospitals of the university, including Rochester General Hospital, Genesee Hospital, Highland Hospital, St. Mary's Hospital, and Monroe Community Hospital in Rochester, New York. Dr. Dolin was and remains an internationally well-recognized virologist, and he eventually returned to his alma mater, Harvard University Medical School, to serve as a dean and continue his pioneering research in HIV and its vaccine development. I respect him and miss him dearly.

**Dr. Raphael Dolin, chair of the Department of Medicine** (*fifth from right*); **William Konar** (*sixth from right*); **and members (in part) of the Konar Center for Digestive and Liver Diseases, Strong Memorial Hospital, including the author** (*fourth from right*); **Kathleen Fulton, RN** (*seventh from right*); **and the rest of the faculty and fellows, 1995.**

I was expected to boost the existing gastroenterology program at the medical center, starting from centralizing in one location all the existing clinical facilities, which were scattered in the medical center, including faculty offices, administrative offices, outpatient clinical facilities, diagnostic and therapeutic endoscopic facilities, and clinical research facilities. In addition, the X-ray equipment and facility were installed in the premises of the GI center for the first time in the history of the medical center. At that time, no more than ten academic gastroenterology units in the country, to my knowledge, had X-ray equipment in their teaching hospitals' digestive disease units. This X-ray equipment was, and still is, an indispensable necessity for safety and efficiency for patients who require invasive diagnostic and therapeutic procedures, and for learning for fellows in training. At the new digestive disease center, all the facilities were located on the fourth floor of the new ambulatory care building. Thus, this was the first time the gastroenterology unit at the medical center was centralized with the state-of-the-art modern equipment and facilities to serve as a proud tertiary referral center in the University of Rochester Medical Center.

**Mr. William B. Konar in the 1990s.**

The establishment of this new center for digestive and liver diseases was made possible mainly by generous gifts of my dear patient and friend Mr. William B. Konar, a successful businessman and generous philanthropist, and his friends. In 1995, in our profound appreciation and in honor of the Konar family, the center was named the William and Sheila Konar Center for Digestive and Liver Diseases, and I had the honor of becoming the founding director. The center became a launching pad for future advancement in the art and science of the digestive and liver disease program at the medical center for many years to come.

**Mr. William B. Konar and Mrs. Sheila Konar, 1990s.**

The benefactor of the digestive and liver disease center, Mr. William B. Konar, was born in Poland around 1930. He was twelve when he and his family were incarcerated in the Auschwitz concentration camp in Poland. After the family were separated in the camp, he never saw his parents again. After being liberated from the camp in 1945, he traveled to the United States of America on a ship for orphans. He was settled in Rochester, New York, and enrolled at Benjamin Franklin High School. During off-hours, young Bill was ambitious and worked hard in local stores and markets. In those days, he used to carry heavy pickle barrels. After graduation, he started his first business, working tirelessly for eighty to ninety hours a week, which lasted throughout his career. He grew the business into a chain of eighty-four discount drugstores that extended to the Eastern United States from Michigan. He served as senior vice president of CVS drugstores for eight years and retired at age fifty-two. Then he founded the successful William Konar Properties, a real estate company catering to both residential and commercial properties, another success in business, in the Rochester area. He was a staunch family man who always believed family should come first. Bill was supported by his loving and caring wife, Sheila; two children—Howard, an attorney-at-law, and Rachel, a businesswoman—and five grandchildren. He was a generous philanthropist. At the University of Rochester Medical Center, he and his family not only established the Konar Center for Digestive and Liver Diseases in 1995 but also recently installed two endowed chairs; they also established the Konar Family Professorship in Geriatric Psychiatry and Geriatric Medicine. Many in the community called him "a beautiful person." He and his wife established a family foundation, the William B. and Sheila Konar Foundation, which supports local philanthropic organizations. Indeed he fulfilled his American dream. Sadly, he passed away in 2015 at eighty-five years of age. He was my unforgettable dear friend and my personal counsellor. I miss him profoundly.

# Continuity of Our Research Program at the Medical Center

Our entire research team and all of our research equipment was relocated in a research building in the medical school to continue productive research work as I moved to the medical center. Trainees in gastroenterology and many scientists, mostly research fellows, from abroad participated in our research program. Under the leadership of the research faculty, including three talented senior research faculty members—Ta-min Chang, PhD; K. Y. Lee, MD, PhD; and myself—the research fellows were chosen from the United States, South Korea, Japan, China, Southeast Asia, East Asia, Europe, Central and South America, and Africa. I was and am very proud of those fellows, who worked hard and were dedicated to their work. We had such an exciting two-hour research conference every Saturday morning, at which we discussed their research data obtained during the week. From their hard work, over three hundred scientific articles were published in respectable peer-reviewed scientific journals and textbooks. Their work, including those of them at the Isaac Gordon Center, was presented at national meetings in major cities of the United States and at international meetings held in many foreign countries, including Canada, Mexico, Japan, South Korea, Taiwan, China, Thailand, Singapore, Indonesia, the Philippines, Saudi Arabia, Italy, France, Germany, Switzerland, Denmark, Norway, Sweden, and England.

The majority of them returned to their home countries after the training in Rochester and held leadership positions in universities and hospitals. Among some thirty research fellows who returned to their home countries, three became deans of medical schools; and four, chief executive officers in university hospitals. We were honored to have these talented, hardworking and dedicated scientists, physician scientists and physician educators. They all came to Rochester, New York, to spend part of their careers and enjoy American culture for a period of one to two years. Some of them enjoyed return visits years later with their children who grew up here.

# Our Overall Research Accomplishments since 1971

O ur main research work and contributions were in the areas of gastrointestinal hormone research. We developed radioimmunoassay methods for secretin, cholecystokinin, gastrin, motilin, and peptide YY, which play important roles in the physiology and pathophysiology of digestive functions of the pancreas, stomach, small intestine, and colon in both experimental animals and humans.

The crown jewel of our research accomplishment was our extensive research work on secretin, the first known gastrointestinal hormone. Secretin, a hormone produced in the duodenum, is delivered to the pancreas through blood circulation and stimulates the pancreas to produce an alkaline juice that delivers digestive enzymes into the duodenum (the first part of the upper small intestine).

We investigated to determine whether or not secretin exists in circulating blood in normal conditions in humans as well as in dogs and other mammals. For the measurement of secretin in the blood, we succeeded in developing a very specific and highly sensitive radioimmunoassay method capable of determining secretin levels as low as one pictogram (one millionth of one milligram) or lower in 1 cc of plasma (the fluid part of blood). The success of this research depended on the successful production of a very potent antiserum to secretin. We were so fortunate as to produce such valuable antiserums in our research laboratories. We succeeded in developing one of the most sensitive and specific radioimmunoassay methods for secretin in the world.

Using this sensitive method, we found for the first time that the blood level of secretin was significantly elevated after the ingestion of ordinary meals in humans, dogs, rats, and guinea pigs. This indicated to us that after eating a meal, the duodenum released secretin into the blood in response to digested food products in a substantial amount. Subsequent experiments in humans and animals showed that the increased secretin levels in the blood paralleled the increase in highly alkaline pancreatic juice production. To further investigate whether or not the increased blood secretin level indeed was responsible for the pancreatic juice increase after meals, we carried out experiments that eliminated active secretin in the blood with potent and specific rabbit antisecretin serums that neutralized active secretin in circulation. If secretin was the genuine stimulant of pancreatic juice production, the antisecretin serums would profoundly suppress the meal-stimulated pancreatic juice production. Indeed, when the antiserum was administered intravenously and blocked the rise in the blood secretin level, the pancreatic juice production was suppressed dramatically, up to more than 80 percent. This was the decisive proof that secretin was the major hormone in meal-stimulated pancreatic juice production in healthy canines. A similar study could not be done in humans. Unfortunately, a specific secretin-receptor antagonist usable in humans was not available at the time of this investigation and is still not available at the time of this memoir's preparation.

Although Bayliss and Stahling claimed that secretin was produced by acid in the duodenal mucosa, they used highly acidic solutions (hydrochloric acid) as much as fifty to one hundred times as acidic as those that exist in either humans or other mammals. Was hydrochloric acid produced in the stomach that entered the duodenum responsible for the elevation of blood secretin level after meal ingestion? The answer was yes. When stomach acid juice production was blocked with omeprazole, a potent blocker of stomach acid production in both humans and canines, it also suppressed secretin elevation in the blood and pancreatic juice production. Thus, the stomach acid delivered to the duodenum after a meal was the major stimulant that elevated blood levels of secretin and thus triggered the production of alkaline-rich pancreatic juice.

Secretin can be released from the duodenum by agents other than acid to increase blood secretin levels. Two representative ones—bile and a plant kingdom product, turmeric (an ingredient used in Indian curries)—were found to increase blood secretin levels and stimulate pancreatic juice production in humans and canines. These may be alternative agents that may stimulate pancreatic juice production when the stomach cannot produce hydrochloric acid, such as in the case of achlorhydria.

After the ingestion of a meal, secretin alone cannot stimulate production of pancreatic juice sufficient in quantity for digestion of the meal. We found that the action of secretin is potentiated (enhanced) by cholecystokinin, which is produced in the duodenum and released into the bloodstream almost simultaneously with secretin. Cholecystokinin alone produces a very small amount of pancreatic juice. Only when both hormones circulate simultaneously in the blood after a meal can the pancreas produce enough alkaline juice for the normal digestion of ingested food and neutralization of acid in the duodenum. Thus secretin and cholecystokinin are essential partners for normal digestion, and thus if either one of the two hormones is eliminated or has its action blocked, pancreatic juice production is profoundly decreased after a meal. The discovery of secretin as the major hormone that drives the production and delivery of pancreatic juice into the upper small intestine after ingestion of a meal is indeed one of our major research contributions to the biological sciences.

When pancreatic juice is diverted from the duodenum or upper small intestine, pancreatic juice production after ingestion of a meal is markedly enhanced. This further increase in pancreatic juice was found to be attributable to enhanced increases in blood levels of secretin or both secretin and cholecystokinin, depending on the animal species and the humans we studied. When pancreatic juice was returned to the duodenum, the enhanced increase in pancreatic juice was blocked. Similarly, when a trypsin or chymotrypsin (pancreatic enzymes) preparation was administered into the duodenum, the increases were also blocked. Conversely, when a trypsin inhibitor was administered, the increases in both pancreatic secretion and blood levels of both secretin and cholecystokinin were markedly enhanced. These observations indicated that protein-digesting enzymes, such as trypsin and chymotrypsin in the duodenum, play an important role in pancreatic secretion and the release of secretin and cholecystokinin. Thus, the feedback mechanism of pancreatic juice production is controlled by protein-digesting pancreatic enzymes in the upper small intestine, including the duodenum. Again, my research team in Rochester, New York, was the first to discover that the release of secretin was controlled by trypsin and chymotrypsin or other protein-digesting pancreatic enzymes.

The above observations led us to search for a protein-like substance in the upper small intestine that stimulates the release of secretin. Cholecystokinin-releasing peptides were also found in the duodenal juice by the two groups of investigators, Dr. Chung Owyang and his associates at the University of Michigan Medical Center, and Dr. Gary Green and his associates at the University of Texas School of Medicine in San Antonio, Texas.

We discovered in the late 1980s a secretin-releasing peptide (SRP) in rat duodenal juice when a dilute hydrochloric acid solution was infused into the duodenal lumen in rats. This small peptide was heat resistant and labile to pancreatic protein-digesting enzymes, such as trypsin or chymotrypsin. We also found a small SRP in canine duodenal acid perfusate. Subsequently, we found more than one SRP in duodenal juice and canine pancreatic juice. We could not investigate whether or not the rat pancreatic juice contained a secretin-releasing peptide, because the purification of pancreatic juice for SRP requires a large quantity of juice, and the purification of such a large amount is currently technically infeasible. In the future, SRP will have to be further purified using more advanced scientific methodologies to succeed in determining the amino acid sequence of SRP for further research to assess the scientific and clinical significance.

These studies indicate that hydrochloric acid delivered from the stomach to the upper small intestine increases blood levels of secretin and that the release of secretin from the upper small intestine is mediated by secretin-releasing peptides released from the duodenum. Future research will determine the chemical structure of SRP and the location of SRP synthesis in the duodenum.

We found that in physiological conditions, the vagus nerve has important roles in the release and action of secretin and secretin-releasing peptides in rats The role of the vagal nerve in similar conditions in other mammals remains to be determined.

Secretin also affects the functions of other digestive organs. Secretin in normal amounts in the blood after a meal affects the function of the stomach and intestine by controlling acid production and the motion of the stomach. Secretin slows the emptying of ingested food and liquid from the stomach. Thus secretin regulates the digestive processes of both the stomach and the pancreas. A similar effect of secretin may be found in the motion of the upper small intestine, including the duodenum.

Insulin produced in the pancreas is an important local hormone in the pancreas that regulates the stimulatory action of secretin and cholecystokinin for production of pancreatic juice. We found that when circulating insulin was neutralized with a rabbit anti-insulin serum in rats, guinea pigs, and isolated, perfused canine pancreases, the action of secretin and cholecystokinin was almost completely blocked. These experimental data strongly suggest that insulin in the pancreas plays a pivotal role in the secretin and cholecystokinin stimulation of pancreatic juice production. Similar studies were not carried out in humans. Dr. K. Y. Lee and our research team made significant contributions to this exciting discovery.

In clinical studies in patients with diabetes mellitus, the pancreatic juice production stimulated by intravenous injection of secretin and cholecystokinin in pharmacologic doses was shown to be significantly less in diabetic patients than in normal healthy subjects. Further careful studies are needed using both hormones in physiological doses that are far less than the doses of the two hormones used in the previous studies. Since physiological doses were not known at the time these clinical studies were done in diabetics, the study ought to be repeated using physiological doses, which turned out to be at least fifty to one hundred times less than the doses we and others used previously.

# Discovery of secretinoma, a tumor in the human pancreas and secretin as a major diarrheal hormone.

We also discovered that secretin is a major diarrheal hormone in some patients with pancreatic tumors (benign or malignant) suffering from watery diarrhea syndrome (or pancreatic cholera). Patients with a certain hormone-producing tumor in the pancreas are known to suffer from massive watery diarrhea, hypopotassemia, and severe dehydration, leading to death. Since 1973, vasoactive intestinal polypeptide (VIP) has been the only recognized hormone that causes watery diarrhea in patients with pancreatic tumors that produce VIP. Subsequently this tumor was also found elsewhere outside of the pancreas.

In addition to VIP, I and some others suspected for years that other hormones produced by pancreatic tumors might cause massive diarrhea. Because of our long-term interest, enthusiasm, and extensive research work with secretin, we had been considering secretin as a potential candidate for massive watery diarrhea, or pancreatic cholera. We already knew that when secretin was given intravenously in human volunteers in large doses, a massive amount of pancreatic juice entered the duodenum and caused watery diarrhea. Thus, secretin released into the blood in excessive amounts by certain pancreatic tumors is likely to produce a large volume of diarrhea.

In collaboration with Dr. Christopher Ellison and his co-workers at Ohio State University Medical Center, and Dr. Konrad Soergel and Milton Schmitt and their associates at the Medical College of Wisconsin, we discovered two patients exhibiting massive watery diarrhea associated with pancreatic tumors who had numerous secretin-containing tumor cells in their tumors. In the first patient, a twenty-four-year-old female, the surgical removal of the tumors resulted in complete cessation of diarrhea for over twenty years. The tumor tissue was loaded with secretin-producing tumor cells. Unfortunately, the second patient, a twenty-six-year-old male, had an advanced cancer of the pancreas that precluded the removal of the primary tumor. He had a blood level of secretin as high as over 5,000 pg per ml of plasma (at least one thousand times higher than normal) and massive productions of highly alkaline pancreatic juice—as much as 550 ccs (more than a half gallon) per hour, which flowed into the duodenum. Such a large volume of fluid (over 13,000 ccs per day, as much as ten times more than normal) would flood the small bowel and produce massive watery diarrhea and dehydration. Continuous nasogastric suction of large quantities of duodenal fluid ceased the massive diarrhea. In the latter case, the pancreas was excessively stimulated by a very high blood level of secretin. No other known hormone is as potent as secretin in stimulating production of such a voluminous amount of highly alkaline fluid produced by the pancreas, which can flood the small and large intestines. It has been reported that when a large dose of secretin is given intravenously in healthy humans, diarrhea occurs in some subjects. In the future, the early diagnosis of secretin-producing tumors may well be possible by measuring the plasma level of secretin to save the lives of such patients throughout the world. We believe the discovery of secretin-producing tumors is another important contribution that resulted from our long-term commitment in secretin research in Rochester, New York.

It is likely that watery diarrhea syndrome with massive watery diarrhea is produced by super-excessive intestinal secretion of fluid by VIP-producing tumor or massive secretion of fluid from the pancreas by secretin-producing tumor of the pancreas.

*Part 6*

# Gratifications

# Visiting Professorship and the Joy of Travels by Invitations

One of the joys for many academic physicians and physician scientists in teaching institutions is the recognition by peers and related medical communities of their achievements in the medical scientific field. I enjoyed being invited as a speaker at numerous national and international meetings and medical institutions, and as a visiting professor, guest speaker, or teaching physician not only in the United States but also throughout the world. The countries I was invited to were many: South Korea (Seoul, Daegu, Inchon, Gwangju, Busan), Japan (Tokyo, Kyoto, Hiroshima, Kobe, Osaka, Kumamoto, Nagasaki), China (Beijing, Xi'an, Tianjin, Shanghai, Hangzhou, Chengdu, Chongqing, Da-Tung in Outer Mongolia), Taiwan (Taipei), Singapore, Thailand (Bangkok, Chiang Mai), Indonesia (Jakarta, Bali), Philippines (Manila), Saudi Arabia (Riyadh, Jeddah), Egypt (Cairo, Alexandria), Italy (Rome, Florence), France (Paris, Provence, Marseille), Germany (Berlin, Munich, Freiburg), Denmark (Copenhagen), Sweden (Stockholm), Norway (Oslo, Beito) and England (London, Cambridge). The most memorable visits were my invitations to the People's Republic of China since 1981. China had then just undergone their cultural revolution. Among the many visitations I made, I would like to share some of my memorable visits to China and the Republic of Korea.

# My First Visit to the People's Republic of China and Beijing

In the fall of 1980, I was delighted and honored when I received an unexpected invitation letter from Dr. Chen Min Zhang, then the superintendent of the Capital Hospital and professor of medicine at Peking Union Medical College, Chinese Academy of Medical Sciences, Beijing, People's Republic of China. The letter indicated that the government would take care of all of my travel expenses, including air fare, with a business-class seat accommodation. I was very excited, for good reason. China has a history of more than four thousand years, with the largest population—one billion four hundred million people—of any country in the world. My grandfather used to call today's China "the big country," and many Asians felt the same. China is also my wife's native country. The country had just recovered from a brutal but historical cultural revolution, and here I was being invited as a visiting professor to the best and most prestigious medical college and hospital in China. I was certainly looking forward to visiting this great country.

It was quite a long journey from Rochester, New York, to Beijing, the capital of the People's Republic of China, by way of Narita International Airport in Japan. In the late evening of April 1, 1981, I arrived in Beijing when the plane, from an American airline with a captain who seemed to have little navigation experience with the destination, approached Beijing International Airport. Most of the passengers were looking down at the airport's dim lights through the windows to see not only the airport buildings but also the runway where we landed. In fact, the entire city was dark. When the plane touched the ground, many passengers were tossed into the air from their seats. One American passenger was quite astonished and said, "I thought I was about to hit the ceiling! Boy oh boy." He then shook his head. We giggled. The energy conservation policy because of the serious energy shortage of the country required restriction of the full usage of energy even at the international airport in the capital.

In the dimly lit and half-dark but large lobby, I was welcomed by a crowd of about thirty smiling people whose faces I could barely recognize. All had dark-colored caps and Mao jackets. I was personally welcomed by Professor Chen Min Zhang with warm hands. One distinguished-looking old gentleman with silver-white hair waved his right arm and hand in the crowd, walked toward me, and introduced himself, saying in perfect English, "I am C. C. Wang. Welcome, Professor Chey. I enjoyed your recent publications very much."

I responded, "Thank you very much, Professor Wang. I am well aware of your valuable original work on canine pancreatic secretion published in the *American Journal of Physiology* in 1951. I enjoyed it very much." I had thought he was no longer with us.

Dr. Wang said quickly, "Yes, yes, thank you. I am still working. Welcome, welcome."

I was led to the hospital's guest car by Professor Chen. The car was a large Russian-made sedan, and I was able to enter it without bending much. The driver drove the car on a highway and city roads or streets without headlights or parking lights on. The driver occasionally flashed the headlights when a vehicle was closely passing on the opposite lane or a cyclist crossed the street right in front of the car, as if about to be hit. Dr. Chen mentioned apologetically that the government was very strict on its energy conservation policy. The street was crowded with many people crossing it in both directions in the dark, late at night. More than once, a cyclist crossing the street appeared right in front of the windshield, as if they were about to hit the glass. Both sidewalks were packed with people. I had never seen so many people in my life. Dr. Chen was calm while riding through the city streets, although I was quite nervous each time a cyclist was right in front of the car. We arrived safely at a well-known Beijing Hotel that was probably the largest hotel in Beijing and had been constructed by Russians. In an elegant bedroom, I slept until I was awakened by a telephone call the following morning at seven o'clock. In the lobby, I met a smiling young doctor, Dr. Wang from the Capital Hospital. He escorted me to a large dining room that was still almost empty. Soon a smiling young waitress served a typical Chinese-style breakfast, which was quite delicious. About the time we finished breakfast, I noticed a Caucasian couple sitting at a nearby table. We looked at each other and smiled. They were Americans from Washington, DC. It was good to meet Americans and talk to them for a while.

Through the window in my bedroom, after returning from the restaurant, I looked down to see gigantic two-way streets where hundreds and hundreds of proud cyclists, both males and females, wearing dark Mao caps and jackets, were moving in a slow but orderly manner on about five lanes on each side of the street. Automobiles used designated lanes in the center portion of the street. Needless to say, it was the morning rush hour and was indeed a spectacular scene that I had never seen before. I realized then that I was here in the great country of China.

The Capital Hospital was the original Peking Union Medical College Hospital, which the Chinese consider the premier medical school in China. The institution was founded in 1906 by American and British missionaries and funded by the Rockefeller Foundation in New York City. I was told that both the medical school and hospital were built in a part of the original imperial court property. Instead of building a Western-style hospital and medical school, they decided to preserve the original external imperial court architecture, including their decorated traditional Chinese roofs, traditional pillars, elegant walls, and stone stairs from the ground to the building entrance. Inside the buildings, they built Western-style hospital and medical school structures, including medical wards, operating rooms, lecture halls, offices, laboratories, and hallways. They selected only fifty of the very best students for each class, with an eight-years curriculum. The majority of professors were recruited from Europe and the USA. The students had been taught in English ever since the school was established. When the medical school and the hospital were reopened after the Cultural Revolution ended in 1976, they apparently resumed medical education in English, but soon this was discontinued and students were taught in Chinese.

**Medical ward rounds at the Capital Hospital with Professor Chen Min Zhang** (*third from right*), **the author** (*second from right*), **and Dr. Chen Yuan Fan** (*fourth from right*), **Beijing, China, April 1981.**

My first lecture was given at a lecture hall around one o'clock in the afternoon on April 2. The entire audience, both men and women, including faculty and students, wore dark blue or black Mao jackets and caps. I was introduced to Professor Zhang, an eighty-four-year-old professor of medicine who was considered a national treasure in China. He spoke perfect English and told me he had visited our medical school in Rochester in the early 1940s. When I returned to Rochester, I confirmed his visit. Professor Chen graciously introduced me. The title of my lecture was "Neuro-Hormonal Regulations of the Gastrointestinal Tract and Pancreas." The lecture was originally scheduled for one hour, but because my talk had to be translated into Chinese by a young female faculty member—Dr. Yuan-Fang Chen, who had recently returned from a hard-labor camp during the Cultural Revolution—an additional period of more than two hours was needed.

Dr. Chen spoke perfect English and was a top student in her class when she was a student at Peking Union Medical College. She was an outstanding staff member before she was drafted to a hard-labor camp. I was told that because of the excellence in her profession as a faculty member and as a top student in her medical school days, she was sent to the camp. She was a typical example of intellectuals who were punished during the hostile and brutal time. Virtually all the junior and senior members of the faculty were punished and were sent to hard-labor camps. Even Professor Zhang, over eighty years old, had been ordered to report to the camp, but fortunately, with the desperate persuasion and begging of representatives of the medical school, he was allowed to work on the school campus, wiping down the entrance and stone stairs leading to the building, while his former subordinates and students passed through every day.

My lecture was very well received by the audience, although it took more than three hours because I had to speak slowly and comprehensively so that the translator, Dr. Chen, could better understand my presentation and could translate effectively for the audience. During the lecture, the audience appeared very interested in my presentation, but they looked serious and stiff. They rarely smiled. Many of them appeared hungry for new knowledge. There was not one dozing person during the lecture; nor was there one woman who left the auditorium for the restroom.

The interest in gastrointestinal hormone research was not new at this great institution. I reminded the audience that as early as about 1935, an eminent physiologist, Professor R. K. Lim, from this institution, and a Dr. Kosaka, from Japan, found a humoral substance in canine small-intestinal mucosa that inhibited acid production in the stomachs of dogs. They called it "enterogastrone," and theorized that it might be a physiological inhibitor of acid production in the stomach. Enterogastrone remained, however, a hypothetical hormone. Unfortunately, they could not continue this exciting work because of World War II. We still do not know the chemical characteristics of enterogastrone even today. As the war started, Professor Lim was slated to become the Surgeon General of Republic of China Army when Sino-Japan war began in late 1940s.

Based on our work in Rochester, NY, it is likely that enterogastrone is a combination of more than one small intestinal peptides that are capable of inhibiting the stomach's production of acid. We found that secretin is an enterogastrone. We found and published that secretin, in the physiological dose range, inhibits stomach acid production in both humans and dogs. This was one of our signature items of research work.

The next day, I was invited to the famous Beijing Medical University. On the campus, there were mostly Western-style buildings. Here I was welcomed by the smiling Professor C. C. Wang in front of a building. He said, "Welcome, welcome, Professor Chey, to Beijing Medical University. You must be hungry. It is just before noon. Let's go to our staff dining room and have lunch first."

In the dining room, I was welcomed by several faculty members of Professor Wang's Department of Physiology. He called in the chief chef from the kitchen, who came to our table promptly. Professor Wang introduced me to the chef, who shook my right hand with both of his hands and said, "Welcome, we are honored," in Chinese.

I responded, "Sie, sie" (thank you, thank you), in my limited Chinese vocabulary. Soon I was treated to a feast of several courses of Chinese meals, which were delicious.

During lunch, I noticed several African students who were having lunch in the staff dining room, whereas many regular students were having lunch in the cafeteria. Dr. Wang told me that they were their national guests and they would return to their home country when they completed education at the university. Professor Wang, early in his career, was mentored by the world renowned legendary physiologist Professor A. C. Ivy, who was then at Northwestern University in Chicago, Illinois, in the late 1940s, and he received his PhD in physiology there. His favored research was the physiology of exocrine secretion of the pancreas—in particular, neurohormonal actions, including that of secretin in experimental animals. I was thus pleased and privileged to present my lecture on his favored subject.

The lecture hall was packed with the students and faculty members who appeared, like the audience at the Capital Hospital and Peking Union Medical College, eager to learn about the neurohormonal regulation of the exocrine secretion of the pancreas. More excited than anyone else was Professor Wang.

Professor Wang was particularly interested when he saw the dramatic suppression of pancreatic juice production after ingestion of a meal in dogs when free-circulating secretin was eliminated with intravenous administration of our precious rabbit antisecretin serum. He spent fifteen minutes on his comment on my presentation in Chinese when I finished the lecture. He explained to the audience the highlight of my presentation and stated that he appreciated my contributions to the advancement of knowledge regarding neurohormonal regulation of pancreatic secretion, especially the importance of secretin, which he had studied in Chicago some four decades prior. He shook my hand and said, "Thank you, thank you." The audience applauded enthusiastically once again.

In the remaining afternoon, I had the opportunity to visit their experimental animal physiology laboratories in a research building. Because of the government energy conservation policy, the hallway was dimly lit, but the exit signs on the walls at both ends of the hallway were better lit. It was chilly. The experimental room was also dimly lit, but sunlight through the windows made the room brighter than the hallway. Experimental tables were brought near the windows, since the lighting there was better than in the rest of the room. The researchers wore Mao jackets with caps and thick overcoats to keep warm. The anesthetized experimental animals, such as white rats and rabbits, were kept warm under table lamps. It appeared that the energy conservation policy permeated even the research laboratories of universities in the early 1980s.

In the evening, I was treated to another feast—an unforgettable, delicious Peking duck dinner in a restaurant that was about five hundred years old—the oldest restaurant specializing in authentic Peking duck in Beijing. The building was so old that there was no elevator, and the wooden stairs squeaked when I walked up the stairs leading to the second floor. The several courses of delicious Peking duck dishes were extraordinary. For the first time, I enjoyed the genuine Peking duck dishes, which I have never had elsewhere. They were proud of this historical restaurant. Four years later, when I looked for the same restaurant, sadly, it was no longer present. It had been replaced by a new, modern restaurant building. The flavor of the Peking duck dishes I tried on that trip was not as good as it had been at the old restaurant.

**Tiananmen Square with Dr. Chen Yuan Fan in Beijing, April 1981.**

During the following several days, the Capital Hospital hosted me for sightseeing tours in the greater Beijing area. They escorted me to many historical landmarks, including parks; emperors' palaces, including Imperial Palace (the magnificent Forbidden City), the underground palace of the Ming Dynasty, and the Summer Palace; the Great Hall of the People; Tiananmen Square—the world's largest square, occupying one hundred acres; and the Great Wall of China. Dr. Chen Min Zhang was kind enough to guide me to the Great Wall, one of the greatest human achievements in history, which many people in the world admire and hope to visit someday in their lifetime. Here I was, accompanied by a future Minister of Department of Health in China. We have shared a memorable friendship since then. I was told that the wall, about one hundred miles long, stretches to the west and north from Beijing. Hiking about three hundred yards of it was quite physically demanding, but it was a worthy experience.

**Great Wall with Dr. Chen Min Zhang** (*right*) **and the author** (*center*), **April 1981.**

In the evening, I had dinner with many hospitable faculty members and senior administrators of the hospital and the medical college, including the president of the college, Dr. Gu Fangzhou. At each dinner, I was treated with different cuisines. My most unforgettable dinner was hosted by Dr. C. S. Hwang, the president of the Chinese Academy of Medical Sciences, one evening. Together with ten senior faculty members, we went to a very special restaurant in a beautiful park. The restaurant was small compared to the ones that I had been invited to previously. This elegantly decorated restaurant was the only one in the park. This special place had been built for an empress of the Qin Dynasty who loved to take walks in the park. The empress used to stop by and enjoy tea, desserts, snacks or light meals. The place was only for the empress and was not open to any other people. The meal and dessert were extraordinary dishes that I had never tasted anywhere else, including Shanghai, Hong Kong, Singapore, or Taipei. It seemed that nobody in the room but President Hwang had experienced such dishes in the same restaurant. After the dinner, one professor said, "Professor Chey, come to China more often."

# Acupuncture and Eastern Medicine

I returned to the Capital Hospital in order to learn about acupuncture practice and how acupuncture and conventional Western medical practice are integrated in the same hospital. As I was walking to the acupuncture center, a senior faculty member of the Department of Medicine asked me, "Professor Chey, I am curious, why are you so interested in acupuncture?" I answered that one of the reasons why acupuncture treatment is used for "indigestion or peptic ulcers in your country may involve a neurohormonal mechanism which may include actions of gastrointestinal hormones and possibly other hormones." He still seemed somewhat confused and skeptical. I pointed out to him that no one had investigated whether or not acupuncture influences blood levels of gastrointestinal hormones, such as gastrin, secretin, and cholecystokinin. For example, in both humans and dogs, gastrin stimulates stomach acid production, whereas secretin reduces the acid production. However, it was not known whether or not acupuncture may affect gastric secretion of acid, for example. If acupuncture affects gastric acid secretion, its action may be neurohormonally mediated.

As we approached the entrance of the acupuncture center, the director of the center, who was there to welcome me, opened her eyes widely, looking at Dr. Chen, the professor of medicine. She said, "Professor Chen, I have been waiting for you to visit our center, how many years?" Then she said, "Welcome, Professor Chey." It was apparent to me that Professor Chen and his department members who had Western medical education had not communicated with the acupuncturists or physician acupuncturists in this institution. I saw about a dozen patients in their outpatient facilities, with ages ranging from about twenty to seventy years old. They were receiving either acupuncture or moxa treatments for anxiety, headache, indigestion, arthritis, and chronic back pain.

Although there appeared to be no close working relationship or communication between the traditional Western medicine group in internal medicine and the acupuncture group in this institution, I saw in a teaching hospital in Shanghai an acupuncture physician at a bedside in a medical ward, writing a prescription for herbal medicine for a forty-year-old male patient with hepatitis and moderate jaundice. He said a combination of acupuncture treatment and conventional Western medical treatment is effective. It was not clear how carefully he had assessed the efficacy of the treatment. In my second visit to the Capital Hospital in the following year, I found that general surgeons were using acupuncture for biliary tract surgery, which facilitates the passage of gallstones through bile duct. They showed me their observational result that electroacupuncture facilitates the passage of large stones, mostly bile acid stones, from the bile duct. I was also told that acupuncture anesthesia was used in chest surgery for lobectomy in some hospitals. Of course, this is beyond my comprehension.

After returning to Rochester, we did investigate conscious dogs to determine whether electroacupuncture affects gastric acid production and blood levels of gastrointestinal hormones. In a nutshell, the electroacupuncture method that we used did significantly suppress a meal-stimulated gastric secretion of acid coincident with the substantial decrease in blood levels of gastrin, which is known to stimulate gastric acid production after ingestion of a meal. More interestingly, both beta-endorphin and somatostatin levels increased in the blood. Somatostatin is known to suppress acid production in the stomach. This was the first report that was published in the highly recognized peer-reviewed scientific journal the *American Journal of Physiology*. This study, for the first time, showed scientific evidence in conscious dogs that may be applicable to acupuncture practice in modern medicine.

# Shanghai Medical University

After I had spent one week of memorable and rewarding experiences in Beijing, Dr. Chen arranged for me to visit Shanghai Medical University, a well-recognized medical university in China, via a Chinese airline. The passengers in the plane were mostly Chinese nationals. Although they were friendly, most of them were heavy smokers and ignored the No Smoking sign displayed in the cabin. As the plane descended, I remembered that my dear wife, Fan, lived in Shanghai for a few years during her childhood in the World War II era, and her father, a legendary general, Tang Un-Bo, was the defending commanding general of the Republic of China for the Greater Shanghai Region against Japanese Imperial Army invasion.

The plane landed smoothly and safely on the runway of Shanghai International Airport. I was welcomed by Dr. Zho Wu-Nan, Professor and Chair of the Department of Medicine, and his companions at Zhongshan Hospital, Shanghai Medical University. They enjoyed their reputation as the best medical school in this part of China. The late Dr. Paul Yu, who had been a professor and chief of cardiology at our medical school in Rochester, was a graduate of this great medical school in the later part of the 1940s.

The next morning, when the hospital's car stopped right in front of the entrance of the university hospital on a curved driveway, Professor Zho and other dignitaries welcomed me with a large white cloth banner displaying black letters written with black ink. He held both ends of the banner with his assistant. It stated, in Chinese characters, "Welcome, Professor Chey William." I noticed that unlike in Beijing, most of them wore Western-style clothing with ties or open collars. In the hospital hallway and lecture hall, I found more people with Western-style clothes, which was quite in contrast to the people in Beijing. They appeared to be more relaxed, and no one had on Mao caps. In my lecture, the audience responded with smiles when I made brief humorous comments relative to my presentation. After the lecture, there were lively discussions and questions from young physicians in the audience from both Shanghai Medical University and the Third Military Medical University, which is also in Shanghai. Those who had questions spoke English well and succinctly. A young woman physician, Dr. Jin Hai-Ou, was so impressive that I fulfilled her dream for a fellowship in my program at the University of Rochester. She was one of our best research fellows and was highly motivated, bright, and productive. Her work was published in highly competitive peer-reviewed journals such as Gastroenterology and American Journal of Physiology.

Dr Jin became a board certified internist and a successful clinical gastroenterologist. Currently she holds Chair, Department of Medical Specialties at University of Maryland South Shore Regional Heath. Dr. Jin has been married to Dr. Yi Robert Ding, an anesthesiologist and a pain management specialist. They have two grown up children; Michael, a medical resident, and Crystal, a specialist in finance. Thus Dr.

Jin and her husband are achieving their American dream. It has been my privilege and honor to have had so many talented Chinese scholars in our research laboratories since. They have worked hard and been dedicated to their profession.

After three days of warm hospitality given by faculty members of Shanghai Medical University, I was escorted by a senior member of the Shanghai City Foreign Affairs Department to the train to visit Hangzhou, a beautiful city about one hour away from Shanghai. For the first time, I had the opportunity to have a train ride in China. At the train station platform, a large crowd of people was rushing to get on the train, reminding me of visiting my grandparents' hometown on weekends in South Korea during my middle school days. The hostess was a middle-aged Chinese senior official, and she insisted on carrying my rather heavy trunk with wheels. She lifted the trunk with one hand and walked faster than I did. In about one hour, the train arrived at Hangzhou Railway Station.

# Hangzhou

Hangzhou has been known historically as one of the most beautiful cities in China. The people in the city consider the place a paradise on the earth, and they are very proud of their city. Indeed, Marco Polo, an Italian merchant, explorer, and writer who visited China in the twelfth century, stated that Hangzhou was the most beautiful place next to heaven. There was another reason why the city was special to me. My wife, Fan, was born in this proud city before World War II. The city was also known for the beautiful girls born there. Through the picture window of my hotel room, I enjoyed the picturesque view of the famous West Lake, which showed gentle golden-red waves at sunset. I looked forward to seeing more of the lake the following day.

The next morning, Mr. Lee, a male host, phoned me from the lobby. Mr. Lee was a mid-fortyish gentleman and spoke English well. We planned to spend most of our time in the West Lake area, temples, and tea farms. The lake was indeed clean, and the water near the shore was almost completely filled with large, lively one-foot-long black carp. They were friendly like pets and showed off their gorgeous bodies. The boardwalk was filled with sightseeing people enviously watching these carp, but they were forbidden to catch them, and they seemed to comply with the rules. Some of these carp were harvested for the restaurants of local elite hotels, where cooks prepared their famous carp steaks for foreign guests and the government's high-ranking cadres. There was indeed an old rock in a garden that was big enough and wide enough for a person to sit on. There was an engraving on the rock stating that Marco Polo had been here around the twelfth century.

**General Tang Un Bo** (*center*) **with President Chang Kai Shek, Republic of China, circa 1940, in a painted portrait displayed in a national museum in Taipei, Taiwan (author's photo).**

About noon, there was a rain shower that forced people to rush to the nearby pagodas with roofs in order to avoid becoming wet. People were packed together, standing. We looked at each other and smiled and smiled again. Several young factory workers were apparently off that day. One young man, about twenty years old, broke the silence and spoke to host, Mr. Lee. He asked him about me, saying that he looked different. He told them I was from the United States. When I asked if they knew General Tang Un-Bo, one young man, opening his eyes wide, stated, "Of course we know him. He was one of our national heroes, a very famous general who led the Republic of China Army and defended Shanghai against the Imperial Japan invasion during World War II." I told them he was my late father-in-law. They looked at me with surprise and talked to each other, nodding their heads. The rain stopped, and again the boardwalk was filled with many people.

In the midafternoon, we visited the famous tea farms on a hillside by driving up winding dirt roads. There was nothing but fresh green tender leaves covering one entire hill. We stopped by a small shack to find four healthy-looking middle-aged woman workers who were just about to have a late lunch. They were quite friendly and smiled at us. One woman said something in Chinese. Mr. Lee said they were welcoming us. We sat on a sheet over the dirt ground. Their meals were rice, sautéed tender tea leaves, and fillets of cooked pork. They offered the meal, which was quite tasty. I asked Mr. Lee to thank them for their kindness and the nice meal. One lady said, "Sie, sie," (Thank you, thank you).

I left Shanghai on April 23 and arrived soon at Hong Kong International Airport. A limousine, a Mercedes station wagon, from the Hilton Hotel was waiting for me. When I entered the car, the soft Western music and fresh air from the air conditioner made me feel comfortable, as if I were at home. I was already looking forward to seeing my parents and family in Seoul, Korea, the next day. In the evening, I had a brief tour on a sightseeing bus. The skyline of Hong Kong was stunningly beautiful.

It was indeed the most unforgettable and exciting trip that I have ever had. I could never have imagined that I would receive such an honorable recognition and invitations by the very best medical institutions in China, a country with a population of one billion four hundred million people. Their hospitality during the visit was overwhelming. They seemed to have enjoyed my visit and interactions with them—particularly the young physicians and scientists—and I immensely enjoyed the visit.

# Seoul, Korea

I arrived at Seoul International Airport in midafternoon the next day, April 24. It was so good to see my parents, who were waiting for me at the airport. I noticed they were slowly aging, but though they were in their early eighties, they came all the way to the airport. I felt sad when I realized they would no longer be able to meet me at the airport on my future trips. As we passed through the main streets of Seoul in the car, I asked Father whether it was a holiday today. I said, "I don't see too many people on the sidewalk."

He said, "This street is as busy as when you were last here." Then I realized that I had just been in Beijing and Shanghai, China, where I was accustomed to seeing huge crowds on downtown streets during day and night. It was good to be at home in Seoul again and meet with the family, including my younger brothers—James, a businessman, and Woo-Shik, a bank executive—and their families. My older brother, Woo-Jik, had moved with his family to Busan, the second-largest city in South Korea. He was the successful president of a life insurance company. On one Sunday, we had such memorable and pleasant occasions at our father's small ranch in the outskirts of Seoul. I missed my sister, Ok-Hee; her husband, Kwang-Joon, a radiologist; and their two lovely daughters, Lisa and Vickie, who live in Rochester, New York. Sadly, it was the last time we were together as a family in one place. I went to Busan to visit my older brother, Woo-jik, my sister-in-law, and my nephews and a niece, Ki-Jin. They had grown up to become adults. Using his limousine and family car, we visited our grandparents' cemetery plots on a beautiful hill facing the east, which was located on the outskirts of Gijang, a small town near Busan where I was born over fifty years ago. When I was a middle school student, I was always looking forward to visiting my grandparents' home by train during weekends. The warm and beautiful memories of my grandparents remain always in my heart.

I had been missing my own family in Rochester: dear Fan and my four children, Bill, Donna, Richard, and Laura. It was always hard to see my parents at the airport. I left Seoul on May 1 and arrived on the same day at JFK International Airport. When I was passing through customs, I said to the officer in the box office, "It is nice to be back home."

The officer responded, "Welcome home, sir."

I said, "Thank you, Officer."

I felt so warm and gratified as a citizen of this great country. It was such a pleasure and a memorable occasion to see my welcoming party, my family, who were waiting for me at Rochester International Airport.

# More Visits to China, Japan, and South Korea

Since my first visit to the capital hospital and Peking Union Medical College in 1981, I was invited three more times to the same institutions, and I was honored to receive the title of "visiting professor" in 1985 from Peking Union Medical College. During each visit to Peking Union Medical College, the president of the medical college, Professor Gu Fang-Zhou, arranged for me to visit many other medical institutions: Tianjin Medical University Hospital, Xi'an Second Military Medical University, Chengdu Medical University, Shanghai Medical University and Hangzhou Medical University.

Banquet dinner at an international conference on brain-gut peptides, Beijing, China, 1988. *From left:* Professor Viktor Mutt, University of Stockholm, Sweden; Professor Chen Min Zhang, Peking Union Medical College and Chinese Academy of Medical Sciences, Beijing, China; William Y. Chey, professor of medicine, University of Rochester Medical Center, Rochester, New York; William V. L. Go, distinguished professor of medicine; and Mrs. Frisca Go, clinical professor of neurology, UCLA, Los Angeles, California.

I was also invited to attend and participate in several international symposia in China to speak on physiology and pathophysiology of digestive and pancreatic disorders. My most significant and exciting experience was to help my former fellow and colleague Dr. Yuan-Fang Chen, at the Capital Hospital, who organized the First Beijing International Conference on Brain-Gut Peptides in November 1988. The four-days conference was very successful. Eminent scientists were invited from both Eastern and Western countries and they actively participated in the meetings. Indeed, in China, this conference was the first of its kind in the field of our interest. Before this meeting was planned, she spent one year in our research laboratories in Rochester, New York, to learn and research in the field of gastrointestinal hormones. We were indeed privileged to have her in Rochester. To help her with the successful international conference, I sponsored it and raised funds from various organizations in the United States, including the Konar Family Foundation in Rochester, New York. At one evening banquet, I had the honor of having a memorable evening with my dear friends, including Dr. Chen Min Zhang, minister of health of China; Professor Viktor Mutt from Stockholm, Sweden; Professors William V. L. Go and his wife, Friska, from the University of California at Los Angeles; and T. Yamada, then from the University of Michigan.

# Xi'an, Beijing, Tokyo, and Seoul
# with my Son, Richard

One memorable trip I made to China was when my son Richard joined me for the visit to both Beijing and the oldest capital of China, Xi'an, in 1982.

On the way to China, we stopped over in Tokyo to participate in the annual meeting of the Pancreas Society of Japan. It was so good to again meet with Professor Tadashi Takeuchi and other friends. It was such a delight to have a wonderful dinner party with many colleagues. My son Richard was a senior in high school, and he enjoyed the special gathering. Then Dr. Takeuchi and his two associates, Drs. S. Watanabe and K. Shiratori, accompanied us to Hiroshima. Richard was quite impressed with the historical Hiroshima Peace Park and Museum. It was our pleasure to invite Drs. Wantanabe and Shiratori to our research laboratories in Rochester, New York, as research fellows in subsequent years.

The hosts were kind enough to show Richard around Beijing and Xi'an while I was engaged at the inviting institutions. I was so glad that Richard and I had this unusual but exciting opportunity of seeing the two great cities. In Xi'an, Chinese archeologists discovered thousands of life-size warriors made of clay and bearing lifelike expressions, as well as clay horses and chariots, that had been buried over the tomb of the first Chinese emperor about two thousand years ago. It was indeed a breathtaking sight. Something I still cannot forget was when Richard turned on his portable electric hair dryer (which was made in the US) one early morning, the electricity in the room and hallway went out and our room became dark in the large Russian-built hotel we were staying in in Xi'an. Richard was perplexed for a moment, but the lighting was restored by the hotel workers a short moment later. Richard did not use the hair dryer again until we left Xi'an.

On the way back home, we stopped over in Seoul. It was so good to see my parents again after one year, and Richard not only got to be with his dear grandparents and our family again but also had the opportunity to see Seoul for the first time, while I was invited to deliver lectures at Seoul National University Hospital, my alma mater; Yonsei University School of Medicine; and Catholic University College of Medicine. In 1983, I was gratified to receive an honorary professorship from the latter medical college. I had the privilege to have four capable and bright faculty members in our research laboratories from the Catholic University College of Medicine; three from Department of Physiology, including Drs. Myeoung-Seok Kim, Hyeoun-Jin Park and Yang-Hyeok Jo and from Department of Medicine, Dr. In-Shik Jeung. After returning to their home country, all three became chairs of the Department of Physiology in subsequent years. Moreover, two became deans of medical schools—Dr. Kim at his alma mater, Catholic University; and Dr. Park at Hallym University College of Medicine in Chuncheon, South Korea. Late Dr. Jeung was professor of medicine and CEO of Catholic University Hospital in Seoul, Korea.

# My Last Visiting Professorship
# in China in 1999

Professor Li Zhong Ming (*right*) welcoming the author at
Chongqing University of Medical Sciences, April 1999.

In the Spring of 1999, I was invited for the last time by Dr. Li Zhong Ming, a former professor of medicine and president, to the well-known Chongqing University of Medical Sciences. This invitation was special to me. During World War II, Chongqing was the wartime capital of Nationalist China in Southwest China, where my-in-laws, Fan, and her two sisters and young brother lived during their childhood to their teens. Her father was one of the leading army generals in Nationalist China who fought against the invasion of the Japanese Imperial Army. The university was the best in Central China and was one of the top-ranked medical institutions in China. Professor Li was a graceful and hospitable host. His late son, Dr. Li Ping, who worked with me in our research laboratories, was an outstanding researcher. He was instrumental in discovering secretin-releasing peptides.

**The author in a lecture and discussions with the faculty and students at Chongqing University of Medical Sciences, April 1999.**

I delivered a series of lectures on my favorite topic, recent advances in gastrointestinal hormone research, to the students and faculty, and I enjoyed lively discussions with them—particularly the many enthusiastic students. I received similar enthusiasm and appreciation from the audience who attended the meeting held by the Chongqing Physiologist Group. One afternoon, I was invited to observe an experiment carried out in an anesthetized rat by graduate students in an experimental physiology laboratory. The laboratory was well equipped, and they no longer had to be inconvenienced by lighting restrictions as they had in the Beijing university I visited in 1981.

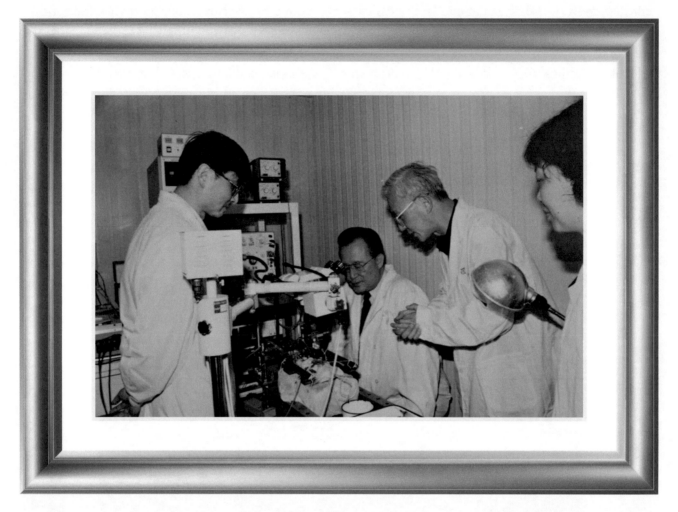

**The author** (*third from left*) **microscopically examining the pancreas of an anesthetized rat and discussing the experiment with faculty and graduate students at a university, April 1999.**

One evening, I was invited to a typical Chongqing dinner by Professor Jin Xian-Ging, president of Chongqing University of Medical Sciences, and his colleagues. Many dishes were characteristically spicy, and the aroma wafting up from the dishes irritated my nostrils, as if they were being mildly burned. Nevertheless, the dishes were delicious, and I thoroughly enjoyed eating the exotic meal. The professor was a wonderful host, and we all enjoyed the memorable evening.

The author (*second from right*) enjoying a delicious Chongqing dinner of
hot, spicy dishes with the professor, and president of the University,
Jin Xian-Ging (*right*) and a faculty member (*left*), April 1999.

Thinking back, I realize that I had exciting, rewarding and memorable experiences at many distinguished institutions in both China and South Korea. I enjoyed delivering lectures and having discussions with young physicians and students who expressed such enthusiasm; I recognized their eagerness to learn. This was probably because they had just experienced the Cultural Revolution, which interfered with their medical education and intellectual stimulation in medical sciences and research in China. It became clearer to me when some of these medical scientists were invited to our research laboratories as research fellows. I saw that they worked hard even on Saturdays and Sundays. They enjoyed being a part of our research team in Rochester, New York. Their works were published in reputable scientific journals. They returned home proud of the recognition of their work, with reprints of their published articles. For my part, I was privileged to be their mentor. They came from outstanding institutions in their home countries. The invitations to these distinguished foreign medical institutions would not have been possible without my commitment to become a physician scientist in competitive learning medical institutions in the US.

# The Fun and Rewards of Research Work, Teaching, and Mentoring

Our programs for both clinical and research fellowship in gastroenterology and hepatology at the University of Rochester School of Medicine and Dentistry and at Genesee Hospital, as well as my subsequent transition to the Strong Memorial Hospital program, produced over sixty highly qualified clinical gastroenterologists and thirty-five gastrointestinal scientists. After clinical training, they became competent, board-certified gastroenterologists. They spread their wings and moved from Rochester to Seattle, Washington; Palm Springs, California; Austin, Texas; Boca Raton, Florida; North Carolina; Detroit, Michigan; Maine; Connecticut; Baltimore, Maryland; New York City and Manila, Philippines. I am proud of them for their successful practice in serving their communities. My sincere appreciation and respect are long overdue for my talented clinician colleagues Ashok Shah, MD; Jorge Gutierrez, MD; Arthur McGuire MD; Chul You, MD; David Hamilton, MD; the late James Stormont, MD; Stephen Stowe, MD; Arthur DeCross, MD; Gregory Potter, MD; the late Fred Klipstein, MD; and the late Rene Menguy, MD, PhD, professor of surgery, emeritus.

Many young, talented, and hard-working academic gastroenterologists and scientists came from all over the world to Rochester, New York, for research training in our research laboratories under the tutelage of dedicated senior faculty members including H. H. Tai, PhD; Ta-min Chang, PhD; K. Y. Lee, MD PhD; Cecilia Chang, MS; and their research technicians. The majority of them were sponsored by their home institutions or scholarships. They came from South Korea, Japan, China, India, Denmark, Scotland, Poland, and Africa. It was our privilege and honor to have them in our Division of Gastroenterology and Hepatology. Especially noteworthy to recognize is that my dear lifelong friend, then professor of medicine and chief of gastroenterology, Dr. Tadashi Takeuchi at Tokyo Women's Medical University, Tokyo, Japan, sent his outstanding protégés to our research program. Drs. Keiko Shiratori, Kyoko Shimizu, and S. Watanabe were hardworking and productive researchers who produced more publications than research fellows in other competitive research universities in the United States.

It was a fun and rewarding experience to have weekly Saturday research conferences with these talented and hardworking research fellows and research faculty. The fellows presented the highlights and progress made in their ongoing research projects. Their work was presented at national meetings and international meetings. They learned how to prepare manuscripts from their tutors, and the manuscripts were published in highly competitive scientific medical journals. Their published articles represented the fruit of their hard work and significant accomplishments. Over 85 percent of them returned to their home institutions. In later years, they earned full professorships in their disciplines. Many became chairs in departments of medicine or physiology. Three of them became deans of medical schools, and another three were promoted to become CEOs of their university medical centers. It was my pride and privilege as their colleague and mentor more than ever to be invited to their home institutions in my later years. This is one of the gratifications that has resulted from my pursuing a career in academic clinical medicine and the physician scientist track in learning institutions, particularly in the United States of America.

I had experienced the golden years for those in academic medicine and physician scientists in the United States. It was indeed my American dream. For those who wished to combine meaningful research and clinical medicine, research funds were available on a highly competitive basis from the National Institutes of Health, National Science Foundation, private foundations, and wealthy patient donors. In recent years, however, I have been sympathetic for young faculty members who have chosen this career path, since such welcome opportunities for funding have been more challenging than in the past. Often, after a hard day of clinical work, they may be up late to prepare a grant application, to meet a deadline for submission, or to perform peer review of research grant applications submitted by peers to the National Institutes of Health or other research funding sources, such as the National Science Foundation. Not infrequently, they may have to wear two hats, engaging in research activities in the laboratory and doing clinical work or procedure room work on the same day. Some leading administrators in medical centers may not recognize their hard work, but these young physician scientists are the future of our proud American medicine.

I found it so gratifying also that some of my wealthy patients made efforts to raise funds to support my research programs in part, as well as clinical services, by donating funds to purchase new equipment. Each time my colleagues and I were assisted by their help, I was deeply touched by their generosity. Rochester, New York, my hometown, has been a special place for me.

Because of our clinical and research contributions, I was recognized locally, nationally, and internationally as a clinician healer, physician scientist, and mentor. The highlights of such recognition includes the W. V. L. and Frisca Go Award for Lifetime Achievement from the American Pancreatic Association (2014), the Distinguished Clinician Award in 2004 and Mentor's Research Award in 2007 from the American Gastroenterological Association, Invited Lecturer for Annual David Sun Lectureship at American College of Gastroenterology in 1987, the Governor's Award for Excellence in Clinical Research in 2000 from the American College of Gastroenterology, the Distinguished Service Award in 2012 from the Rochester Academy of Medicine, and the American Top Physicians Award in 2008 from the Consumers' Research Council of America. In addition, I received an honorary professorship from Catholic University College of Medicine, Seoul, Korea, and an appointment for a visiting professorship from Peking Union Medical College in Beijing, China, which is one of China's premier medical institutions.

*Part 7*

# Joy of Post-Retirement Medical Practice, Family and Parents' Visits

# The Joy of Private Medical Practice, A Challenge after Retirement

After retirement from my full-time position as a professor and director of the Konar Center for Digestive and Liver Diseases, I decided to have a private practice, which would again give me the opportunity to have direct interactions with patients who had challenging diagnostic or therapeutic problems. As a division director with multiple responsibilities at the university medical center, I had missed out on opportunities for the direct patient care that I enjoyed. This meant that I was now engaging in the last part of my career as a healer—a dream that I had had since I committed myself to becoming a young physician who took care of the sick and protected them from harm to the best of his ability. My dear friend and patient William Konar was one of my closest confidants, and he was like my brother in our later years. He supported my next move in my career, and he was ready to help me so that my dream could become a reality. It was so sad that he passed away from advanced dementia and stroke at age eighty-five. I was and am eternally grateful for his generous support and help for so many years. He achieved his American dream, which everybody admires, respects, and appreciates. I miss him profoundly.

I opened a private practice in gastroenterology on one floor of the Genesee Hospital Professional Building. It was nice to be back at the Genesee Hospital campus again, where I had started my career four decades prior. We remodeled one floor for gastroenterology practice and a limited clinical research space having doctors' offices, a nurse practitioner's office, a spacious waiting room, a nurses' office, endoscopy facilities, a fluoroscopy room with X-ray equipment, rooms for diagnostic motility testing and clinical research, examining rooms, a conference room, a reception area, and an office manager's room. I was so grateful to my former colleagues from Strong Memorial Hospital Gastroenterology Division, who joined me for the last move. They included my former head nurse, Mrs. Kathryn Fuiton, RN; a research nurse, Mrs. Deborah Corcoran, RN; the division administrator, Mrs. Dorothy O'Leary, as the office manager; and two research faculty members including Ta-min Chang, PhD and K. Y. Lee, MD, PhD. I was so pleased to have them with me like a family. In addition, we had a new gastroenterologist, Dr. George Kunze, one of my former fellows who had finished training at Strong Memorial Hospital; and a nurse practitioner, Ms. Maxine Lubkin, who joined us later.

My medical practice family in 2008. Kathy Fulton, RN, nurse supervisor (*right, front row*); Debbie Corcoran, RN, research coordinator (*second from left, second row*); the author (*left end of third row*); K. Y. Lee, MD, PhD (*second end of third row*); Maxine Lubkin, MSN, ANP (*right end of third row*); George Fox, NP; and Cameron Hoellrich, BS, research assistant (*fourth row, from right*).

We were the first in the greater Rochester area to establish an independent outpatient endoscopy practice separate from an in-hospital practice, and a freestanding ambulatory endoscopy facility. We felt it was highly desirable and appropriate to have such an endoscopy unit off the hospital campus for efficiency and convenience for patients and their families. Moreover it is cost-effective. Several groups of gastroenterologists in the community have followed a similar practice since. It was also the first independent endoscopy unit that was approved for the certificate of need (CON) from New York State, which allowed us to receive reimbursement fees for the endoscopy services rendered to patients with Medicaid who could not afford private health insurance. This meant that our practice accepted all the patients who had either private medical insurance or Medicare, or underprivileged patients with Medicaid. Although it was costly for us to modify the structures of our office and facilities to meet the New York State requirements for the CON, we felt it was the right thing to do. I was so grateful to my friend and patient Arnold Gissin and Dennis Grutadaro, Esq. for their dedication in spending the much time required to process the difficult CON application for a successful approval from the New York State Department of Health.

It was gratifying for me to have many of my former patients return to our services, along with new patients in the Rochester community as well as those from Upstate New York. Our practice activities consisted not only of office visits but also endoscopy; fluoroscopy of the esophagus, stomach, small bowel, and colon when needed; and special tests for motility disorders of the gastrointestinal tract, such as swallowing problems and severe constipation. It was indeed a dream practice. It was such a fun and rewarding experience to help many patients with challenging diagnostic and therapeutic problems. In doing so, we discovered a clinical condition that had been overlooked by clinicians, including myself. There is a group of many female patients with severe constipation and lower abdominal pain who also have urogynecological symptoms, such as frequent urination, stress-urinary incontinence, and dyspareunia. This group of patients was found to have a large cecum (the beginning of the colon located in the lower right side of the abdomen) filled with feces. The heavy cecum can thus move down to the pelvis, where it can irritate or put pressure on pelvic organs, such as the urinary bladder, uterus, vagina, and ovaries.

This large cecum can be readily found by fluoroscopy after ingestion of a barium meal. I did not know such a clinical condition existed. In fact, no one did, including my esteemed general surgeon, Dr Vincent Chang. After surgical resection of the colon, including the cecum, the patients were relieved not only of severe constipation but also of their urogynecological symptoms. They were so grateful to us for relieving these embarrassing, humiliating, and uncomfortable urogynecological symptoms. In collaboration with my son, Dr. William D. Chey, a professor of medicine at the University of Michigan Medical Center, and Dr. Vincent Chang, we published our new observation in a peer-reviewed medical journal. It was such a fun and rewarding experience to discover this yet unknown or overlooked clinical condition, which would help many patients for years to come. The patients suffering from this condition silently beg for help after having had incorrect treatment, including incorrect surgical operations. This is why medical practice is fun and rewarding; it is indeed a noble profession.

After ten years of practice, it was about time for me to retire as a physician healer, physician scientist and physician educator. It was indeed a heartbreaking experience to leave my dear patients and dedicated and loyal colleagues. I was indeed privileged to have taken care of my patients for so many years in my limited practice. I am eternally grateful to my late dear friend, a beautiful human being, Bill Konar. Without his thoughtful and generous support, I could not possibly have helped so many patients who needed proper care, which they well deserved. This last chapter of my career was indeed one of my American dreams that came about by way of the help of the man who came to this great country without a penny in his hands and became a multimillionaire and a generous philanthropist—another successful American dreamer.

# Our Family

In the Spring of 1957, I met an attractive and beautiful young woman, Fan, in Washington, DC, when I was visiting my brother-in-law at a hospital. At first sight, we were attracted to each other and became close friends. As I came to know her, I found her a beautiful person with whom I could share my life. She was affectionate, compassionate, understanding, and caring. Like me, having been born in Korea, she was an immigrant who had been born in China. Although marriage between Chinese and Koreans in those days was not common, I proposed marriage to Fan in the spring of 1959, and she accepted. It was the most memorable and exciting day in my life. She was so happy and deeply touched, with tears in her eyes. We both realized we had a hard road ahead because of our ethnic differences. We married on May 20 in the same year and promised each other we would share our lives together for many, many years into eternity.

**Our family, 1990.** *From left to right:* **Donna, the author, Fan, Richard, Laura, and Bill.**

Fan had been the pillar and matriarch of the family. We had four lovely children born in the following decade, Bill, Donna, Richard, and Laura. They were born in Philadelphia, Pennsylvania, and have been the pride and treasure of our lives. They all married happily and gave us nine lovely grandchildren and, recently, two lovely great-grandsons, whom we all adore and love.

Our family, winter 2014. *Front row, left to right:* LiLi Warren, Paris Chey, Megen Chey, Wyatt Warren, Samuel Chey, Russell Chey. *Second row:* Cameron Hoellrich, Fan Chey, the author. *Third row:* Allison Injaian, Janine Chey, William D. Chey, Ric Warren, Laura Warren, Dale Hoellrich, Donna Hoellrich, Richard Chey, Josephine Chey.

# William D. and Janine's Family

O ur first child, Bill, was born in Pennsylvania Hospital and was a beautiful baby boy who was the pleasure of our lives. Soon we moved to a two-bedroom apartment near the suburbs of Philadelphia. He was such a good-natured child whom we were so proud of. His mom was so affectionate and totally devoted to our son. Bill made our daily life fulfilled. So frequently on Saturday afternoons, we three used to go to Schuylkill Park and enjoy looking at the scenery of the river and the magnificent Philadelphia Museum of Arts buildings. As he grew up, Bill became a dependable and good big brother for his brother and two sisters.

He chose to pursue a medical profession as his career, and I was very pleased about this. He studied hard and received a bachelor of arts degree from the University of Pennsylvania and a doctor of medicine degree and training in internal medicine at Emory University School of Medicine. After completing a fellowship in gastroenterology at the University of Michigan Medical Center, he remained as a faculty member at the university in Ann Arbor, Michigan, since 1993. He is currently the Timothy T. Nostrand Collegiate Professor of Gastroenterology. He was awarded a joint appointment in the Department of Nutrition Sciences in 2015. His research interests focused on the diagnosis and treatment of functional bowel disorders, acid-related disorders and *H. pylori* infection. He is a medical innovator and holds two patents. He co-founded My Total Health, a company developing novel health information technology solutions for persons with gastrointestinal problems.

He has been a prolific writer, authoring more than three hundred manuscripts, reviews, chapters and books. He served as coeditor-in-chief of the *American Journal of Gastroenterology* (2011–2015) and founding coeditor of *Clinical and Translational Gastroenterology* (2011–2014). He led the American College of Gastroenterology (ACG) *H. pylori* practice guidelines published in the *American Journal of Gastroenterology* (AJG) in 2017. He also served on the editorial board for the Rome IV Criteria for Functional GI Disorders published in 2018. He was a member of the ACG IBS Task Force, which was responsible for an updated evidence-based monograph published in 2018. Bill is currently a member of the Board of Trustees of the American College of Gastroenterology, the Board of Directors of the Rome Foundation, and the Council of the American Neurogastroenterology and Motility Society. He is also chief scientific adviser for the International Foundation of Functional Gastrointestinal Disorders.

He is a gifted speaker and enjoys numerous trips nationally and internationally as a visiting professor and an invited speaker. He has received numerous awards. Some representative ones are the Dean's Outstanding Clinician Awards at the University of Michigan and the Distinguished Clinician Award from the American Gastroenterological Association. Recently he received the second Dean's Award for

Innovation and Commercialization at the University of Michigan. Bill is a past president of the Clinical Excellence Society in the Department of Medicine at Michigan Medicine. Very recently, the American College of Gastroenterology announced that William D. Chey, MD will receive the 2020 Berk/Fise Clinical Achievement Award, a highly prestigious award, in recognition of distinguished clinical practice in gastroenterology and contributions in patient care, clinical science, clinical education, technological innovation, and public and community service.

**Bill and Janine's family.** *From left to right:* **Janine, Russell, Josephine, Samuel, Bill.**

He and his attractive wife, Janine, a physician's assistant, have three lovely children: Samuel, Russell, and Josephine. Janine is devoted to and unselfishly supportive of her husband and children with her unconditional love. Sam, their eldest son, earned his MPH from the University of Michigan and wishes to pursue his career further in a healthcare profession, and both Russel and Josephine are in college. We are very proud of them.

# Donna and Dale's Family

Our second child, Donna, was a cute and lovely baby girl born at Temple University Hospital in 1963. We were so happy to have a boy, Bill, and a girl, Donna. As she grew, she was a kind and caring daughter and big sister. She helped her mom; took care of her baby sister, Laura; and was a good playmate of her sister. She was always protective of her sister and her younger brother, Richard. During her senior year of high school, she expressed her disinterest in advancing to college education, although she was an earnest and smart girl who could have entered a medical school to become a very good physician. To her, it was important that she stay home so that she would not be separated from her boyfriend, Dale Hoellrich, a fine and hardworking young man who was not interested in a college education. We were heartbroken when we failed to persuade her to pursue higher education. I wanted all my children to have the highest possible education, but both her mother and I respected her decision. Dale is a grandson of a German immigrant who lived in our community. His father was a college graduate and believed in honesty, integrity, and hard work for the family.

**Donna and Dale's family.** *From left to right:* **Cameron, Dale, Donna.**

While living on the second floor of Dale's father's convenience store after they were married, Donna became pregnant and delivered a beautiful baby boy, Cameron, our first grandson. Cameron was adorable and such a good-natured boy; we all loved him very much. The newborn child moved Donna further away from considering higher education. She believed firmly that her job was to be a good mother for Cameron full-time at home. Even now, thirty years later, she is a strong believer that there is a need for a full-time mom or dad at home for growing children. Dale worked hard day and night for his father's business, and they moved to a good newly built home in a good neighborhood of Syracuse's suburbs.

Two years later, after Cameron was born, they had their second son, Brandon, our second grandson. Brandon was another good-natured, beautiful, and friendly little boy with curly blond hair. He was such an affectionate and friendly child who loved to hug me and his grandma. Everybody adored him. We felt as if he were a gift of god. Unfortunately, he began to suffer from sudden episodic occurrences of severe headaches, seizures, and joint pain. He was evaluated by specialists, including a professor of neurology at the university hospital, and underwent extensive diagnostic tests, but without a definitive diagnosis. One day when he was five and a half years old, his father and he went for a follow-up visit with his pediatrician. The pediatrician told his dad the child was fine. As he left the office, Brandon screamed, "Daddy, Daddy, help me!" and he screamed again before having a severe general seizure and falling unconscious. He was rushed to the hospital by ambulance. His consciousness never returned. Magnetic resonance imaging (MRI) of the brain showed massive infarction (a brain catastrophe). In an isolated room of the intensive care unit, while he was receiving intravenous fluid, Brandon was held in his grandmother's arms, with his hands in my palms, until he passed away. It was an unforgettable tragedy, especially for our precious child, who suffered so much. My agony and sadness, then and now, was expressed in part in my eulogy written on July 11, 1996:

> … Brandon was an extraordinary, lovable and affectionate, gentle and caring child. He was indeed God's gift to us. God allowed us to have him for more than five years.
>
> I can still see Brandon with his charming smile and affection, running toward me so often with his two arms and hands raised, saying "Papa," wishing for me to hug and hold him. What a thrill and a sweet time we experienced on each occasion whenever I had him.
>
> Brandon, you have given us such joy and beautiful memories in our lives, such pleasure and pride to your brother, mom, dad, cousins, uncles, aunts, papa, and mama. Each time when you were ill, you strengthened our family bond and gave us courage. We thank you for being a part of our family. We will always love you and cherish our memories. You will remain in our hearts. Farewell, my son, until we meet again.

Donna became a full-time mother for Cameron in order to make certain that he was well brought up. After Cameron entered primary school, she worked as a teacher's assistant at an elementary school in Baldwinsville, New York. She taught computer skills to children from ages five to ten. In 2015, she moved to the high school, helping in eleventh-grade English. This year she was chosen as the favorite teaching assistant by the senior class and was an honored guest at graduation.

Her husband, Dale, worked very hard day and night as the owner of a small business who believed in good, honest hard work. Without any family inheritance, in less than twenty years, his dream became a reality. He is now a successful businessman. Dale believes that with honest and hard work, there are opportunities in this great country to become rich and enjoy a meaningful life—an American dream.

Cameron, sadly having had missed his brother, was brought up with the tender, loving care of his mom and dad. He successfully finished primary, middle, and high school and entered Syracuse University College of Arts and Sciences to study near his parents. He was highly interested in a career in social work. After graduation, He served in AmeriCorps for one year. While serving in AmeriCorps, he fell in love with a charming and attractive AmeriCorps member, Allison Injaian. After finishing their service, both of them were accepted to the University of Michigan for graduate studies—social work for Cameron and ecology and evolutionary biology for Allison—in Ann Arbor, Michigan. Both successfully completed their graduate work to receive graduate degrees: a master's of social work and a master's of ecology and evolutionary biology, respectively. They were engaged and, in July 2015, had a beautiful wedding in the hometown of Alli in a Philadelphia suburb in the presence of Alli's family, including her over-ninety-year-old grandparents, Dale's family, and our family. My sister, Ok-Hee; my brother-in-law, Dr. Kwang- Joon Nam; their two daughters, Lisa and Vickie; and Vickie's husband, Marc, came for this special occasion from near San Francisco, California.

After the wedding and honeymoon, they drove in a new car—a gift from Cameron's father, to cross the country to settle in Davis, California, where Alli was accepted by the University of California at Davis for her PhD work. Cameron found a position as a social worker in a nearby state prison hospital. Cameron was quite content with his daily work. Alli completed her PhD work, and they returned east in three years with a beautiful baby boy, Pierce, our first precious great-grandson.

**Pierce Brandon Hoellrich, one year old.**

In Ithaca, New York, Cameron has been recruited by Cornell University and Alli has begun her postdoctoral work at Cornell. Pierce is, as his father used to be, a happy, adorable, and good-looking baby boy whom people can't keep their hands off of. On April 30, 2020, we had another adorable newborn baby boy, Clark, in the house of Cameron and Allison.

**Clark, three months old, and Pierce, two years old.**

# Richard and Maura's Family

Richard is our third child. He was a lovable and cute baby boy born in September 1964. Rich became a caring and thoughtful boy who hung around his big brother and was friendly with his sisters. He got along well with his neighboring friends, particularly David, when he was five to six years old when we lived in Wyncote, Pennsylvania. He was always as interested in extracurricular activities as he was in his studies. Another thing he was always interested in was business. When asked what he wanted to be when he grew up, he would say that he wanted to own a bank. He worked at the local grocery store, Super Duper, during his high school days and borrowed $500 from his parents so he could buy a lawn mower and start a lawn mowing business. Although he was accepted by several highly competitive universities, Richard chose Colgate University because of its size and its proximity to home.

As Bill left for college, he alone mowed our large yard. He became such a reliable, dependable, responsible, and self-disciplined young lad. As he biked on sometimes busy roads on the hill near our house, I often became anxious in fear of an accident. Drivers on the road become reckless from time to time. It was another sad moment when he drove away from home. We felt as if we had an empty house for a while. At the school, he joined the Phi Tau fraternity and held numerous offices, including social chairman, house manager, vice president, pledge master and president. Rich realized he enjoyed leadership roles and business more than medicine. After graduation from the Colgate University College of Arts and Sciences, he became interested in pursuing a business career. After gaining experience as an employee in various business corporations for about one year, Rich decided to go to a business school. Among many outstanding business schools where he was accepted, he chose the Wharton School of Business at the University of Pennsylvania. He majored in marketing and entrepreneurial management. He paid his tuition by working at the Small Business Development Center (SBDC) for two years while he was at Wharton. He provided consulting services for small businesses and conducted business plan writing workshops. After receiving an MBA degree from Wharton, Rich accepted a job with MBI, Inc., a privately held direct-marketing company in Norwalk, Connecticut as assistant product manager. He worked hard there long enough to realize that he was not suited for the corporate world.

He saved his money and began looking for a business to purchase in a new environment as a challenge. Richard purchased a couple of dry cleaners and a laundromat in Atlanta, Georgia, to start his new career in the fall of 1991. He ran the dry cleaners for three years but soon realized this was not a long-term career for him. One of the things he missed in Atlanta was the food he had enjoyed in the Northeast. Top among that list was bagels. In April 1994, he shipped off to Burlington, Vermont, for six months to apprentice with Ron Goldberg, a second-generation bagel baker. When he returned from Vermont, Rich opened Highland Bagel Company with his childhood friend, Pierce Page. They opened a second bagel bakery in 1996.

Another thing Rich missed were the noodle shops he had learned to love during his trips to Asia with his father through work, and in New York City and Philadelphia. He opened Doc Chey's Noodle House in 1997 in the Morningside neighborhood of Atlanta. He opened a second location near Emory University in 1999; a third location in Asheville, North Carolina, in 2001; and a fourth location in Atlanta in 2009. Rich attempted to franchise the Doc Chey's concept around 2005. They then opened three franchised restaurants: one in Georgia, one in South Carolina, and one in Florida. Unable to ensure the quality of the original Doc Chey's restaurants, Rich decided to shut down his franchise operations in 2009.

His tenacious and relentless hard work during all these turbulent times led to the fruition of a lifelong dream. In 2003, Rich closed Highland Bagel Company and opened Osteria 832 and Pizza in the same place. Osteria 832 serves affordable pasta and pizza. Indeed, it was delicious, and I hoped I could find similar delicious cuisine in Rochester. He converted the Emory Doc Chey's into a new concept, Dragon Bowl, in 2014. He currently owns and operates four restaurants in Atlanta. Rich has spent the last ten years running his four restaurants in Atlanta. He has focused on serving affordable food to neighborhood families and serving his community through charitable events. He was awarded the Distinguished Service Award by the Georgia Restaurant Association in 2011 for his outstanding service to the Atlanta community. His restaurants have been voted onto many "best of" lists in Atlanta over the years.

**Richard and Maura's Family.** *From left to right:* **Maura, Paris, Megen, Richard.**

He found a charming and attractive young lady, Maura Bauman, a physician's assistant, at his brother's wedding in May 1990. They dated long distance (Rich was in Connecticut and Maura in Atlanta) for a year and a half before Richard moved to Georgia. They married in April 1994 and have two beautiful daughters, Megen and Paris. Both attended Catholic schools and played soccer at a competitive level. Megen won two Georgia high school state titles at St. Pius X Catholic High School. Paris won four state titles at St. Pius and a state championship with her club team. Megan graduated from Emory University in May 2019 with dual degrees in environmental science and media studies. She is passionate about the environment and music. Paris is an honor student at the University of Georgia and will graduate in 2021 with dual degrees in biology and psychology. She plans to enter a medical school and pursue a medical career. She has already been accepted to two reputable medical schools for 2021.

# Laura and Ric's Family

Laura was our last child, born in Philadelphia in December of 1965. She was an adorable and happy baby. My wife said Laura always knew she was child number four, as she had given birth to all four of our children in six years. As a baby, she would happily await Fan's arrival to lift her from her crib in the morning after she had gotten the other three ready. Laura grew up in a warm home under the devoted and loving care of her mother and enjoyed the companionship, help, and the protective love of her older siblings. Fan called her a social butterfly because of her love of people. Laura is organized and enjoys planning, which was demonstrated by her holding several student government titles from fifth grade on. After graduating from Penfield High School in 1983, she went on to pursue a liberal arts degree at Hobart and William Smith Colleges in Geneva, New York. She was hired by Bankers Trust Company in New York City, where she worked for five years and left as an assistant vice president of sales and marketing of mutual funds.

One afternoon in the autumn of 1992, I was invited to deliver a lecture titled "Scientific Basis for Acupuncture" at New York University Medical Center. Laura had written her college baccalaureate essay exploring acupuncture from two disciplines, science and history, so I invited her to come along. She was fascinated by my well-received lecture. One week later, Laura came home to Rochester and expressed her desire to study acupuncture and Chinese medicine. This was an unexpected surprise, but her mother and I reluctantly accepted her desire and supported her career change. She was accepted to Pacific College of Oriental Medicine in San Diego, California.

I remember the emotional moment when she drove away in our Toyota sports coupe for a cross-country adventure before settling in Southern California, such a long way from home. She graduated with her master's degree in Chinese medicine in 1996 and returned to Rochester with her fiancé, a fine young man who was a professor and expert acupuncture clinician. Ric is a marine and served this great country like I served mine. He attended Ohio State University on the GI Bill and was the first in his family to attend college. Imagine the rivalry in our extended family, with both Buckeyes and Wolverines! Who knew we would be a part of this type of American tradition. Both Laura and Ric are licensed acupuncturists and board-certified Chinese herbologists. They opened Balance Acupuncture Center in 1996 and have been practicing since. Balance was voted the best acupuncture clinic in Rochester by the people's choice awards of Rochester's city newspaper. Laura married Ric Warren in 1997. They have two beautiful children: Wyatt Tang Warren, born in November 1999, and LiLi Chey Warren, born in July 2001. Laura received her doctorate of acupuncture and Chinese medicine (DACM) in 2017. Yes, she is yet another Dr. Chey.

**Laura and Ric's Family with LiLi and Wyatt.**

Our youngest grandson, Wyatt, is a student at Hobart College (class of 2022). He is pursuing his political and Asian studies degree with an eye toward entrepreneurship. Wyatt is a charming and bright young man with a magnetic personality. Our LiLi is the youngest grandchild. Her talent and drive earned her accolades in vocal performance, and she has performed at New York City's Carnegie Hall. LiLi also received the World Tour Scholarship from Berklee College of Music, where she is in the class of 2023. Both of my grandchildren graduated from Pittsford Mendon High School, where they were involved in student government, athletics, and the arts. Pittsford, New York, is a small community on the Erie Canal and is the epitome of a classic American town. Wyatt and LiLi benefited from all this country has to offer, including excellent public schools and a safe environment. This plus their multicultural backgrounds have helped them evolve into strong, compassionate, and resilient individuals.

# Ok-hee and Kwang Joon Nam's Family

In October 1971, the newly wed Nam family—my sister Ok-Hee and her husband, Dr. Kwang Joon Nam—arrived in Rochester for a new life as immigrants and joined our family. We were so delighted to see the beautiful young couple. Our children were excited to meet their new aunt and uncle they had never seen before. We welcomed them in our home until they settled. Fan and our children were very happy to have new relatives at our home. I, too, felt warm in my heart to have one of my siblings in the United States with her husband as a family. Dr. Nam is a graduate of YonSei University College of Medicine, one of the top medical schools in South Korea; and my sister graduated from the prestigious Ewha Women's University in Seoul and majored in art. Both pursued further graduate work and contributed to their newly adopted country, the United States of America. I found out that Dr. Nam's father began his career as a professor of chemical engineering at Seoul National University but felt that he would contribute more to his new country by serving as a senior engineer in the cement industry for reconstruction of industrial infrastructure in Korea. As the leader of the cement industry, he was instrumental in successful development and construction of modern highways and buildings. He was indeed the grandfather of the successful modern Korean.

Before Dr. Nam came to this country, he had served as a flight surgeon for three years in the ROK Air Force. In Rochester, he had an unusual opportunity to have a six-months period of an externship in pathology under the tutelage of Dr. John Abott, chief of pathology, and his staff at Genesee Hospital, a major teaching hospital of the University of Rochester. This helped him to get familiarized with some aspects of the American medical culture. After completing a straight internship in internal medicine at Prince George General Hospital in Maryland in June 1993, he and his family returned to Rochester. He completed a three-year diagnostic radiology residency at Rochester General Hospital, a major teaching hospital of the University of Rochester School of Medicine and Dentistry. His mentor, the late Dr. Theodor van Zandt, professor of radiology, was an outstanding teacher whom we respected and admired. Dr. Nam, a board-certified radiologist in diagnostic radiology, decided to serve as a full-time radiologist of the Canandaigua VA Medical Center and Rochester VA Outpatient Clinic. He established the Department of Radiology and was the chief of radiology. Dr. Nam felt strongly that his service for veterans came first in his mind, before he would think of a lucrative private practice in radiology. After his retirement from the VA Medical Center in 2006, he enjoyed a private practice in radiology until 2014.

My youngest sister, Ok-Hee is an attractive and beautiful woman. She is a painter and storyteller. She and her husband, Kwang-Joon, raised two adorable and beautiful baby girls, Elizabeth (Lisa) and Victoria (Vickie). Ok-Hee was a devoted and dedicated mother in this unfamiliar land. She managed to earn her master's in fine art from the Rochester Institute of Technology. She worked as a graphic designer at a firm in Rochester. She then switched gears and opened her own interior design studio. When she retired, she decided to dedicate her life to painting. Her artistic goal has been to create visuals that interweave and connect memories of growing up in Korea with the diverse experiences she had had as an adult mixing and melting into life in America. She believes that her painting should spur a range of human emotions from wonder, happiness, and exuberance to sadness, loneliness, and even anger. During the past few years, her work has been shown at the Armory in West Palm Beach, Florida; the gallery at the Palm Beach International Airport; the Lighthouse Art Center in Jupiter, Florida; the gallery at Contemporary Living in Palm Beach Gardens, Florida; and at the Santa Cruz Art League gallery in Santa Cruz, California. The most exciting exhibit is currently on at the Tauni De Lesseps Gallery.

Their two daughters grew up in Pittsford, New York, under the loving care of their parents. They had excellent middle school and high school educations in the Pittsford School System.

**Ok-Hee and Kwang-Joon Nam's family.** *From left to right:* **Marc Chow, Elizabeth Nam, Victoria Chow, Yuna Nam-Chow, Ok-Hee, and Kwang-Joon Nam.**

# Elizabeth

———————————◦◦◦———————————

Lisa is a 1994 graduate of Wellesley College and received her juris doctorate from Boston University in 1997. She is a member of the New York State Bar and is a specialist in wills, trusts, and estates. After beginning her career as an attorney and spending several years as a professional trustee, Lisa is now an executive director of family office resources at Morgan Stanley, where she provides planning, philanthropy, and family governance advice. Specifically, she works with the firm's West Coast clients to integrate their wealth creation and financial planning activities with the efficient and thoughtful transfer of wealth. Her professional goal is to encourage constructive dialog within families so that wealth is a positive force, not a destructive one, in relationships. Lisa currently lives in the San Francisco Bay Area with her poodles. She loves hanging out with her family, attends worship services at church on Sundays, is an avid traveler, enjoys playing golf, and loves to cook and eat. Lisa became a hula dancer in 2018 and dances with South San Francisco–based Hālau O Keikiali'i, under the instruction of Kumu Hula Kawika Alfiche. She also works on her Korean language skills by binge-watching Korean dramas on TV.

# Vickie and Marc's Family

Vickie and Marc live in Santa Cruz, California. They have an adorable and cute baby daughter, Yuna, who is two years old. Vickie, with the full support of Marc, is a totally devoted mother for Yuna. Like her sister, Vickie is a 1997 graduate of Wellesley College, magna cum laude. She received a PhD in psychology from the University of California–Monterey Bay in 2016. She authored a book titled *YELL-Oh Girls! Emerging Voices Explore Culture, Identity and Growing Up Asian American*, published by HarperCollins. She was the 2001–2002 Asian Pacific American Leadership Institute discovery leadership fellow.

Marc Chow, a Chinese American born in the San Francisco area, is a totally devoted husband and father whom we all are proud of. Marc was a 1997 graduate of the University of San Francisco and received a bachelor of arts degree in sociology. Then he earned a master's of science in health policy at the George Washington University School of Public Health in Washington, DC. He is currently CEO and president of the Kidney Collaborative, executive director of the National Renal Administrators Association, executive director of the Renal Services Exchange, and vice chair of the board of directors of the Asian Pacific Islander American Health Forum.

# Our Parents' Visits to Rochester and After

O ur parents had visited with us, including Nam's family, in the summers of 1977 and 1980. They arrived in Rochester the first time they met with our family. It was indeed a moving moment for all of us when we met with them for a long time at Rochester International Airport in July of 1977, which was indeed a long-awaited happy occasion. This was the first time they met their precious grandchildren, including Lisa and Vickie. It was also the first time they met my wife, Fan, who was so delighted, and the first time they stayed in our home with their son, daughter-in-law, and grandchildren. We all were overwhelmed by such happy occasions. They enjoyed having their grandchildren around them.

One afternoon, our parents, Lisa, and two small girls from our neighborhood were sitting around the kitchen table. On the table, they saw several live red lobsters, and they were all fascinated, watching them move their claws and legs, and touching them timidly. The two children laughed and screamed from time to time when the lobsters moved. It was fun to watch the lobsters before they were cooked by Fan for a picnic dinner in the backyard. Indeed this outdoor meal with us was an experience my parents had never had before.

My parents were interested in sightseeing both at Niagara Falls, one of the natural wonders of the world, and in New York City. One Saturday, my parents and my entire family went in our station wagon to the Canadian side of the falls. It meant so much for me and Fan to travel with our parents together with our children. It was such fun to be with them. They were absolutely astounded by the magnificent views of the three falls. They enjoyed seeing their grandchildren standing wet on the street, soaked by mists coming from the falls in the late afternoon, with a background of gigantic waterfalls and beautiful, colorful rainbows behind them. After early dinner in a restaurant overlooking the falls, we returned home tired. We all enjoyed this memorable trip to the falls.

**Misty Niagara Falls with a beautiful rainbow on a late Saturday afternoon. With their grandparents, Donna, Bill, Laura, and Richard got wet but enjoyed the cool mist.**

My parents and I visited New York City by airplane. We went to Manhattan by taxi from LaGuardia Airport and checked into the Hilton downtown. Both father and mother enjoyed immensely the ride across clean and gigantic highways and bridges, and viewing the magnificent Manhattan skyline. After lunch and a short nap in the early afternoon, we started the sightseeing tour, which lasted for four days. The highlights of the tour included a walking tour of downtown, including Radio City Music Hall, Rockefeller Center, the mighty Empire State Building, Central Park, the Metropolitan Museum of Art, Chinatown, and a boat tour of Manhattan Island that included all of Manhattan island, part of New Jersey, Queens, Brooklyn, and Roosevelt Island (formally Welfare Island) on the East River, where I had my internship at the City Hospital of New York in 1954–55. My parents enjoyed the tour immensely and were overwhelmed. They were exhausted at the end of the tour, but they were still excited. On the way back to Rochester, my mother said, "I feel like I've been having a beautiful dream with my son for the past several days."

I said, "Thank you, Mother. When you and Father return next time, we will go to Philadelphia and Washington, DC. It was a sad time when we saw Mother and Father off at Greater Rochester International Airport after their memorable three-week visit.

**My parents' second visit to Rochester, in 1980.** *From left to right:* **the author, Fan, Lisa Nam, Donna, Father** (*sitting*), **Richard, Laura, Bill, Mother** (*sitting*), **Kwang-Joon Nam, Ok-Hee Nam, and Vickie Nam.**

Our parents returned in September 1980. one year after I visited Seoul on my return trip home from Beijing, China. My family and Nam's family were so glad to see them back again. They were so pleased to meet with Fan and our four grown-up teenage children, Ok-Hee, Kwang-Joon (Dr. Nam) and their daughters, Lisa and Vickie, who were elementary school students. After one week of rest at our home, we visited Philadelphia and Washington, DC, for sightseeing. In one afternoon, both parents and I flew to Philadelphia and checked into the Maine Line Marriot and planned to rent a car for sightseeing in the two cities.

At seven o'clock the following morning, I was awakened by a phone call. "Dr. Chey? This is Bill Goodwin"

I said, "Bill, how did you find me here?"

He laughed. "Yesterday I called your office in Rochester for an appointment for my wife, Marion. Your secretary told me that I could find you in this Marriott. I am here in the lobby."

I recalled I had seen her at my office at Temple University Hospital more than ten years prior for irritable bowel syndrome. I thought he would have a cup of coffee with me and talk about her medical problem. In the lobby, he was so glad to see me, and he pointed his right hand toward the parking lot. Right near the hotel building, Bill smilingly showed me a new black Cadillac and a cream-white Lincoln Continental. I felt awkward and asked him why these two beautiful cars were here. "I thought you might choose one of the two for sightseeing in both Philadelphia and Washington, DC. I took care of the automobile insurance for you. All you have to do is select your favored car and leave it at the national airport in Washington, DC, before you leave for Rochester, New York." I couldn't believe this unexpected generosity by a former patient's husband. I told Bill that I had planned to rent a car for myself that morning. "There is no need for that, Dr. Chey. After what you did for Marion, this is at least I can do. This is a special occasion for you. Your parents came all the way from Seoul, Korea." Then he winked at me.

I was deeply touched by his kindness and generosity. Then I recalled his wife, Marion, who was referred to me by her family practice physician for unexplained abdominal pain, indigestion, and irregular bowel habit. For these symptoms, she was recommended for cholecystectomy by a local surgeon. After my careful evaluation of her condition, I dissuaded her from having the surgery, and she was treated for irritable bowel syndrome. Bill told me, "Marion has been feeling well for as long as she has followed your diet and used the medicine you recommended when she needs it. We have been so grateful to you." I was very gratified. I chose the black Cadillac, since my father was more familiar with the name Cadillac than Lincoln Continental. Father was very pleased that for the first time in his life, he and Mother had the pleasure of riding in a Cadillac while sightseeing. We visited Independence Hall and other historical and interesting sites, including the DuPont Garden. After three days in Philadelphia, we drove to Washington, DC.

We stayed in one of the Marriott hotels in Washington, DC. The highlights of the sightseeing were the White House, Capitol Hill, and Arlington National Cemetery. We enjoyed the guided tours of both the magnificent White House and Congress on the Hill. Mother was particularly eager to visit John F. Kennedy's grave and observe the eternal flame. One interesting episode worthy of mention was that at the gate of Arlington National Cemetery, two young, good-looking marines in full uniform with bayonets fixed to their rifles saluted us. I opened the window and told them that we were interested in visiting John F. Kennedy's grave and the eternal flame. One marine kindly directed us where to go. He said, "You can drive slowly up there at a speed of five miles per hour, sir." As I slowly drove up the winding road, all the people were walking on the roadside to avoid our car. Some of them were friendly and waving at us. Then I realized that the marines at the gate must have thought that we were VIPs from a foreign embassy. Our parents enjoyed the beautiful scenery of the national cemetery, and we paid our respects to the great president John F. Kennedy. Mother kneeled on the ground in front of the grave and gave a deep bow. As we were driving down, both Father and Mother were very pleased. Mother said, "This visit to Arlington National Cemetery alone made coming to this great capital worthwhile." A dignified-looking person like my father, driving a new Cadillac passenger car, could impress the soldiers at the gates in those days.

After returning to our home in Rochester, they spent time with Nam's family at their home for several days and visited a Canandaigua lake resort to enjoy the beautiful lake with their youngest daughter, Ok-Hee, Dr. Nam, and their two lovely granddaughters, Lisa and Vickie. It was indeed another sad occasion for all of us when they left Rochester International Airport to return home to Seoul. On their return flight to Seoul, they stopped over in Tokyo. My dear friend Professor Tadashi Takeuchi from Tokyo Women's Medical University hosted them. They were escorted by Dr. Takeuchi to a hotel in downtown Tokyo. He entertained them with a delicious dinner and expressed his sincere appreciation for my contributions in the faculty development of some of his junior staff at his department. Of course, Father and Mother spoke Japanese well, and they must have had a wonderful time in the evening. I treasure Takeuchi-san as my lifelong friend.

**Certificate of the Republic of Korea Presidential Medal of Honor, August 14, 1980.**

**Father's Republic of Korea Presidential Medal of Honor.**

After returning home to Seoul, Father received his long-awaited presidential recognition and medal for patriotism and contributions to Korean independence from the government of the Republic of Korea. Many years later, both my father and mother passed away from old age. Both my father and mother are resting in peace in the Republic of Korea National Cemetery, a beautiful, serene, and sacred place. I know they are proud of us. What we have here in the United States is the fruit of our parents' hard work, sacrifice, and strong determination for education that started eight decades ago in a small rural town in Korea. I appreciate sincerely their love and sacrifice for all of us. I am proud of them and miss them profoundly. Once again, I thank them and love them dearly.

My parents' plots in the Republic of Korea National Cemetery.

# Reflections

This book depicts the life of an immigrant who was fortunately able to come to the United States and fulfill his American dream. It is the story of his journey from a small rural town in South Korea to Rochester, New York. Rochester became the root of my resilient and strong family.

I grew up in a small rural town of South Korea close to Busan in South Gyeongsang Province. My parents' lifetime goal was to educate their children to the best of their ability. Their hope, however, was hampered by Japanese colonialism because my father was not allowed to receive a graduation certificate from the high schools he attended, owing to his political crime on March 1, 1919, at the age of nineteen, when he and his many schoolmates protested for Korean independence under Japanese colonial rule in Korea. He was imprisoned for one year. Under Japanese rule, one had to have a high school graduation certificate in order to have a decent job. After hard work for years, my father eventually became a deputy manager of a small bank branch in a rural town where the school education was at substandard level. As World War II began, we were forced to take on Japanese names, which was indeed an unforgettable humiliation to all Koreans. At age thirteen, I had to leave home to live in a small boarding house in a city where I could have a better primary school education, which helped me to pass the entrance examination in a highly competitive middle school—one of the best for pupils of Korean natives in the province. Japanese students had their own school system in the same school district. My middle school education by Japanese teachers was harsh—without passion or enthusiasm, and often unpleasant. Many of them exhibited attitudes of superiority over Koreans. Every day, we lived with national humiliation in a country with over three thousand years of history. Most Koreans saw no fair future under Japanese colonialism.

I still don't understand why I deserved to suffer physical punishment by a Japanese physical education teacher for my red, swollen, and itchy lower lip, which was found years later to be caused by a sun allergy. It is still difficult to forget the teacher who slapped my face so hard. The teacher accused me of coloring my lip with red lip paint. Many of these teachers had no understanding, affection, or respect toward students as persons, just because we were Koreans. When I met many Japanese in the post–World War II era, they were gentle, courteous, intelligent, and pleasant people. In fact, one of my best friends is a Japanese man who is now a retired professor in Tokyo. They were then, and still are, just like us—ordinary Asian people. How could this happen to those who were mostly well educated and were brought up in a well-mannered, gentle, and courteous home environment? At the turn of the twentieth century, many of the leaders in the military–political establishment pumped the idea to the public that Japanese people are superior to people in neighboring countries, particularly Koreans and Chinese. Their military government leaders told lie after lie about other countries, such as the United States, England, China, and Korea. Many of the good-hearted people in Japan began to believe that what their leaders told them day in and day out was real—a dangerous precedent in any country. This was an ugly form of propaganda in Japan before World War II started. In hindsight, I realize that this trend must have become a national fever and nightmare for them in the prewar era. This kind of political and social epidemic illness can occur in any country, including the United States, when a national leader uses propaganda made of many lies, ignoring the country's constitution, morality, and honest values that the populace are so proud of. Today Japan is one of the most civilized countries under democracy in the world, and I admire this country.

When World War II ended and Korea was freed from Japanese colonialism in August 1945, my Korean name was restored, as were those of all other Koreans. I again spoke the Korean language freely, and I eventually attained my medical school education because my father could afford it in free Korea. I was so fortunate to complete medical education during the Korean war in March 1953; this was a dream of my parents as well as me.

The long-awaited freedom in Korea, however, was unfortunately short-lived, as the North Korean People's Volunteer Army invaded South Korea on June 25, 1950. During the first three months of the brutal occupation of Seoul under the egregious and atrocious dictator Kim Il-Sung, his cronies, and their brainwashed soldiers, people soon realized how precious and important the freedom was—that freedom is the fundamental right and need of civilized humans. My family survived the nightly terror and brutality. I survived by escaping from a group of troops marching to North Korea as so-called Korean People's Volunteer Army soldiers, making a miraculous escape from North Korean secret policemen's skillful nightly intrusions and the last inspection of our home in a late September night 1950, and enduring fierce Chinese artillery attacks in combat only several days before the fighting ended on July 27, 1953. It is almost a miracle that I survived these atrocious times. Even now I shiver sometimes when I recall those atrocious days. We can't allow this to happen in this great country at any cost. But it can happen even in a mighty country like ours if the government becomes irreversibly corrupted under wrong political leadership or if the people no longer fulfill their responsibility to the country. History has given us many such examples.

After the truce was declared by both the allied forces and the two communist countries, North Korea and China, I was told that the president of the Republic of Korea, Syngman Rhee, sent the official letter to commanding generals of military divisions on the front line encouraging them to help soldiers and young officers to obtain scholarships or other financial aid for study in advanced countries, such as the United States of America. Unfortunately, however, the letter was ignored by most of the military leaders on the front line. It was fortunate for me that I had an excellent rapport with my regimental commander. With his help, I was granted release from active duty for study in the United States. The colonel had respected me ever since I saved a very ill young soldier suffering from acute appendicitis by successfully performing an appendectomy in a combat zone medical facility. I still wonder how I did this at night under candlelight. I didn't even have an internship when I was drafted for active military duty only four months earlier. This was because young doctors were desperately needed in combat when the northern savages fiercely attacked South Korea in the early dawn of June 25, 1950. Without the colonel's cooperation and help, I couldn't possibly have gone to the United States with an internship in a hospital that helped me gain advanced training in medicine. This was indeed the turning point in my life and career for achieving my American dream. I am proud that I was probably the first medical officer to come to the United States for postgraduate medical training after the war ended in July 1953.

It was such an exciting time to start my rotating internship at City Hospital on Welfare Island (now known as Roosevelt Island) in New York City. However, I soon realized that I needed more inspirational learning experiences than the ones I had at the hospital. Whenever and wherever I could, I attended medical meetings and conferences held during my off-hours in institutions in Manhattan, such as the New York Academy of Medicine and the world-class teaching hospitals like Mount Sinai Hospital and the Cornell Division of the legendary Bellevue Hospital. In doing so, I became more proficient in managing patients with challenging diagnostic and therapeutic problems. For example, these learning experiences helped me to suspect a young African American woman had a rare but exciting relatively new disease at the time, when she presented with episodic hypertension and severe headache. As it turned out, she indeed had a pheochromocytoma (a tumor) of the right adrenal gland. Two major teaching hospitals in Manhattan had overlooked her condition. The removal of the tumor by the surgical team at Columbia Presbyterian Hospital had completely relieved her agonizing symptoms for which she had a working diagnosis made by others of essential "hypertension and hysteria or anxiety neurosis." It was indeed my diagnostic and therapeutic triumph when this patient, who needed help so desperately, received a correct diagnosis. I felt then that I served well as a physician healer.

My diagnosis of this rare and new exciting disease impressed not only my peers in the hospital but also all the attending physicians, none of whom had ever heard of such a new disease except for one—Dr. Lester Tuchman from Mount Sinai Hospital, who happened to be a senior visiting physician at City Hospital. I also made a diagnosis of another rare medical condition as an intern—cancer of the ampulla of Vater in the duodenum in a fifty-five-year-old Caucasian male, which other colleagues overlooked. My performance on these two patients brought the attention of two prominent attending physicians: Doctors Lester Tuchman and Morris Steinberg, both attending physicians of Mount Sinai Hospital who were highly respected by my peers and other attending physicians at City Hospital. I often walked extra miles to learn more and enrich my medical knowledge, which helped me to become a better-informed and intelligent physician.

I was eager to move upward to achieve my high-standard professional goal. With a special fellowship award recommended by Drs. Lester Tuchman and Morris Steinberg, I was fortunate to enjoy an exciting year at Mount Sinai Hospital studying pathology and pathophysiology of many varieties of diseases and being tutored by eminent pathologists, including Doctors Hans Popper and Sadao Otani. Equally exciting and important at that time was that my bright peers were graduates from leading medical schools in the United States. They were young, smart, and hard-working physicians who were equally eager to learn as I was. It was indeed exciting and instructive for me to interact with them every day. In addition, I had so many opportunities to learn by attending many other teaching activities in the same institution, such as well-prepared clinical conferences and lecture series, which included Dr. Popper's hepatology lectures. The experience at Mount Sinai inspired and encouraged me to pursue further graduate studies, including advanced degree work for a doctorate of medical science at the University of Pennsylvania Graduate School of Medicine in Philadelphia, Pennsylvania. By this time, it was clear to me that my professional goal was to become a physician scientist and physician educator in learning institutions in the United States—another American dream.

I was very fortunate to meet in Washington, DC, in the Spring of 1957 a young, attractive, and beautiful lady, Fan K. Tang, who was born in Hangzhou, a beautiful city in China. Fan had just graduated from a nursing school in Boston and was working in a local hospital. We fell in love, and we both dreamed of having a good, happy, and stable family. We were so happy to have four lovely children: Bill, Donna, Richard, and Laura—the children of our dreams—while I was working as a faculty member at Temple University Medical Center in Philadelphia. Fan was totally devoted and dedicated to our children, who were so happy with us as a wonderful dream family. I was also so grateful for her unselfish support, which made it possible for me to pursue my demanding work in an academic medical career and as a physician healer.

I was lucky to find a combined fellowship training program for both clinical and research gastroenterology at the Temple University Medical Center Samuel Fels Research Institute in Philadelphia. Dr. Harry Shay, the director of the institute, was a nationally and internationally recognized physician scientist in gastroenterology. His program was the best in the city for my circumstances at that time. He gave me the impression that he was like my father at my initial interview, as he was warm and kind. He sponsored me for my advanced degree work in his research laboratories and helped me to become a faculty member at the medical center to continue my clinical and teaching activities. Dr. Shay was a visiting faculty member at the University of Pennsylvania Graduate School of Medicine. He was indeed my genuine mentor and guardian who encouraged me to stay and pursue my academic career in the United States. I was deeply indebted to his kindness and help, which made it possible for me to do graduate work for advanced degrees, including a master of medical science (MSc) in gastroenterology and a doctor of medical science (DSc) from the University of Pennsylvania. In 1968, I was promoted to associate professor of medicine, a rank below full professor, with tenure, and director of research at the Division of Gastroenterology at Temple University Medical Center. Moreover, I became a citizen of the United States in 1970. Without the efforts initiated by the late Dr. Harry Shay and Temple University—particularly without his help—I could not possibly have pursued my dream—a career in academic medicine.

Dr. Shay was born in South Philadelphia in 1898. Unfortunately, when he was a little boy, his father passed away and he was brought up by a hardworking widowed mother. Young Harry was bright and studied hard to enter one of the most prestigious universities in the country, the University of Pennsylvania School of Medicine. He worked harder than ever after his medical school graduation, with the dream of becoming a good physician healer and scientist, although he realized such opportunities were quite limited for him at that time. His impossible dream became a reality when an elderly patient wearing a shabby jacket walked into his humble practice office for a consultation regarding indigestion. Dr. Shay helped him and relieved the patient's indigestion. The patient turned out to be a wealthy and successful businessman and was the president of a soap manufacturing company, Fels and Co., and a generous philanthropist. With his encouragement and support, the young Dr. Shay established the Samuel S. Fels Research Institute at Temple University Medical Center with the title of professor of clinical medicine and chief of gastroenterology. I found that Dr. Shay's longtime dream had been realized at the time when I joined his program. He was indeed an American dreamer who had worked very hard in his profession to achieve his goal ever since his childhood. I envied Dr. Shay's success as a physician scholar and admired his compassion, empathy, and skillful care for patients. I also recognized the generosity of patients such as Mr. Fels, who appreciated the caring and kind services provided by their physicians.

One of my dreams as a gastroenterologist was to have a well-balanced program in a learning institution where I could independently organize clinical services in the same location, including an endoscopic procedure room, an X-ray room, and both outpatient and inpatient services. In addition, I wanted research laboratories located in the vicinity of clinical facilities. The generous gift of a local philanthropist, the late Mr. Isaac Gordon, made it possible for me to establish such an exciting digestive center, named after him, in Rochester, New York. This dream became a reality when I was slated to develop the Center for Digestive Diseases and Nutrition at Genesee Hospital and the University of Rochester School of Medicine and Dentistry, a very good medical school. The successful development of the Gordon Center was, in part, attributable to the unrelenting support of Dr. Alvin Urelese, chief of medicine and professor of medicine, for many exciting years to follow. It has been my privilege to have him as one of my dearest friends and as a mentor.

My talented and hardworking faculty colleagues helped so many patients with diagnostic and therapeutic challenges. I am so proud of them. Our research work at Genesee Hospital, a part of teaching medical institutions of the University of Rochester, was quite productive and recognized by peers nationally and internationally. So many physician scientists and scientists came to the center from places all over the world—including South Korea, Japan, China, Europe, and Africa—to learn and contribute their hard work to our research program. The majority returned to their own countries and held leadership positions in their respective learning institutions. It was such a rewarding and indeed golden year for academic medicine. It was also an exciting time in my career and for my family. Our four children had grown up well and had begun to fly out their old nest one by one for further education. We loved them dearly and were very proud of them. After twenty years of tenure at Genesee Hospital, I was slated once again by the University of Rochester Medical Center's Strong Memorial Hospital to become the director of the Gastroenterology and Hepatology Division to strengthen the digestive and liver diseases program. My dear patient and friend, the late Bill Konar, a generous philanthropist, and our other patient friends helped us to establish a center for digestive and liver diseases that combined clinical and research programs at the University of Rochester Medical Center. The center was named the William and Sheila Konar Center for Digestive and Liver Diseases in 1995. Thus my research program started at the Isaac Gordon Center at Genesee Hospital in 1971 was continued at the William and Sheila Konar Center for Digestive and Liver Diseases in the medical center. It was indeed an exciting and gratifying experience and was another American dream for me. Without Bill's generosity and help, the William and Sheila Konar Center for Digestive and Liver Diseases could not have been established at the medical center. I am profoundly grateful to my dear friend Bill Konar and his family. This is another example of a grateful American generosity.

I was always gratified when our work was recognized by our peers nationally and internationally. In particular, our long-term research with secretin (the first hormone proposed to exist in the digestive tract, in 1902) was started during my gastroenterology fellowship days in 1960 under the tutelage of Professor Harry Shay at the Temple University Medical Center. Because we succeeded in producing the very best antisecretin sera in the world, my research team was able to define secretin as a genuine gastrointestinal hormone in 1978. One of our later exciting bits of research was the discovery of secretin-producing tumors in the pancreas in some patients with devastating symptoms of massive watery diarrhea and dehydration. The early detection of this tumor by radioimmunoassay measurement of secretin in blood can save these patients' lives. It is such a satisfying and rewarding experience as a physician scientist to take part in meaningful research like this.

I also enjoyed being invited to national and international meetings for our work done in Rochester, New York. More enjoyable and rewarding were when my former fellows or trainees invited me to their home institutions as a visiting professor and to their institutional and national and international scientific meetings as a guest speaker. One of the most memorable visits that I enjoyed was when I was invited by Professor Chen Min-Zhang to Peking Union Medical College and the Capital Hospital, the Chinese Academy of Medical Sciences, a premiere medical institution of China in Beijing, in April 1981. I was probably the first gastroenterologist to visit Beijing from the United States since their cultural revolution. Subsequently, I received invitations to many medical learning institutions throughout China. They were eager to learn and very hospitable everywhere I was invited. I also enjoyed seeing their culturally rich historical sites and landmarks.

After retirement from the university, I was fortunate to work mainly as a clinician healer, again in a private practice setting. It was such a pleasure and a rewarding experience for me to take care of suffering patients closely again. This final chapter of my professional career was possible because of the kindness and generous help of my dear friend, the late Bill Konar. How many retired academic physicians could have such a satisfying professional career? This can happen in this great country, the United States of America. Bill was indeed my dearest friend and a generous philanthropist who had an American dream, just as I did. There was nothing else pleased me more than when our patients were helped and protected with no harm coming to them. In my final analysis, a physician's role—a sacred mission—is to take care of the suffering and sick with compassion and protect them from harm.

Finally, I have been so blessed to share my life together with my dear wife, Fan, for over sixty years. She was the firm pillar holding up the Chey family. I am proud of my children, who worked very hard and achieved their own American dreams. Two of them, Bill and Laura, are health care professionals with advanced degrees, and my two grandchildren are aiming for future careers in medical professions. I am excited that we may have three generations of medical professionals in our family. I am proud of them dearly. The latest arrivals to our family are our two great-grandsons, Pierce and Clark. They are adorable and good-looking two-year-old and six months-old boys who brighten us every time they are around. Their proud parents, Cameron and Allison, love them and fulfill their lives every day.

Parents' portrait (circa 1975).

# *Conclusion*

With the relentless effort and sacrifice of my parents in difficult times in Korea in the early part of the twentieth century, I received a medical education and graduated from one of the best medical schools, a dream of my parents and myself, in 1953. I served as an ROK Army medical officer fighting in fierce combat against the Korean People's Army and Chinese Volunteer Army. Although I initially felt I had an impossible dream in a bunker in a Korean war zone, I was fortunate to come to the United States, my dream country, in 1954. Moreover, I was incredibly fortunate to be nurtured and helped by many teachers, mentors, and generous friends. Many of them were American dreamers in their own right and found success through their hard work and merit. I fulfilled three goals in my career: having a wonderful family, becoming a successful physician healer and physician scientist in a very good university medical school with a title of professor of medicine, and being a proud mentor of those who came to Rochester, New York to study hard and fulfill their own career goals. I achieved my American dreams, which are still alive for those who work hard and set clear goals in life in this great country, no matter where they come from. I am proud of my children and their families, who worked hard and achieved their own American dreams.

**Family with our grandchildren in 2010.** *From left:* **Paris, Wyatt, Samuel, the author, Cameron, Grandma Fan, Russell, Josephine, Megen, and LiLi.**

## *About the cover artist*

**O**k-Hee Nam resides in West Palm Beach, Florida. As a college student in Seoul, South Korea, Ok-Hee studied fine art at Ewha Woman's University, and later, received her Masters of Fine Art from the Rochester Institute of Technology. She subsequently worked at a commercial design firm and ultimately, opened her own interior design studio, where she focused on residential interiors. Ok-Hee and her husband raised their family in Rochester, within 10 miles from where Dr. Chey raised his.

With her business wound down, Ok-Hee transitioned to retired life in Florida and returned to the work that had originally captivated her – storytelling through visual art. With mentorship from Professor Sam Perry of Palm Beach Atlantic University, she delved deep into her own personal history to share her testimony about life as a first-generation immigrant to the United States, and her joys – as a mother, as an American, as a Christian, as an artist, and as a lover of nature – on canvas. In 2018, Palm Beach Atlantic University hosted Ok-Hee's solo exhibition, entitled "The Narrative in Paint," featuring more than 30 of her original paintings.

In recent years, Ok-Hee has rekindled her interest in sketching and drawing. In particular, she has discovered the power of pencil and pen to render the emotional dimensions and momentous history of members of her family. In 2018, she sketched a portrait of her father-in-law, Ki-Dong Nam, for the cover of his autobiography, "I Am 100 Years Young", which was published and released in South Korea. In 2019, she drew, and then subsequently painted, a portrait of her late father, Ki-Bok Chey, who is memorialized as a national patriot in the liberation of Korea from Imperial Japan. And, in 2020, inspired by her older brother and sole surviving sibling, William Y. Chey, and his mission to document the stories from his dramatic and passionate life journey, Ok-Hee sketched the cover for this book.

The illustration, based on photos, shows Dr. Chey at two different points in his life. On the left, Dr. Chey is an adolescent in Korea, at the traditional home where he grew up. On the right, Dr. Chey has arrived to the U.S. to begin a new life, and is shown with his fellow interns in New York City.

# *References*

KOREA: Old and New, A History by Carter J. Eckert, Ki-Baik Lee, Young Ick Lew, Michael Robinson and Edward W. Wagner. ILCHOKAK, Publishers, Seoul Korea, for the Korea Institute, Harvard University. Distributed by Harvard University Press, 1990.

THE KOREAN WAR, An International History, by Wada Haruki, Published by Rowmann and Littlefield, 2014

SECRETIN: Historical Perspective and Current Status. Chey WY and Chang TM. Pancreas 2014; 43: 162-182

PRIMARY PANCEATIC SECRETINOMA; Secretin is a Diarrheogenic Hormone. Chey WY, Frankel W, Roy S, Sen CK, Dillhoff M, Muscarella P, Soergel KH, Tomkins RD, Chang TM, Bradley III EL, Ellison EC. Annals of Surgey 2017; 266: 346-352

Printed in the United States
by Baker & Taylor Publisher Services